Marcia Munson
Judith P. Stelboum, PhD
Editors

The Lesbian Polyamory Reader: Open Relationships, Non-Monogamy, and Casual Sex

The Lesbian Polyamory Reader: Open Relationships, Non-Monogamy, and Casual Sex has been co-published as *Journal of Lesbian Studies,* Volume 3, Numbers 1/2 1999.

Pre-publication
REVIEWS,
COMMENTARIES,
EVALUATIONS . . .

"**P**rovocative, thoughtful, and well-written, *The Lesbian Polyamory Reader* explores the adventurous sexual heart. It offers a good antidote to the assimilationist championing of same-sex marriage and encourages us to continue deconstructing the patriarchal model of sexual ownership.

Ranging from searing personal narratives to lucid scholarly analyses, from poetry to prose, and from the serious to the humorous, these pieces all challenge the two-by-two paradigm of Noah's–or Sappho's–Ark."

Nancy Manahan, PhD
Editor, Lesbian Nuns: Breaking Silence *and* On My Honor: Lesbians Reflect on Their Scouting Experience

More pre-publication
REVIEWS, COMMENTARIES, EVALUATIONS . . .

"*The Lesbian Polyamory Reader: Open Relationships, Non-Monogamy, and Casual Sex,* edited by Marcia Munson and Judith P. Stelboum, revisits the passion that feminist-lesbians in the '70s brought to our confrontations with patriarchal forms of relationship and love. However, here we have stories and poetry based on personal experience that now spans decades of herstory and wisdom. These are interspersed with clear academic feminist analyses as well as solid descriptions of working models of polyamorous relationships. A conscious collection, this "Reader" gives challenge and permission to stretch our minds and see sexual expression and love in relationships as valid within and without the bounds of our society's view of monogamous "coupledom." Pain and struggle are not denied here, but the freedom and joy of learning who we are and what we desire to choose is affirmed. We are reminded that, with honesty, together we can continue to create alternative forms of commitment, friendship and sexual relatedness. Hopefully this book will shake up some minds as it reminds us that how we are with each other when we know what we want and take responsibility may not look at all like we thought it would. As Donna Allegra says in the Foreword: 'This anthology lets us look at a familiar landscape, the standard configurations for sexual relationships, with new eyes.' Provocative, well-written and entertaining, I highly recommend this be read by lesbians, bi's and other adventurous individuals. A definite must for women's reading and discussion groups."

Molly Gierasch, PhD
Licensed Psychologist, Private Practice Boulder, Colorado

"This ground-breaking collection provides the reader with a fascinating look at trangressive lesbian relationships. Stelboum and Munson have brought together writers of diverse background and writing style. I was alternately amused, saddened, angered and aroused. Those seeking inspiration for new ways of experiencing intimacy and sexuality will not be disappointed."

Karen F. Kerner, MD
New York, New York

More pre-publication
REVIEWS, COMMENTARIES, EVALUATIONS . . .

"**W**arning! Be prepared to have the dishes pile up in your sink, or just be left on the table. Your bed will be unmade, and barely slept in and dust will cover your furniture. Even more serious, all the other books you have started will remain closed and you won't be able to tear yourself away from *The Lesbian Polyamory Reader* for such mundane things as work and evenings with friends. This is the way it worked with me.

I found the book to offer reasonable, logical and persuasive explanations for a style of life I had not seriously considered before. Especially telling was the section with the political arguments. The section on friendship being the core relationship in life was powerful, too. I also learned some new ways to have safe sex.

This book is a terrific read and I will be lending it to many friends."

Beverly Todd, BS
English Education
Acquisitions Librarian
Estes Park Public Library
Estes Park, Colorado

"**A**s a life-long serial monogamist, I found the *Reader* to be entertaining, informative and thought-provoking. The combination of theoretical and personal essays is potent: the first forced me to question my long-held assumptions about love and relationships; the second showed me real-live lesbians actually navigating the uncharted waters of a polyamorous world. This book amused me, disturbed me, and opened my monogamous eyes. But I still can't figure out where these girls find the time."

Terry Baum
Playwright, Producer

The Lesbian Polyamory Reader: Open Relationships, Non-Monogamy, and Casual Sex

The Lesbian Polyamory Reader: Open Relationships, Non-Monogamy, and Casual Sex has been co-published as *Journal of Lesbian Studies,* Volume 3, Numbers 1/2 1999.

The Lesbian Polyamory Reader: Open Relationships, Non-Monogamy, and Casual Sex

Marcia Munson
Judith P. Stelboum, PhD
Editors

The Lesbian Polyamory Reader: Open Relationships, Non-Monogamy, and Casual Sex, edited by Marcia Munson and Judith P. Stelboum, was issued by The Haworth Press, Inc., under the same title as a special issue of *Journal of Lesbian Studies*, Volume 3, Numbers 1/2 1999, Esther D. Rothblum, Editor.

Harrington Park Press
An Imprint of
The Haworth Press, Inc.
New York • London

ISBN 1-56023-120-3

Published by

Harrington Park Press, 10 Alice Street, Binghamton, NY 13904-1580 USA

Harrington Park Press is an imprint of the Haworth Press, Inc., 10 Alice Street, Binghamton, NY 13904-1580 USA.

The Lesbian Polyamory Reader: Open Relationships, Non-Monogamy, and Casual Sex has been co-published as *Journal of Lesbian Studies,* Volume 3, Numbers 1/2 1999.

Cover design by Jessie Gilmer

Cover photo *Three Is Not a Crowd* by Shoshana Rothaizer

Library of Congress Cataloging-in-Publication Data

The lesbian polyamory reader : open relationships, non-monogamy, and casual sex / Marcia Munson, Judith P. Stelboum, editors.
     p. cm.
    Includes bibliographical references and index.
    ISBN 0-7890-0660-X (alk. paper).–ISBN 1-56023-120-3 (alk. paper)
     1. Lesbians–United States–Sexual behavior. 2. Group sex–United States. 3. Free love–United States. 4. Lesbian feminism–United States. I. Munson, Marcia. II. Stelboum, Judith P. III. Journal of lesbian studies.
HQ75.6.U5L385 1999
306.76′63–dc21
                                                        99-10965
                                                         CIP

INDEXING & ABSTRACTING

Contributions to this publication are selectively indexed or abstracted in print, electronic, online, or CD-ROM version(s) of the reference tools and information services listed below. This list is current as of the copyright date of this publication. See the end of this section for additional notes.

- *Abstracts in Social Gerontology: Current Literature on Aging*

- *BUBL Information Service, an Internet-based Information Service for the UK higher education community*

- *CNPIEC Reference Guide: Chinese National Directory of Foreign Periodicals*

- *Contemporary Women's Issues*

- *Feminist Periodicals: A Current Listing of Contents*

- *Gay & Lesbian Abstracts*

- *GenderWatch*

- *HOMODOK/"Relevant" Bibliographic database, Documentation Centre for Gay & Lesbian Studies, University of Amsterdam (selective printed abstracts in "Homologie" and bibliographic computer databases covering cultural, historical, social and political aspects of gay & lesbian topics)*

- *Index to Periodical Articles Related to Law*

- *PAIS (Public Affairs Information Service) NYC*

- *Referativnyi Zhurnal (Abstracts Journal of the All-Russian Institute of Scientific and Technical Information)*

- *Sociological Abstracts (SA)*

- *Studies on Women Abstracts*

- *Women's Studies Index (indexed comprehensively)*

(continued)

Special Bibliographic Notes related to special journal issues
(separates) and indexing/abstracting:

- indexing/abstracting services in this list will also cover material in any "separate" that is co-published simultaneously with Haworth's special thematic journal issue or DocuSerial. Indexing/abstracting usually covers material at the article/chapter level.
- monographic co-editions are intended for either non-subscribers or libraries which intend to purchase a second copy for their circulating collections.
- monographic co-editions are reported to all jobbers/wholesalers/approval plans. The source journal is listed as the "series" to assist the prevention of duplicate purchasing in the same manner utilized for books-in-series.
- to facilitate user/access services all indexing/abstracting services are encouraged to utilize the co-indexing entry note indicated at the bottom of the first page of each article/chapter/contribution.
- this is intended to assist a library user of any reference tool (whether print, electronic, online, or CD-ROM) to locate the monographic version if the library has purchased this version but not a subscription to the source journal.
- individual articles/chapters in any Haworth publication are also available through the Haworth Document Delivery Service (HDDS).

Illustrations

Three Is Not a Crowd   Cover

The Three of Cups   69

Healing Hands   70

May Day Celebration   123

Festival Showers   124

Traveling Amazons   177

The Henna Heads   178

All photographs by Shoshana Rothaizer and used here by permission.

ABOUT THE PHOTOGRAPHER

Shoshana Rothaizer is a native New Yorker who often looks for lyrical and humorous qualities in her photographic subjects. Shoshana's photos (and in some instances, her writing) have been published in *Garden Variety Dykes, Cats (and Their Dykes), The New Our Right to Love: A Lesbian Anthology, Becoming a Woman: The Socialization of Gender, Women's Lives: Themes and Variations in Gender Learning, American Women Artists: A History of Women Working in Three Dimensions* and *Lesbian Land* (including the cover image). Her work has also been in periodicals such as *The Advocate, off our backs, The Bay Guardian, Womanews, Womanspirit, The Blatant Image,* and *Pagan Place.* In addition, she has often been included in group photography exhibits.

A brochure of Shoshana's photo postcards is available by mailing a self-addressed stamped envelope to Shoshana Rothaizer, 147-44 69th Road, Flushing, NY 11367-1784.

ABOUT THE EDITORS

Marcia Munson is a writer, researcher, and sex educator. Her articles have appeared in the periodicals *On Our Backs, Weird Sisters, Girljock,* and the journal *Women & Therapy.* She has contributed to the anthologies *On My Honor: Lesbians Reflect on Their Scouting Experiences, Dyke Life,* and *Lesbian Friendships.* Her essays on single lesbians, safer sex, and lesbian sex are included in *The Encyclopedia of Lesbian Histories and Cultures.* Marcia has a BS in biology and a Certificate as an Advisor/Instructor of HIV/STD Prevention from the Institute for Advanced Study of Human Sexuality. She has led workshops on lesbian sexuality at the Michigan Women's Music Festival, the University of Colorado Women's Week, and the Billy DeFrank Community Center.

Judith Stelboum, PhD, is Associate Professor of English, Women's Studies, and Lesbian Studies at the College of Staten Island, City University of New York. She is also the Editor of the *Harrington Lesbian Fiction Quarterly*, published by Harrington Park Press, and a reviewer/ essayist for the *Lesbian Review of Books*. Her essays, fiction and poetry have appeared in *Common Lives/Lesbian Lives*, in *Sinister Wisdom*, and in the anthologies *Sister and Brother, Dyke Life, Resist: Essays Against a Homophobic Culture, Not the Only One, Heat Wave, Tangled Sheets, Hot Ticket,* and *Best Lesbian Erotica '98*. In addition, Dr. Stelboum has written a brief, critical biography on two American Lesbian poets, Olga Broumas and Marilyn Hacker, for the *Oxford Companion to Twentieth Century Literature in English*, and her essay *Monogamy–Non–monogamy* is included in *The History of Homosexuality: Vol. 1: Lesbian Histories and Cultures.*

CONTENTS

Foreword: Rhomboid Pegs for Oblong Hearts
  Donna Allegra   xv

Introduction: The Lesbian Polyamory Reader: Open
  Relationships, Non-Monogamy, and Casual Sex   1
  Marcia Munson
  Judith P. Stelboum

CHOOSING ALTERNATIVES

The Polyamory Quilt: Life's Lessons   11
  Anne Dal Vera

If This Is Tuesday, It Must Be Dee . . . Confessions
  of a Closet Polyamorist   23
  Nanette K. Gartrell

Lesbians as Luvbeins   35
  JoAnn Loulan

Patriarchal Monogamy   39
  Judith P. Stelboum

Turning Down the Jezebel Decibels   47
  Marny Hall

Poly Wants a Lover   63
  Ellen Orleans

FRIENDS AND LOVERS

Poly-Friendships   71
  Esther (Polyester?) Rothblum

Seven Poems for Three   85
  Amanda Kovattana

Addressee Unknown   97
       Karla Jay

Bad Friend Book   105
       Katharine Matthaei Sprecher

The Spontaneous Imaginative Life   111
       Joanne Hetherington
       K. Linda Kivi
       Catherine Fisher
       Lyn Merryfeather

LIVING THE DREAM

Matriarchal Village   125
       Thyme S. Siegel

A Boomer's View of Non-Monogamy   135
       Molly Martin

Impossible Body   143
       Lisa Lusero

Paradigms of Polyamory   151
       Margarita Zambrano

If Love Is So Wonderful, What's So Scary About MORE?   157
       Ellen L. Halpern

A Long Journey Towards Polyamorous Bliss   165
       Cynthia Deer

SO MANY WOMEN, SO LITTLE TIME

Kitaka's Experiment; or, Why I Started the Ecstasy Lounge   179
       Kitaka

("Denny's Tune") I'm Not Monogamous Anymore, But . . .   185
       Alix Dobkin

Dinah, Sam, Beth, and Jolyn Say   189
       Merril Mushroom

Gays to Marry? Let's Not!   197
       Martha McPheeters

Canary in the Coal Mine   205
       Teri

Safer Sex and the Polyamorous Lesbian   209
       Marcia Munson

Models of Open Relationships   217
       Kathy Labriola

The Flexible House: A Fairy Tale   227
       Kathryn Werhane

Index   235

Foreword:
Rhomboid Pegs for Oblong Hearts

Many who profess to worship at the altar of monogamy with a picket fence surrounding hearth and home also want the leeway to slip out the back door and have a little something on the side. Naturally, they think they must lie to the Mrs. or else risk losing that primary relationship and its hope of happily ever after.

Like most people, I was nursed by television, radio and film on models for sexual love that told of love-at-first-sight-unto-forever-and-ever amen. Still, many lesbians and non-lesbians alike experience the anguish of sexual interest refusing to settle down until death-do-us part from a one-and-only.

This is good news.

In the good old days of yore, feminist thought focused on identifying the constructs of patriarchy and dismantling its prison cells. The second wave of feminism explained how marriage, and its younger brother, monogamy, stemmed from women's oppression.

It's no small task to stand aside from Noah's Ark relationship structures and uproot them from our consciousness. But for lesbians to

Donna Allegra writes fiction, poetry, and essays. Her recent work is anthologized in: *Dyke Life: From Growing Up to Growing Old–A Celebration of the Lesbian Experience,* edited by Karla Jay; *Close Calls: New Lesbian Fiction,* edited by Susan Fox Rogers; *Queerly Classed–Gay Men & Lesbians Write About Class,* edited by Susan Raffo; *Best Lesbian Erotica 1997,* edited by Tristan Taormino and Jewelle Gomez; and *Does Your Mama Know?–An Anthology of Black Lesbian Coming-Out Stories,* edited by Lisa Moore.

Address correspondence to Donna Allegra, 60 East 4th Street, Apartment #3, New York, NY 10003.

[Haworth co-indexing entry note]: "Foreword: Rhomboid Pegs for Oblong Hearts." Allegra, Donna. Co-published simultaneously in *Journal of Lesbian Studies* (The Haworth Press, Inc.) Vol. 3, No. 1/2, 1999, pp. xxi-xxiv; and: *The Lesbian Polyamory Reader: Open Relationships, Non-Monogamy, and Casual Sex* (ed: Marcia Munson and Judith P. Stelboum) The Haworth Press, Inc., 1999, pp. xv-xviii.Single or multiple copies of this article are available for a fee from The Haworth Document Delivery Service [1-800-342-9678, 9:00 a.m. - 5:00 p.m. (EST). E-mail address: getinfo@haworthpressinc.com].

aspire no further than the heterosexual-style couple reminds me of the goldfish taken out of its bowl and set free in a pond: the fish swam in circles no larger than the size of its previous tiny glass enclosure.

What to do? Admit that monogamy isn't the whole kit and caboodle. Then, go through the difficult process of re-inventing the wheel of relationships that probably turned the world before patriarchy shackled women to one man at a time.

The fact is, human beings can and do want to have a variety of sexual relationships with different people. Why is it so hard to be honest about this? Do I have to hate someone I once loved when she beds another? Our culture tells us that having more than one lover constitutes sexual betrayal to the formerly monogamous pair. We often have a hard time talking about our behavior when we are defying cultural norms. The human fact is that sex is a big deal, but whether it is the sex itself, or the dishonesty so often accompanying the act, that constitutes the betrayal is a matter up for discussion. Some of that discourse takes place in this groundbreaking collection of essays and personal accounts by women who have stepped aside from Sappho's ark.

Two-by-two in relationships doesn't cover the territory the way we have been told it is supposed to. A multi-billion dollar industry in self-help books and workshops–and a side industry in drugs, prescriptive and recreational–testifies to the fact that we're trying to fix a modus operandi that doesn't fit libidos.

We often want more than one sexual partner for any number of reasons. Structures for those sexual relations shouldn't be drawn to a flat world when we inhabit a round globe. How can we have and hold more than one woman without so much fuss and broken hearts, broken homes and messed-up bank accounts, not to mention custody for pets and CDs? Just how do you split a waterbed?

Part of the problem with approaching alternatives to pair-bonding is that we have no welcoming language for this ground in Eve's garden. The popular labels "slut," "homewrecker," and "cheat" aren't coveted nicknames that invite the seeker.

Even so, lesbians have grown in emotional intelligence to recognize that the relationship universe goes beyond monogamy to wider possibilities than an idealized pair of lovebirds cooing happily ever after. Many in lesbiandom are at that difficult and strange frontier of acknowledging that the marriage model isn't an accurate map for the heart's terrain.

This anthology lets us look at a familiar landscape, the standard configurations for sexual relationships, with new eyes.

Being outside the pale of legal sanctions, lesbians have a certain freedom to look for an ergonomic design that encompasses our relationship truths. We are not legally bound or economically dependent in our unions, unless we choose to go those extra miles, creating contracts, wills and powers of attorney. Even when we take the legal steps available to us, what we get is a far cry from the privileges married heterosexuals enjoy, as any court case will prove.

As lesbians approximate marriage in our partnerships, many of us hold to concepts of infidelity, adultery, and promiscuity to accuse the sexually adventurous and unconventional among us.

How liberating it would be, instead, to view the commonplace stories of our sexual partnering in new fashions. Familiar data would be given happier and broader possibilities for interpretation.

These essays answer questions I didn't know I had because no one was holding discussions on other manners with which to approach the life of the sexual heart. The propositions around polyamory feel totally new and make absolute sense. They widen the globe again. The language is awkward around "polyamory," but that will develop as the topic is explored. I remember the resistance to the word "lesbian" and the internalized homophobia feeding many people's reluctance to name ourselves. Perhaps our stumbling over the word polyamory reflects our discomfort with the concept.

I delight in the irreverent and subversive insights that feminists bring to any staple of heterosexual culture. We see through the masks that the emperor's new clothes put on over naked sexism. Polyamorous narratives become like feminist re-writings of fairy tales. In this volume, patriarchal myths are turned on their heads. A wizard's spell is broken and we are set free from the smoke and mirrors that mesmerized us to believe in the power of monogamy.

This volume dares to think beyond the mundane blinders that the social structure of patriarchy sets on us all: those dust motes of sound that stifle our music. Who says that the fast girl on the block, the unwed mother, or the other woman has to be a bad girl? The notion of polyamory as feminists conceive it sings to a wider range of connections that entail sexual love.

This is the first anthology to serve as a guide for lesbians in the throes of inventing a new wheel. We need to hear from scouts who've traversed the way. What can be found along the unmarked path where we link with multiple lovers without scandal or shame? How exhilarating, heady, lusty to find testimonials that desire for more sexual love need not be saddled to the two-some or reined-in by its attendant unspoken rules. Uncharted realms beckon us to reconfigure our designs for love to better suit the heart.

Donna Allegra

Introduction:
The Lesbian Polyamory Reader:
Open Relationships, Non-Monogamy,
and Casual Sex

This anthology contains personal accounts of the joys, problems, struggles, and successes of living life with multiple intimate involvements. Also included are theoretical articles and analytical essays addressing the political and social significance of choosing a lovestyle other than monogamous coupling. Not all lesbians practice or idealize lesbian coupling, and not all successful long-term couples are monogamous. Not all sexual partnerships are limited to two people, and not all satisfying love affairs lead to primary relationships.

The term "polyamory" literally means "many loves." While loving several people simultaneously is the reality of most people's lives, the term polyamory usually implies sexual involvement with more than one person.

In the 1980s, the term "non-monogamy" was used to describe multiple concurrent sexual involvements. In the 1970s, after the release of Nena and George O'Neil's book *Open Marriage*, people referred to "open relationships." In the 1960s, the term "free love" described the uninhibited, outside-of-marriage sexual connections suddenly made possible with the invention of the birth control pill, and the new ability of medical science to treat all known sexually transmitted diseases (STDs). In the 1950s, sex outside of a monogamous

[Haworth co-indexing entry note]: "Introduction: The Lesbian Polyamory Reader: Open Relationships, Non-Monogamy, and Casual Sex." Munson, Marcia, and Judith P. Stelboum. Co-published simultaneously in *Journal of Lesbian Studies* (The Haworth Press, Inc.) Vol. 3, No. 1/2, 1999, pp. 1-7; and: *The Lesbian Polyamory Reader: Open Relationships, Non-Monogamy, and Casual Sex* (ed: Marcia Munson and Judith P. Stelboum) The Haworth Press, Inc., 1999, pp. 1-7. Single or multiple copies of this article are available for a fee from The Haworth Document Delivery Service [1-800-342-9678, 9:00 a.m. - 5:00 p.m. (EST). E-mail address: getinfo@haworthpressinc.com].

1

couple relationship had simply been referred to as "cheating." The centuries-old double standard around sexuality was rooted in biology. Women who cheated were "loose." Men, less likely than women to acquire STDs from heterosexual intercourse, and not at all likely to become pregnant, were said to be "sowing wild seeds" when they had multiple sexual involvements.

The term "monogamy" means sexual involvement with only one partner, usually for life. The term "serial monogamy" refers to exclusive sexual coupling with one person at a time. The term "polyamory" includes many different styles of multiple intimate involvements, such as polyfidelity or group marriage; primary relationships open to secondary affairs; and casual sexual involvement with two or more people.

Polyamory compels us to question traditional definitions of fidelity, family, and intimacy. For instance, if a lesbian has other lovers while living with a woman, is she presumed by others to be unfaithful? Should we define fidelity for women within the restrictive male definition of sexuality? How do we broaden concepts of honesty or accommodate individual privacy? How do we face our jealousies, insecurities, and rage?

Before the Industrial Revolution of the late 1800s, most Americans lived an agrarian lifestyle. Extended families were the norm; sharing of tools and supplies by neighbors was common; work roles were not necessarily divided along gender lines. The long hours and grueling conditions of factory work created the necessity for wage earner/homemaker partnerships, giving rise to what we now consider "traditional family roles." Corporate profits required expanding markets, so the idea of "owning your own everything" was popularized through advertising. Martha McPheeters, in "Gays to Marry? Let's Not!" describes how ownership of a spouse is related to a consumerist mentality. She attacks the homogenization of lesbians into straight society through the institution of marriage, and warns us that "pair bonding that requires a license certainly leads to a society that is easier to control."

The subject of polyamory needs to be discussed using a new frame of reference. Feelings such as jealousy, possessiveness, control, and privacy all have to be understood from a new perspective. Lesbian bed death and the realities of lesbian merging are two other elements that enter into any analysis of polyamory: multiple intimate involvements can offer relief from both these problems. Kathryn Werhane portrays the importance of including an intense and passionate affair in a stable, otherwise traditional coupled life in "The Flexible House: A Fairy Tale."

In her chapter "Turning Down the Jezebel Decibels," Marny Hall tackles the "big J" which she breaks down into "little j's" by analyzing the feelings behind jealousy: fear of loss, poor self-esteem, a sense of powerlessness. She describes techniques which can be helpful in overcoming, or at least coping with, jealous feelings that can threaten any relationship.

The question of how to best communicate with multiple partners is a recurring theme in this collection. Ellen Orleans, in "Poly Wants a Lover," assures us that she knows from her reading that polyamory requires "no sneaking around." In her story "If This Is Tuesday, It Must Be Dee . . ." Nanette Gartrell describes how, over the years, she has learned to use discretion in sharing details of her love life. Cynthia Deer, in "A Long Journey Towards Polyamorous Bliss," writes of the night she felt the truth/privacy continuum bending until the ends of the line met, creating a circle of communication skills that included "tact, honesty, intimacy, privacy, truth, fiction, kindness, and common sense."

Another recurring theme in this volume is the question of knowing what you want and seeking it out, versus letting relationships evolve. Kathy Labriola's theoretical article "Models of Open Relationships" wisely suggests that for any kind of relationship to work, it's best to know what you want, then find someone who wants the same thing. However, the true-life adventure stories paint a different reality. Molly Martin, in "A Boomer's View of Non-Monogamy," talks of experimenting with different relationship styles over her two decades as a lesbian, being influenced by partners' desires and shifting community norms. Amanda Kovattana's "Seven Poems for Three" portrays love relationships growing and changing in ways none of the partners would have predicted.

The U-Haul Syndrome, a long-joked-about tendency of lesbians to move in together on the second date, is a logical progression of events for two women who have been taught to believe that sex is only good if you are in love, that love and marriage go together, and that good women don't "cheat" on their spouses. Adding these three common beliefs to small doses of touch starvation and horniness can lead a lesbian to move in with a new lust object without much dating, discovery, experimentation, or consideration of options.

Lesbian polyamory offers an alternative to the U-Haul Syndrome. The casual sex with dates, play partners, or friends described in this volume may sometimes have a less intense emotional component than exclusive sexual involvement with one lover, but should not be dismissed as devoid of intimacy, or lacking the possibility of future fulfillment. One of the most intriguing entries is Kitaka's account of why she started the Ecstasy Lounge, San Francisco's 1990s lesbian sex club.

Anne Dal Vera, in "The Polyamory Quilt: Life's Lessons," tells how multiple involvements lead to increased intimacy. She urges readers "to continue to make intimate, passionate, wild connections between women, not to restrict relations due to fear and absolutism."

In "Matriarchal Village," Thyme S. Siegel writes about her experiences living on lesbian land with a community of country dykes who believed in sharing everything. Shoshana Rothaizer's photos, and several of the articles, remind us that open relationships were the norm in many lesbian feminist communities of the 1970s. Karla Jay's story informs us that current visions of polyamory may also include academic conferences, and Ellen Halpern writing as a bisexual woman expands the context of polyamory even further.

In reading this collection, many lesbians will think that polyamory is an interesting idea, and wonder how to make it work. After all, there are daily conflicts and problems, logistics of arranging schedules, possible feelings of anger or guilt. Katharine Matthaei Sprecher, in *Bad Friend Book*, demonstrates that many conflicts simply cannot be resolved.

A group of Canadian lesbians write about their day-to-day travails and the necessity for the four of them to keep open minds and hearts along with their open relationships. "The Spontaneous Imaginative Life" reveals their thoughts and feelings over a period of several months in a journal shared by the four lovers.

Some of the writers tell of lesbian friendships that included sexuality at one time in their histories. Many lesbians can relate to this topic through the legendary link of lesbians and ex-lovers and ex-lovers' lovers who have all maintained varying degrees of friendships over the years. But a sexual connection is not necessary for passionate love to exist. In her essay "Poly-Friendships," Esther Rothblum decries the emphasis the culture places on sexuality as the ultimate intimacy, while ignoring the value of loving friendships.

Many women go through stages of polyamory and stages of monogamy during their lesbian lives. Alix Dobkin, in "I'm Not Monogamous Anymore, But . . ." wrote about the time she was totally smitten with a new lover, soon after declaring herself non-monogamous. Margarita Zambrano, in "Paradigms of Polyamory," describes her transition from monogamy to a life of multiple relationships. Merril Mushroom's "Dinah, Sam, Beth, and Jolyn Say" captures varied lesbian attitudes towards non-monogamy. JoAnn Loulan, in "Lesbians as Luvbeins," reminds us that lesbian love is to be cherished in its many varied forms.

Writing about lesbian polyamory seems particularly important in the late 1990s, as the efforts of gay rights activists around the U.S. are focused on seeking domestic partnership benefits and legal marriage between same-sex couples. Gay assimilationists try to present the image that we are just like heterosexuals, except for our choice of same-sex partners. In the 1970s, radical lesbian feminists rejected all patriarchal institutions, including monogamy. In the 1980s, as lesbians and gay men joined forces to fight AIDS, many lesbians were influenced by gay men's freer, more exotic, and playful sexual style. This happened at the same time that many gay men saw health reasons to curb their uninhibited sexuality.

Lesbian and gay male sexuality is currently evolving in opposite directions. Will it some day defy hormonal and cultural differences to meet on middle ground and become similar? In the 1990s, we hear gay men promoting monogamy as a way to gain acceptability in mainstream culture, and to prevent the further spread of AIDS. For example, Gabriel Rotello in *Sexual Ecology* and Michelangelo Signorile in *Life Outside* view non-monogamous behavior as infantile and dangerous.

At the same time, in the 1990s, lesbians have published a plethora of books celebrating uninhibited, non-traditional sexuality. Examples include Shar Rednour's anthologies *Virgin Territory I and II; The Persistent Desire*, edited by Joan Nestle; and *Making Out*, by Zoe Schramm-Evans. Celeste West's innovative book *Lesbian Polyfidelity* was released soon after we began collecting articles for this anthology. It is popular myth that polyamory is practiced by only a few lesbians. When 106 members of TLC, a lesbian social group in Boulder, Colorado, were surveyed in 1987 and again in 1997, two-thirds of the women with sexual partners defined themselves as monogamous, while the other third chose some other description for their current involvement, most commonly, "committed, open relationship." Clearly, a significant minority of these lesbians, in both decades, were living lives that might be considered polyamorous.

This anthology assumes a premise that lesbian lives are different from those of men or heterosexual women, and that lesbians can be models of alternative ways of living. We present personal and theoretical writing about loving partnerships that do not fit the traditional "monogamous couple" model.

The contributors to this volume represent a diversity of lesbian lives as well as a variety of professional and personal experiences. They include academics and scholarly writers, psychologists, a physician, fiction writers, a musician and performer, a poet, a playwright, an owner of a lesbian club, a wilderness ranger, several lesbian mothers, and an environmental educator. Their experiences reflect both rural and urban viewpoints. Single and coupled lesbians in their 20s, 30s, 40s, 50s, and 60s are included. Diversity of class, age, race, ethnicity, and geography was on our minds as we collected the pieces for this volume. The openness and honesty of all the contributors is only a beginning. Our hope is to encourage those who have not written to do so in future collections.

Finally, we are full co-editors. Our names are listed in alphabetical order.

Marcia Munson
San Francisco
Judith P. Stelboum
Manhattan
January 1998

REFERENCES

Munson, M. (1987). How do you do it? *On Our Backs*, 1, 12.
Nestle, J. (1992). *The persistent desire*. Boston: Alyson Publications.
O'Neil, N. & O'Neil, G. (1972). *Open marriage*. New York: Avon Books.
Rednour, S. (1996). *Virgin territory I & II*. New York: Masquerade Books.
Rotello, G. (1997). *Sexual ecology*. New York: Dutton Books.
Schramm-Evans, Z. *Making out*. San Francisco: Harper Collins.
Signorile, M. (1997). *Life outside*. San Francisco: Harper Collins.
West, C. (1996). *Lesbian polyfidelity*. San Francisco: Booklegger Publishing.

FOR FURTHER READING

Anapol, D. (1992). *Love without limits: Responsible non-monogamy.* San Raphael, CA: Intinet Resource Center.

Duggan, L., & Hunter, N. (1995). *Sex wars.* New York: Routledge.

D'Emilio, J., & Freedman, E.(1988). *Intimate matters: A history of sexuality in America.* New York: Harper and Row.

Eisler, R. (1987). *The chalice and the blade.* San Francisco: Harper Collins.

Fisher, H. (1992). *Anatomy of love: The natural history of monogamy, adultery, and divorce.* New York: Ballantine Books.

Gimbutas, M. (1989). *Civilization and the goddess.* San Francisco: Harper Collins.

Hall, M. (1998). *The lesbian love companion: How to survive everything from heartthrob to heartache.* San Francisco: Harper Collins.

Hoagland, S. (1988). *Lesbian ethics: Toward new value.* Palo Alto, CA. Institute of Lesbian Studies.

Johnson, S. (1991). *The Ship that sailed into the living room.* New Mexico: Wildfire Books.

Kassoff, E. (1989). Non-monogamy in the lesbian community. *Women & Therapy, 8,* 167-182.

Klaw, S. (1993). *Without sin: The life and death of the Oneida Community.* New York: Penguin.

Nearing, R. (1992). *Loving more: The polyfidelity primer.* Hawaii: PEP Publications.

Raymond, J. (1986). *A passion for friends: Toward a philosophy of female affection.* Boston: Beacon Press.

Stansell, C., & Thompson, S. (Eds.) (1983). *Powers of desire.* New York: Monthly Review Press.

Stein, A. (1997). *Sex and sensibility.* Berkeley: University of California Press.

Stone, M. (1976). *When god was a woman.* New York: Harcourt, Brace.

Vance, C. S. (Ed.) (1989). *Pleasure and danger.* London: Pandora Press.

Vaughan, P. (1989). *The monogamy myth.* New York: Newmarket Press.

CHOOSING ALTERNATIVES

The Polyamory Quilt:
Life's Lessons

Anne Dal Vera

SUMMARY. A patchwork quilt of panels made by friends is the metaphor for the lessons of life, love and polyamory of the author. She discusses intimacy, jealousy, friendship, and honesty in the context of monogamy and polyamory. She also offers hope for lesbians to have continuing connections based on deep, lasting unconditional love. *[Article copies available for a fee from The Haworth Document Delivery Service: 1-800-342-9678. E-mail address: getinfo@haworthpressinc.com]*

Life is a patchwork quilt of experiences, each part fitting into a pattern. The patchwork of my life experiences, like a quilt, is a result

Anne Dal Vera is a wilderness ranger in Colorado and has worked and skied in Antarctica. She was a member of the 1992-93 American Women's Antarctic Expedition (AWE), the first all-women expedition to ski to the South Pole. She has published stories of the AWE expedition in *Another Wilderness: New Outdoor Writings by Women* (Seal Press, 1994, Susan Fox Rogers, editor), *Travelers' Tales, A Woman's World* (Travelers' Tales, Inc., 1995, Marybeth Bond, editor), and *Women's Voices in Experiential Education* (Kendall Hunt Publishing, 1996, Karen Warren, editor).

Address correspondence to Anne Dal Vera, P.O. Box 1157, Frisco, CO 80443.

The author would like to thank all her friends for being a part of the story of her life. Many of the names and some of the details of events have been changed to respect the privacy of individuals who are very special to the author. Abundant thanks are also extended to Better-Me-Than-You Research Services for editing assistance and for locating some of the references quoted in this article.

[Haworth co-indexing entry note]: "The Polyamory Quilt: Life's Lessons." Vera, Anne Dal. Co-published simultaneously in *Journal of Lesbian Studies* (The Haworth Press, Inc.) Vol. 3, No. 1/2, 1999, pp. 11-22; and: *The Lesbian Polyamory Reader: Open Relationships, Non-Monogamy, and Casual Sex* (ed: Marcia Munson and Judith P. Stelboum) The Haworth Press, Inc., 1999, pp. 11-22. Single or multiple copies of this article are available for a fee from The Haworth Document Delivery Service [1-800-342-9678, 9:00 a.m. - 5:00 p.m. (EST). E-mail address: getinfo@haworthpressinc.com].

of knowing many women as friends and lovers. In the pioneer days of America, women gathered together to quilt, using the remnants of material they had on hand to create beautiful patterns stitched intently as they talked about their lives. Just as each piece of the quilt adds to the pattern, color, and texture of the whole, each of the women I've loved has contributed to my understanding and experience of polyamory, and love, and life. The quilt of my life continues to evolve as I continue loving women.

EARLY LEARNINGS ABOUT MONOGAMY

I remember growing up in a nuclear family and thinking that was the only way people lived. It meant a stable and secure life, with someone (Dad) who brought home the money and someone (Mom) who took care of the kids and cooked the food and made sure that things went smoothly at home. The kids did chores and washed the dishes. I was happy and secure in this situation, although the Catholic Church tried to make me feel plenty of guilt and shame about simply being female.

My father, like most American men of his time, dominated the family. He got his way all the time. Whenever my mother had a good idea about the family, she would manipulate my father into thinking it was his idea. She learned early in their relationship that he would not accept her ideas as valid. I certainly didn't want to repeat those patterns of relating. I wanted something different when I grew up.

In high school I was supposed to date boys. But I was not interested in boys. My emotional life was full of my friends' struggles and traumas. All my friends were girls. That was all I cared about. Besides, I had a huge fear that if I went out with a boy it would lead to more dates, and then going steady and then marriage. And then kids, and being stuck. I definitely didn't want that! So I figured I'd better not even get started. It all seemed to me to be about owning a woman's body, mind and spirit. And I certainly didn't want to be a possession of some man.

I saw how women were expected to go from being named with their father's name to their husband's name. That is one sign of possession—naming. Then I saw that my mother couldn't even be credited with coming up with her own good ideas. And I saw the expectation that a woman would be monogamous with her husband and I asked, "Why? Does he own her body?"

BECOMING A POLYAMOROUS LESBIAN

When I finally did come out in the early seventies, I was thrilled with the newness of being a lesbian. I was 21 and life was full of possibilities. I was also discovering feminism. The idea that lesbians could create new ways of having relationships not based on possessiveness was very appealing to me. Many women-identified women were exploring non-monogamy, creating a world different from and better than the patriarchal limits we grew up with. "Lesbian-feminists were convinced that monogamy was bad not because it inhibited wild sexual exploration, but rather because it smacked too much of patriarchal capitalism and imperialism. It was men's way of keeping women enslaved. People are not things to own, lesbian-feminists said. No lesbian should want to have the right to imprison another human being emotionally or sexually. The most popular lesbian-feminist novels, such as Rita Mae Brown's *Rubyfruit Jungle* (1973) and June Arnold's *Sister Gin* (1975), reflected the community's distrust of monogamy, which the authors presented as inhibiting a free exploration of self and detracting from one's commitment to the lesbian-feminist community, since it led to nesting rather than involvement in political work" (Faderman, 1991, p. 233).

Non-fiction writing of lesbian-feminists of the seventies also reflected a desire to create new lifestyles independent of the restrictions of patriarchy. In *Our Right to Love, a Lesbian Resource Book,* Jeri Dilno (1978) wrote of the difficulties of finding alternative lifestyles:

> The issue of monogamy versus non-monogamy is being debated in women's communities everywhere. It would seem a logical step for lesbians to extend their rejection of the standards of heterosexual marriage to include monogamy. It isn't that easy. The society that brought us up, that we live in most of the time, and that provides us with the cultural reinforcement that helps to shade our identities, is strongly couple-oriented. (Dilno, 1978, p. 57)

Still others were creating collectives of lesbian separatists who worked to overthrow capitalism and fight classism, racism, sexism, and heterosexism.

We must move out of our old living patterns and into new ones. Those of us who believe in this concept must begin to build collectives where women are committed to other women on all levels–emotional, physical, economic, and political. Monogamy can be cast aside, no one will "belong" to another. Instead of being shut off from each other in overpriced cubicles we can be together, sharing the shitwork as well as the highs. Together we can go through the pain and liberation of curing the diseases we have all contracted in the world of male dominance, imperialism and death. Women-identified collectives are nothing less than the next step towards a Women's Revolution. (Brown, 1976, p. 67)

Reading all these interesting points of view was very exciting for me in the 1970s. I began to question the principles I had grown up with. Rejecting the ideal of "saving myself sexually for marriage," I learned about myself as a sexual being with friends. Sex was exciting and confusing and full of wonder and fear. In my early twenties, I couldn't imagine that I would be involved with more than one woman at a time, because that seemed to be too frightening.

Still, I knew I had feelings of attraction for many women. What if I acted on those feelings? Perhaps it would be fun. While I was in my first long-term relationship, I got involved with a younger single woman. And my lover June slept with another woman a couple of times. We both knew of these involvements and we knew that we were primary to each other. Still, being in this multiple relationship scheme did reveal a lack of assertiveness on my part. As a result, the two women I felt strongly about didn't know what I wanted or how I felt about each of them.

I didn't feel jealous about the fact that June had slept with someone else. And I didn't feel jealous later when she had a clandestine affair with a man. Instead, I felt crazy having the perception that they were having an affair, when June would not speak the truth of her involvement with him. I thought June would tell me if she was sleeping with him. But days went by and nothing was said. Finally I asked. She broke into tears and admitted it, saying, "I was going to tell you, but I couldn't figure out how to tell you." My main reaction was one of relief to finally know what was going on. She went through a lot of confusion and soul searching for six months. After that she broke off our relationship of 8 years, her confusion resolved. Still I thought that lesbians could do things differently. We didn't have to give up on one relationship to have another.

THE GIFT OF A QUILT

About a year after I came out, I was given a magical quilt, made by my best friend Sunshine. She had cut the many pieces by hand from pieces of neck scarves from summer camps where we had worked together. In 1972 I didn't know how to deal with the love I felt for Sunshine. We became as close as two friends could, and when my desire to express my love for her became sexual, she got scared. She didn't want that. We drifted apart. For several years we each went our own way. I cherished the quilt, and it aged with me. Many lovers shared that quilt with me and came to know me in ways that Sunshine never did.

Gradually, the fear and anger that Sunshine and I had subsided. We each found peace in our lives and resumed our friendship. She visited me with her small son and I showed her how I still loved the quilt, though it had become threadbare. She thought she could repair it, and she took it home to Washington.

After some time, Sunshine sent me a new, beautiful quilt, lovingly sewn together. Friends and former lovers from all over the country had contributed panels for the quilt. In each panel I could see the character of a friend, a lover, someone who still cared for me after years of friendship. The love that emanated from that quilt gave me the strength to take on the next big adventure and the stability to deal with challenges.

Even now, as I look at that quilt, I am drawn to examine the web of friendships around me. I am also thrilled by the memories of women I have loved and still love. The times we share are so exquisite, so full of magic! The boldness of these women is expressed in the creations they made for me, in the patterns of their work.

While not all of these treasured friends have been lovers of mine, a surprising number have been. Sex can be a way to share friendship. Sex is a basic need, like food, water, shelter, community, fresh air, and spirituality. These are all things we enjoy sharing with our friends. Friends can share sex too. The ties that we form as friends and lovers are strong bonds. Some of the roles we play in our lives change as well.

LONG-TERM POLYAMOROUS RELATIONSHIP

For eight years I was in a mutually open relationship with Martha, a bold and adventurous woman. She or I would occasionally have an "alter-honey," a woman lover who was involved with one of us. Martha and I discovered that we had different tastes in women (we are very different from each other). Early on in our relationship we agreed that we could not and would not be expected to meet all of each other's needs. We affirmed what we each cherished about each other and were honest about the things we did not do for each other. We had some structure or boundaries to the way that we found an "alter-honey." We agreed that on any given night we would first sleep with each other if that were at all possible. This was to avoid the uncertainty of wondering where each other's loyalties were. An alter-honey would need to live at least 50 miles away. Martha and I sometimes spent several weeks apart working in different states. So that did allow for some extended time to enjoy another exciting adventure with a willing woman. We also were clear with our alter-honeys that the relationship Martha and I had was important and strong; ours was a primary relationship. This meant that our relationship would have priority if decisions became difficult.

At times, if either Martha or I was feeling insecure, because of unemployment, or moving to a new place, one could ask the other to refrain from acting on other attractions for awhile. For myself, I enjoyed life with Martha. We shared a lot of the same values and were great outdoor adventure buddies. Our sex together was superb. Having alter-honeys added variety and excitement to our lives and met some of those needs that we couldn't provide for each other. After 8 years, Martha and I split up to go our separate ways. This was hard, but not a failure. We realized that we had each changed, and we were following different paths.

MANAGING POLYAMORY

Since then, I have enjoyed the affection of friends who have become lovers. Knowing someone before entering the realm of intimacy does not mean that there will not be surprises and changes of heart. I once embraced a fun, no commitment, intense, emotional and sexual connection with a lovely friend. Gradually she began to wish for our lives to be intertwined forever and to have a strong desire for a commitment to lifelong monogamy. Although I was tempted to grasp the security that seemed to offer, a small voice inside asked me, "Are you doing this out of fear?" And I had to admit I was. I was fearful of losing her if I didn't pledge monogamy. But if I did, would I be true to myself? I couldn't agree to making such a serious commitment out of fear. To me, commitment means doing what I say I will do. I have to be trustworthy to myself before I can be trusted by another. Time and experience with each other, knowing that each is good to her word, develops trust.

Honesty is an important value of mine. I never learned to lie, and I feel that secrets eat at a person until she is no longer aware of who she is. Besides, lies don't work. As Celeste West says in her book *Lesbian Polyfidelity,* "NEVER underestimate the fabled Lesbian radar, *laydar.* Lesbians seem born with a deeply-set crystal for sensing any foreign body vibration. With high decoding powers, laydar ultimately hits target" (1996, p. 74). In addition, I don't want to be part of a deception that leads to a feeling of resentment and betrayal. Betrayal is a deep and lasting hurt. I would rather deal with the consequences of an honest disclosure, made with respect for the listener's feelings.

Saying all this, it was with great apprehension that I once became the "odd woman" in a secret affair, one where my lover's partner didn't know about my involvement. This was very hard for me. I struggled with the secret, worrying that I was party to a deception. I didn't want to split the two of them apart. Couple-ness is so strongly assumed to be the norm in the U.S., even within the lesbian community. Often, the "odd woman" in a threesome is assumed to have an agenda of splitting the original couple apart in order to form a new couple. I didn't want that. The dynamic of being in a secret love relationship finally eroded my trust in myself and my lover. I asked for a disclosure of our love, and my lover was able to do that in a way that respected her own integrity and her primary relationship.

From my relationship with Martha I learned how to be honest without going into excessive detail. I didn't need to tell her what I did with my alter-honey or how good the sex was. What was important for her to know was that I loved her for who she was and for the unique things she brought to my life. Martha also loved other women, and for their uniqueness as well. She didn't compare us. I knew that she would not leave me. Once, when she was seriously tempted by a proposal for a monogamous commitment with another woman, I felt lost and alone and frightened. But I did not feel betrayed, because I knew what was up. Later, Martha chose to stay with me rather than be locked into monogamy with the other woman.

INTIMACY

My friends tell me that there is still circulating a myth that women are polyamorous because they are avoiding "healthy adult intimacy." I first heard this over 12 years ago. I think this dogma is a way to keep women in a certain prescribed set of monogamous behaviors which may not be true for them.

Intimacy is a closeness or bond that one feels as a result of mutual sharing of a part of oneself with another. It can be sharing a challenging physical adventure; emotional bonding, as friends share personal feelings; intellectual intimacy from working on a tough mental problem together; or a deep spiritual connection. A sexual experience can be part of any of these times of intimacy. Or it can stand as its own intimate connection between women. Intimacy happens with friends, lovers, confidants, peers, mentors, and therapists to name a few. There are levels or circles of intimacy that we choose with different people in our lives. All can be healthy, sane and mature.

I say it is a myth that only those who choose serial monogamy can achieve "healthy adult intimacy." This myth is based on a scarcity model that simply doesn't hold true. If anything, I've seen monogamous couples become less intimate over time because they develop set expectations of one another and they think they know all there is to know of the other person. They don't search for the unexpected. I did this myself with June, and I called it complacency. (With hindsight, of course.) When she changed, I didn't want to join her in the direction her life was taking her.

With polyamory, there is an abundance of opportunity to explore intimacy. Different lovers are interested in looking at various aspects of who I am. They ask a diversity of questions. With each intimate there is a medley of conflicts; distinct concerns surface. Even the friction that arises over issues brought up by multiple sexualoves can create situations where we learn about each other.

Intimacy should not be confused with exclusivity. Exclusivity is keeping people away. Intimacy is welcoming someone closer. Monogamy is an attempt at exclusive intimacy. (Is that a contradiction of terms?) At the least it operates out of a scarcity model. A feeling of "I have only enough intimacy for one other in my life." Or perhaps it is felt that "if I share myself intimately with more than one person it reduces or negates the intimacy I have with each of them." I don't find that to be the case in my experience. In fact, during one of the most difficult times of my career, when I chose to confide in many friends, I found an increase in intimacy with each of them as they confided in me their difficulties and struggles and gave me support. I think many women have had that sort of experience.

The bond we feel with another person who is close to us is an essential basic need. It is as fundamental as clean air and water and a connection to the earth. Terry Tempest Williams encourages us to make the connections we need with each other and wilderness in *An Unspoken Hunger*: "But what kind of impoverishment is this to with-hold emotion, to restrain our passionate nature in the face of a gener-ous life just to appease our fears? A man or woman whose mind reins in the heart when the body sings desperately for connection can only expect more isolation and greater ecological disease. Our lack of inti-macy with each other is in direct proportion to our lack of intimacy with the land. We have taken our love inside and abandoned the wild" (1994, p. 64). We owe it to ourselves and to each other and the earth to continue to make intimate, passionate, wild connections between women, not to restrict relations due to fear and absolutism.

Sexual intimacy is, by its nature, no more demanding of exclusivity than is emotional intimacy. It is true that the level of sharing between lovers may be different. But intimacy with one does not mean the bond with another will necessarily decline. Sexual closeness can bring strong emotions to the surface. It can be intense. Sometimes real risks are taken. Hopefully, women can assess the risks and choose the ones they are ready to take, based on their skills, and willingness to be fully present and responsible. Those should be the guiding factors, not some assumption that monogamy is the only way to achieve "healthy adult intimacy," whatever that jargon means.

SEXUAL FRIENDSHIP IN THE MAGIC OF WILDERNESS

I've been fortunate to have dear, close friends who are curious about the world and wild places. Sometimes the wilderness worked its magic on us, and we found a curiosity about each other as well. The introduction of sexuality into our friendship seems natural. I liken this to a story a friend once told me about a sea kayak trip that she took in Maine. After she and her friend found a campsite on a small island, a three-masted wooden Windjammer schooner anchored off the island and about 45 tourists disembarked onto the island. The guide apologized to my friends for the inconvenience of having disturbed their solitude and invited them to a lobster picnic, complete with fresh baked apple pie! Pam didn't want to accept, but her friend, Tanya, said, "Pam, when a lobster picnic lands in your lap, enjoy it!"

If the magic of the wilderness works to bring two (or more) women together to explore each other, may they have a wonderful picnic! Once, Pam and I were sea kayaking off the coast of New Zealand, thoroughly enamored with the rhythm of the ocean tides and wind patterns. The miracle of wildlife–bottlenose dolphins checking out our yellow kayaks, and little blue penguins trumpeting to their families at dusk–gave us a heightened sense of awe of life. Our bodies, strong from weeks of daily paddling, relished each day's challenges and discoveries. Toward the end of the expedition she proposed having an affair. I was hesitant, then reminded myself of her story. We had a delicious "lobster picnic" of our own.

Yes, others are affected by the magic of a new affair. Old lovers usually sense the intensity of a new romance, whether or not it is openly discussed. Friends may be called on to be nurturing and supportive of the growth and discoveries that occur early in a new relationship. Processing honest feelings and realizations often is a stretch for everyone. But the bottom line is that for the polyamorous woman, it is not assumed that because a lover sleeps with someone else, she is no longer available in the original relationship. Everyone is asked to stretch in communication and self-knowledge.

POLYAMORY AS AN OPTION

Because we are culturally conditioned in the U.S. today to believe that monogamy is desirable, valuable and "the norm" (whatever that means), we may have assumed that it is the only way to be in relationship. This is simply not true. It may take some work to rearrange a world view that is sanctioned by society. Yet I nurture hope that the lesbian community will value the diversity of experience that includes polyamory.

Polyamory may work for many lesbians who are frustrated with the pattern of serial monogamy, where they fall in love, have a passionate affair for two to three years (the common time women are strongly bonded), fall "out of love," break up and repeat the cycle. Monogamy tends to isolate two people into an exclusive relationship. I think initially, when two women become sexually involved, they are fascinated with each other. It is an intense time of discovery, joy, passion, longing, desire. . . . During that phase the couple is usually very exclusive. And expectations or hopes for lifelong monogamy are assumed or discussed. Then the relationship moves beyond the "limerance" stage. Other feelings emerge. One or both women recognize their needs are not being met in the relationship. Power struggles may develop or a difference in sexual desire might exist. If polyamory is an option, the relationship might open up. If not, the two individuals try to compromise, adjust their hopes and dreams, sneak around with someone else, or break up the relationship. If they break up, they each try to find the "perfect " one to fall in love with next time. The pattern gets repeated until the lessons are learned or the childhood wounds get healed.

With polyamory, instead of assuming that two women need to compromise or break up to get their needs met, it is accepted that others can help meet those needs. The pressure to meet all of each other's needs is taken off the relationship. Space is made to acknowledge all that each one does bring to the relationship and to each other. Acceptance of the uniqueness of each woman, her needs and her gifts, is possible. This creates a peaceful, deep knowledge and appreciation–unconditional love.

WARMTH OF THE POLYAMORY QUILT

I've had adventures with friends and lovers, and have my stretch marks and bruises. Probably not more or less than if I had tried to be monogamous. I am a feeling, breathing woman. And I will continue to enjoy life's challenges and the comfort and warmth of the quilt of friendship and polyamory that life pieces together.

I cherish the quilt of life that has been created by my community of lovers and friends and the love we share. When I look at my quilt stitched by Sunshine and the many women who created panels, I feel very happy that they have touched my life. When I touch the different images, they remind me of specific women and experiences and many different feelings–joy and sadness and curiosity and wonder and ecstasy and pain and peace. Altogether the quilt makes a varied, many-textured pattern of love and caring that comforts and sustains me.

REFERENCES

Arnold, J. (1975, reissued 1989). *Sister gin.* Plainfield, VT: Daughters Inc. New York: Feminist Press.

Brown, A. (1973, reissued 1977). *Rubyfruit jungle.* Plainfield, VT. Daughters Inc. New York: Bantam Books.

Brown, R. M. (1976). *A plain brown rapper.* Oakland: Diana Press. (First published in *Women, A Journal of Liberation,* June 1971.)

Dilno, J. (1978). Monogamy and alternative life-styles. In G. Vida (Ed.) *Our right to Love: A lesbian resource book.* (pp. 56-63). Englewood Cliffs, NJ: Prentice-Hall, Inc.

Faderman, L. (1991). *Odd girls and twilight lovers: A history of lesbian life in twentieth-century america.* New York: Columbia University Press.

West, C. (1996). *Lesbian polyfidelity.* San Francisco: Booklegger Publishing.

Williams, T. T. (1994). *An unspoken hunger.* New York: Pantheon Books.

If This Is Tuesday, It Must Be Dee . . .
Confessions of a Closet Polyamorist

Nanette K. Gartrell

SUMMARY. The author discusses the evolution of non-monogamy in a 24-year lesbian relationship. The couple's initial agreement stipulated that outside liasions be concealed as much as possible. More recently, the couple has established a complex system for incorporating other paramours into their lives. *[Article copies available for a fee from The Haworth Document Delivery Service: 1-800-342-9678. E-mail address: getinfo@haworthpressinc.com]*

When a topic is acceptable enough to appear in your Curriculum Vitae (CV), it is time to move on to other, more controversial issues.

–Esther Rothblum

Nanette K. Gartrell, MD, is Associate Clinical Professor of Psychiatry at the University of California, San Francisco, where she teaches feminist psychotherapy theory. She has been documenting sexual abuse by physicians since 1982 and conducting a national longitudinal lesbian family study since 1986. She has a private psychotherapy practice in San Francisco.

Address correspondence to Nanette K. Gartrell, 3570 Clay Street, San Francisco, CA 94118.

Dr. Gartrell would like to thank Dee Mosbacher and Jasna Stefanovic for their love and support, along with Esther Rothblum, Jane Futcher, Joan Biren, Marny Hall and Minnie Bruce Pratt for their assistance in the preparation of this article.

[Haworth co-indexing entry note]: "If This Is Tuesday, It Must Be Dee . . . Confessions of a Closet Polyamorist." Gartrell, Nanette K. Co-published simultaneously in *Journal of Lesbian Studies* (The Haworth Press, Inc.) Vol. 3, No. 1/2, 1999, pp. 23-33; and: *The Lesbian Polyamory Reader: Open Relationships, Non-Monogamy, and Casual Sex* (ed: Marcia Munson and Judith P. Stelboum) The Haworth Press, Inc., 1999, pp. 23-33. Single or multiple copies of this article are available for a fee from The Haworth Document Delivery Service [1-800-342-9678, 9:00 a.m. - 5:00 p.m. (EST). E-mail address: getinfo@haworthpressinc.com].

As I write about my own non-monogamy for this special volume on polyamory, I recall the anxiety I felt applying to psychiatric residencies in the early 1970s, having decided to include my research on lesbian-themed topics in my resume. I had carefully crafted my CV as a screening device, hoping to filter out the homophobic programs and to be selected for the more progressive. Now more than twenty years later, career opportunities may be enhanced by having multiple citations concerning lesbianism in one's Vitae. Likewise, I no longer experience trepidation when I include other controversial topics–such as exposure of health professionals who exploit their patients–among my publications.

In coming out as a "polyamorist," I am once again positioning myself on the thinner branches of acceptability. Aside from those who share or aspire to a similar lifestyle, most lesbians I encounter clinically or socially are strongly opposed to non-monogamy. Even flagrant philanderers are often remorseful about their own behavior, equating polyamory with an inability to settle down, to establish intimacy, or to generate longevity. Non-monogamy, they think, guarantees misery, drama, and trauma.

I suspect that experiences with non-monogamy are as varied as the individuals involved. In this article I will be telling my story–or my version of my story, since the others involved would probably tell it differently. As I look back at the essential ingredients of my thirty-year love life, I realize that I could not have managed without organizational talent and communication skills. And, surprising as it may seem, I do not consider honesty, integrity, and commitment the guiding principles of my intimate life. Certainly they offer a framework, but honesty and integrity are relative concepts. I have found that discretion (concerning potentially hurtful feelings or behavior) is sometimes more helpful than candor. I also consider "commitment" a terribly elusive construct. (Commitment to what? My feelings 10 years hence? For how long? "For better or for worse . . . "? Why should I stay with a lover if I am miserable?) I learned long ago when my sister Yvonne died that I could not make assumptions about my future: I had planned on spending my senior years with her, even if none of my lovers endured. Ever since Yvonne's death I have lived one year at a time. (My organizational talents prohibit me from confining myself to a day.) I have committed myself to making each block of time I spend with each lover as glorious as it can be.

Monogamous is what one partner in every relationship wants it to be.

-Strange de Jim

My first intimate relationship was memorable only in that I wish I could have skipped it and gone on to the next. After promising faithfulness as we watched the sun set on our first day of lovemaking, Ann (a pseudonym) proceeded to bed countless women and men during the tumultuous eight years we were together. Although I had not considered myself particularly prone to jealousy before Ann, her liaisons, along with detailed accounts of their highlights (provided to me out of a belief in 60s-style "honesty"), reformatted my tolerance. I became obsessively jealous whenever Ann was having an affair, which was most of the time. A few dalliances of my own did nothing to diminish my possessiveness. When I left Ann for good (after numerous false starts), I resolved never to become involved with a non-monog again.

A firm believer in trading up with relationships, I worked my way through several short, progressively healthier involvements before I met Dee in 1975. Dee had the reputation of being a heart-breaker at the time I met her, since she had never wanted to commit herself to any of her previous partners. Because of her history, I anticipated that any liaison with her would be brief. As our relationship unfolded, we were surprised to find so many ingredients that each of us had unsuccessfully sought in other partnerships. We had a prolonged, joyful honeymoon. We laughed and played and loved. Our respective families were thrilled that we had found each other. I couldn't imagine being happier.

During that first year we talked about the concept of commitment. Dee said that she anticipated staying with me as long as we were happy with each other. While her statement initially seemed hollow and bizarre (staying together through the usual "thick and thin" had been my un-thought-out preference), I grew to appreciate the importance of living in the present, valuing consistency in love, growth and happiness. Without an assumption of permanence, I realized that we might be less likely to take each other for granted.

In our second year Dee raised the issue of non-monogamy. Until that point, we had been strictly monogamous. We also had agreed not to flirt with other women when Dee and I were together, since flirting could lead to hurt or insecure feelings. Additionally, we had promised never to lie to each other. Withholding information was acceptable, but outright lies were not. At the time that she initiated what turned into a year-long discussion of non-monogamy, Dee had been contemplating the marvels of our relationship. She explained that she had begun to assume that we were going to be together for a very long time. Since few relationships survive affairs, Dee suggested that we chart a course through those predictably stormy waters.

I agreed that each of us was likely to have numerous other attractions, but argued that we needn't act on them. In further discussions, we realized that neither of us had ever faced that situation. It seemed unlikely that we would be more successful at suppressing inopportune lust than countless other lesbians who had tried and failed to do so.

Nevertheless, I was extremely reluctant to agree to non-monogamy. I did not want Dee to have affairs. Although I understood the importance of figuring out how to handle outside attractions long before they were likely to occur, I wasn't interested in giving Dee the green light. Whereas neither of us had felt jealous or insecure about our independent friendships, I imagined that a non-monogamy contract would make any woman fair game for sex. I was unconcerned about how I might handle my own attractions, because I was certain that nobody would measure up to Dee. She felt the same way about me, but her heart-breaker history worried me.

Over time we worked out an agreement that seemed fair and manageable: (1) Affairs would be allowed, as long as they were concealed; (2) lying to camouflage such liaisons was acceptable; and (3) outside romance must not interfere with the primacy of our relationship. We also anticipated that it might be very difficult to reestablish our own sexual relationship if we let it slide during an infatuation, and therefore planned to maintain as much sexual constancy as possible. Various unreasonable amendments, such as "no falling in love" and "no vacations with a paramour" were tacked on during premenstrual dysphoria and inevitably later withdrawn. I was convinced that Dee would take the first plunge, and that I would be more talented at the deception required by our new agreement.

We were monogamous for four years. During that time, I became more confident that our relationship could handle infidelities–as long as they weren't too frequent, very serious, or all-consuming. After a passionate first year together, we settled into a pattern of two-to-three-times-per-week, good, sweet, loving sex–unlike the typical "Lesbian Bed Death" scenario we were to hear so much about a decade later. Although a new infatuation would undoubtedly be associated with greater sexual intensity, we believed that our post-limerent sexual dance was as pleasurable and compatible as it could be.

In the spring of 1979, I completed my psychiatric residency, and Dee earned her Ph.D. in social psychology. I was offered an exciting job in Boston, and Dee was admitted to medical school in Houston. I really wanted to stay in Boston, and Dee really wanted to go to Baylor. Neither of us wanted to commute. I reluctantly agreed to move to Houston.

Three weeks before we were scheduled to leave Boston, I met Milena (a pseudonym). I was instantly attracted to her, and she to me. Strongly motivated to complicate my feelings about moving even further, I began to pursue Milena. I explained the parameters of my agreement with Dee. Milena felt uncomfortable with the secrecy requirement, but she promised to respect it. We assumed that our liaison would end when I left town.

I concealed the affair from Dee for eight days. I could have kept it from her longer, but I felt overwhelmingly guilty. We had not factored guilt into our agreement. I have since learned that responsible management of guilt is obligatory for the dallier. When I unburdened myself to Dee about my involvement with Milena, Dee responded very kindly and lovingly–after pointing out the irony in my taking the first plunge. Although she felt hurt and sad, Dee encouraged me to take whatever time I needed with Milena. Dee was convinced that our relationship was strong enough to survive my remaining in Boston with Milena, while Dee attended medical school in Houston.

I returned to Boston after four months in Texas, because I could not stomach the sexism and homophobia of Houston's psychiatric community. My affair with Milena turned into a longer-term loving relationship. Dee kept her jealousy toward Milena in check by focusing her attention elsewhere, but Milena tormented herself with thoughts of Dee. I became progressively more silent about Dee when I was with Milena, and mum about Milena when I was with Dee. Such secrecy helped to contain my guilt, and to reduce their pain. I learned to avoid comparisons. I made enormous efforts to keep both lovers happy, because I valued the unique pleasures I experienced with each.

I was exhilarated with the pace of my life. Aside from weather delays, I enjoyed commuting to Houston every other Thursday for a four-day weekend. My time management skills were honed to perfection: I worked long hours, punctuated by two-, three-, or four-times-per-day phone calls to Dee. I spent nights with Milena when we were both free. (Fortunately, Milena had her own time limitations as an on-call physician.) I worked on planes to and from Houston. I managed household responsibilities for Dee–partly out of guilt, and partly out of surplus organizational energy. When Dee was liberated from her medical school responsibilities, we played fast and furiously, squeezing in as many activities as we could in the available time.

The intensity of my loving feelings toward Dee grew exponentially during my relationship with Milena. I felt enveloped by Dee's kindness, support and generosity. I also appreciated her ability to exercise denial. Not being constantly grilled about my affections enormously enhanced our time together. I aspired to handle Dee's affairs as supportively as she had mine.

Not surprisingly, my relationship with Milena was much more tumultuous. She wanted a primary, monogamous commitment from me. She sashayed back and forth between being resistant to and tolerant of the many limitations. Milena often threatened to leave, and occasionally did. This perpetual uncertainty, along with time restrictions, partings and reunions, kept the spark alive for us.

Rarely did I wish to end one of the relationships and settle down in the other. Such thoughts occasionally crossed my mind after too many hours of processing with Milena, or too much frustration with the commute to Houston. Sometimes I relished the thought of a day or a week to myself. But mostly I enjoyed living my life to the max. My heart stretched to embrace the love I felt for Dee and Milena, and I joyously gobbled up their adoration and devotion.

No one worth possessing/Can be quite possessed

–Sara Teasdale

During the height of my romance with Milena, Dee had a secret affair. I was so preoccupied with Milena that I didn't notice. I figured it out months after it had ended. Despite all my preparation and my own infidelity, I felt devastated. I was convinced that Dee couldn't maintain her love for me while opening her heart (or body) to someone else, despite the fact that I had been able to do just that. Even though Dee was extremely reassuring, I worried about losing her. That her paramour was long gone seemed inconsequential. Undoubtedly, some of my insecurity came from the recent loss of my sister. The remainder felt like it had been encoded in my DNA. It took more than a year for me to get over it.

At about that time Milena left for good. Her goal of a primary, monogamous commitment was not being met with me. She had pursued other women, only to find that her feelings about others never measured up to the intensity of her experience with me. It was hard for Milena to believe that our relationship might not seem as stimulating if we were together full-time. The ending was very painful for both of us, especially since Milena forbade contact for a very long time. Milena needed to distance herself as much as possible in order to find a new lover.

Dee and I each had a brief fling a few years later. By then, Dee had returned to Boston, where living under the same roof made it impossible to conceal liaisons. My jealousy became slightly more manageable with each incident. I realized that I was far more successful at maintaining a semblance of emotional steadiness during my own affairs than Dee was during hers. I kept a lid on my ebullience in Dee's presence, whereas Dee couldn't contain her enthusiasm. Dee's candor, which inadvertently contributed to my jealousy, had become an anticipated impediment to my sense of security during her dalliances.

In 1987, Dee and I traveled for a year before relocating to San Francisco. We were uncertain whether the close quarters of travel would foster intimacy or claustrophobia. Happily, we reconnected at a new and deeper level. We shared peak experiences, and celebrated our magical existence. It was a year filled with adventures that broadened the foundations of our love and appreciation for each other.

Our arrival in San Francisco marked the beginning of a five-year hiatus in outside romance. We attributed this change to multiple factors: our renewed attachment to each other; enjoying the relative simplicity of our lives; and having fewer erotic fantasies. (We speculated that sexual fantasies might be hormonally induced, and wondered if our testosterone levels had taken a plunge as we approached our fortieth birthdays.) Other than the involuntary shift in fantasy frequency, the hiatus was largely volitional. Our lives seemed sufficiently stimulating and interesting that neither of us missed the complicated dance of new intrigues.

All that changed for me after my father's suicide in 1991. As I recovered from that devastating loss, I began to long for a new infatuation to distract me from my pain. Eventually, I found one. Or rather, she found me; but I was a willing participant.

Jasna and I met five years ago through tennis. She had been a European champion in her youth. I aspired to be a professional athlete in my next lifetime. We had known each other for several months before she seduced me. Initially, I thought we were so different that our romance would be sweet, but brief. Jasna is eleven years younger (from a generation that gags rather than swoons at women's music), hot-headed and impulsive, strongly opinionated and dramatic. However, she is also generous, protective, patient, helpful and kind. Much to my surprise, I had an available template for just that set of attributes.

Our passionate affair has turned into an intense long-term involvement. Despite its time limitations, Jasna considers it the best relationship she has had. Unlike Milena, Jasna accepts my commitment to Dee. She has also developed a casual friendship with Dee, which has facilitated our endless negotiations about time and space. Jasna is disinclined to pursue other partnerships, because she finds non-monogamy too draining. Her loyalty and commitment to me have been wonderful. I relish her love and companionship.

In 1992, Dee temporarily left psychiatry to pursue a career in filmmaking. Within a short time, she had garnered an Oscar nomination and a new lover. I was thrilled with the nomination, but ambivalent about Kim (a pseudonym). I was pleased to have more time with Jasna. Dee and I worked it out that Jasna could stay at our house when Dee spent time with Kim. Since my office is attached to our home, Dee agreed to meet Kim elsewhere.

It soon became apparent that Dee was more infatuated with Kim than she had been with previous paramours. In addition, Dee was rarely detail-oriented enough to mop up the evidence of her time with Kim before returning home. Once again, her disclosures triggered my jealousy, and I became mistrustful. We began to fight over insignificant issues. Dee seemed guarded, and I felt hurt. After several months of strife, we decided to seek couples therapy.

Finding a couples therapist who was non-judgmental about nonmonogamy was a difficult task. The difficulty was compounded by our also needing a therapist whom neither of us knew. I obtained the names of three allegedly excellent women therapists–two psychologists and one social worker–whom colleagues assured me would be open to our lifestyle. Considering myself savvy to the tricks of the trade, I set about interviewing them. Each assured me in our first meeting that she could "handle this issue." Sensing some discomfort in their respective responses, I decided to smoke them out by making four appointments with each. Within several sessions, one woman asked why I elected non-monogamy over intimacy, and another suggested that Dee and I sign up for a retreat she was conducting on strengthening the bonds in long-term relationships. The third kept her word, and we signed on with her.

In therapy, we realized that living together and being seriously involved with other partners was a new challenge. Sharing a household seemed to complicate our transitions between lovers: neither of us allocated sufficient time to close down the connection to one, and prepare for reentry with the other. Eventually, Dee figured out that she needed her own place. She leased an apartment for six months. During that time, we were apart five nights each week. I spent those nights with Jasna, and Dee with Kim. Although I cherished the opportunity to take my relationship with Jasna to a more intimate level, I felt very sad about Dee's absence.

In the throes of these changes, Jasna told Dee that she would happily fill the temporal space that Dee was vacating in my life, but that she expected at least 50% of my time when Dee returned. Jasna also told Dee that she would be making an enormous mistake if she left me for good. Atypically, I absented myself from these conversations–hoping that a peaceful compromise could be reached while I waited in the wings.

Dee's return marked the beginning of a new era in our relationship. In true "French Twist" fashion, I now spend three nights of the week with Dee, and three with Jasna. Sundays are my nights off. I move back and forth between the home I share with Dee, and Jasna's apartment. I celebrate my birthday twice, and I vacation with each partner, spending Judeo-Christian holidays with Dee and Greek Orthodox holidays with Jasna. Dee sees Kim frequently but irregularly, since Kim is disinclined to participate in four-way scheduling.

There are advantages and disadvantages to this type of arrangement. Among the advantages are the excitement of reunions (with either Dee or Jasna); exposure to different activities (Jasna enjoys trying new restaurants, whereas Dee prefers quiet meals at home); and the constant uniqueness of the voyage. An example of the unique opportunities non-monogamy affords has been the chance to sample 90s-style lesbian sex with women who have had many more contemporary experiences than Dee or I. Disadvantages to this lifestyle include insufficient time to myself, complicated negotiations regarding important events, and sometimes having to see the same play or film twice.

Despite all the obstacles, we are finding our way. Dee and I have emerged from the most serious challenges to our relationship with a sense of togetherness that is as strong as ever. Each of us has savored the magic of infatuations, and felt the richness of being deeply loved by two women. In the realm of relationships, we have the best of all worlds, and the most difficult of all worlds.

As I write that last sentence, I hear the voices of the 154 lesbian moms I have interviewed in the longitudinal lesbian family study I am conducting. Year after year, I am told that having children has been the most wonderful and stressful experience of their lives. My feelings about my own non-monogamous lifestyle echo their sentiments about motherhood. The joys far outweigh the hardships. If I were given the opportunity to do my life all over again, I would again elect to be non-monogamous.

> No matter how coupled we are, we rarely remain in actual twosomes for very long. Typically, pets or parents, children or friends, are constantly joining our magic circle.

> –Marny Hall

It is puzzling that I am so often questioned about my ability to love two women simultaneously. I would never think to challenge a parent's capacity to love a partner and a child, or multiple children at the same time. I believe that each of us is capable of loving as many humans and animals as our hearts can stretch to embrace. My myocardium currently houses two lovers, two Maltese dogs, and seven especially dear lifelong friends.

If I have learned anything about myself in the 24 years since Dee and I resolved to be non-monogamous, it is that my joy in life comes from expanding, not narrowing, my circle. I suspect that may be true of most people. My own experience also suggests that more lesbians dabble in non-monogamy than acknowledge it. Perhaps if more of us speak out about our sex lives, polyamorism will become just as passé on my resume as lesbianism is today.

REFERENCES

Hall, M. (1998). *The lesbian love companion*. San Francisco: Harper Collins.

Rothblum, E. (January 7, 1997). Fat oppression. Lecture at the University of California Medical School, San Francisco.

Strange de Jim. (February 7, 1997). Herb Caen's Eulogy. Grace Cathedral, San Francisco.

Teasdale, S. (1934). Advice to a girl. *Strange victory*. New York: The MacMillan Company.

Lesbians as Luvbeins

JoAnn Loulan

SUMMARY. Lesbians who do not follow the imperative of monogamous, live-in lovers with one other woman are seen as traitors, heretics, and generally fallen women. In a community that often demands conformity, we must find language that includes other ways of being. Thus the idea that luvbeins (a new word that means any or all or more of the following: those that love being, love lesbians, a play on the language for lesbian, a sexual loving woman loving) can become a permutation of the word so that sexually innovative lesbians have another way of communication about themselves. The real fear is always am I loved, am I lovable, can I love? *[Article copies available for a fee from The Haworth Document Delivery Service: 1-800-342-9678. E-mail address: getinfo@ haworthpressinc.com]*

Lesbians traditionally associate love with sex, sex with love and relationships with being lovely roommates. We confuse the idea of lesbians as luvbeins. *(A new word introduced into the written, published*

JoAnn Loulan is a psychotherapist in private practice, a writer, and a lecturer. She is the author of *Lesbian Sex* (1984), *Lesbian Passion* (1987), and *The Lesbian Erotic Dance* (1990), all Spinsters Books, Duluth, MN.

Address correspondence to JoAnn Loulan, 4370 Alpine Road #205, Portola Valley, CA 94028.

The author would like to thank all the members of the lesbian community who have put up with her provocative behavior for years and years now. Here we go again. Thanks to all my friends who have stuck by me. I know you're all talking about me, but I know you love me, too.

[Haworth co-indexing entry note]: "Lesbians as Luvbeins." Loulan, JoAnn. Co-published simultaneously in *Journal of Lesbian Studies* (The Haworth Press, Inc.) Vol. 3, No. 1/2, 1999, pp. 35-38; and: *The Lesbian Polyamory Reader: Open Relationships, Non-Monogamy, and Casual Sex* (ed: Marcia Munson and Judith P. Stelboum) The Haworth Press, Inc., 1999, pp. 35-38. Single or multiple copies of this article are available for a fee from The Haworth Document Delivery Service [1-800-342-9678, 9:00 a.m. - 5:00 p.m. (EST). E-mail address: getinfo@haworthpressinc.com].

language right here which means any of the following: loving being, loving lesbians, love and lesbian combined, in other words a darling play on the language, used to connote a sexual, loving woman loving.) The community often defines a loving and good lesbian as one that is a companion with a long-term partner. However, there are many ways luvbeins may express themselves in a loving and sexual way.

There are reasons we confuse sex and love, and often prefer to go for the love. Sex seems to be a painful topic for many of us. That pain may be due to incest, sexism, sexual harassment, not having much information, or just plain not liking it. Due to the history of women on the planet, sex seems to have been down on our list of problems to be solved. We've been traditionally trained to worry about everything and everyone else. Our bodily pleasure has been used against us in many ways and we have often been intimidated into believing that good girls don't.

Lesbians have been seen as not being good girls. The world still sees us this way just because we're lesbians. While that is changing, we ourselves often have problems believing that sex is a wonderful activity that could be enjoyed in many ways. Creating an open and informative dialogue about sex in the lesbian community usually has been lively and met with great resistance. Whether the topic introduced is vibrators, dildoes, s/m, or non-monogamy, put something new outloud to the community and everyone freaks.

The outloud part is the problem. Lots of sex activities have been done by lesbians for a long time. The crime, as usual, is saying it loud and proud. Or even worse saying it loud and with a lot of shame. Then the community really freaks. Like the "don't ask don't tell" military solution, lesbians (and the rest of the world) often are practicing sex activities but just not telling anyone about them. Judgments are hard to accept, especially within a small town community like the lesbian one.

The idea of being sexual with more than one person is viewed by the whole culture as tawdry, negative, hurtful and taking something from someone. It's the taking something from someone that seems to be the problem with lesbians. We don't want to hurt anyone; we don't want to make our primary partner feel unimportant in a world that discounts lesbian relationships. We want to honor each other, and to do this we believe we need to use the model of the heterosexual imperative. That is the married, monogamous one.

After enjoying a slight respite from this grindingly limiting model in the 1960s through 1980s, this heterosexual monogamous ideal is becoming more embedded in the culture in the 1990s. In deference to the radical right wing, President Clinton has announced a program to teach children not to have sex outside of the married heterosexual paradigm. Interesting for someone with the reputation of Billy boy. The Presbyterian Church has announced no one can be a deacon or a minister that has *ever* had sex outside this model. I wonder if they think they can come up with cures for the majority of the population that does not want to or cannot fit into that narrow category.

The dilemma the polyamorous (I love this word, so much more sexy and alluring than "non-monogamous") luvbein faces is formidable. Not only must she stand up the to the radical hetero nut cases, she must stand up to her own community that sees polyamory as an affront to the sacrosanct union of two women struggling against the tides of the evil world. She is a heretic within a community of heretics.

I always think it important to remind our outlaw lesbian community that assimilating has never worked for an oppressed group. Trying to do it their way is not going to give us a foot up. Doing it our own way makes it possible to create a difference in our lives and the reality of the world.

Polyamorous lesbian luvbeins are women who want to have sex and possibly love more than one person at the same time. This is a possibility. There really is endless sex and endless love in the world. It doesn't mean that all lesbians want to practice this or act like this. For those who do, it doesn't mean that this will crush a relationship or a community. How the women who want to be polyamorous do so in a loving manner is probably the real question. Without the room to explore and talk about it, there will be a vacuum that doesn't create solutions. The definitions of sex and love and relationship are challenged here. What a healthy and exciting prospect.

The basic principle here is that sexual feelings are part of our lives from birth to death. How we deal with those feelings and what they mean are endless questions. When luvbeins experience sexual feelings that are enjoyable, and they want to act on these with more than one person, many issues come to mind. If she is in a relationship already with a person that she lives with, does that mean she must tell, does it mean she doesn't have enough in her current relationship, does it mean that she is in danger of going off with the new attraction? If said luvbein doesn't live with her lover, issues are slightly less complicated, but the above questions remain. If a luvbein is simply playing the field, as we used to say in the 1950s, is she obligated to answer any questions?

The fear is always am I loved, am I lovable, can I love? Questions that are never answered, at least never answered the same way from day to day. Fears that are never totally left to rest, which is why people invented monogamy, heterosexuality and static sex. They wanted to feel secure and thought this was the way. Anyone who has tried to create security that way and been honest knows that is not the answer. The answer is inside. Security comes without anyone else mucking about. We cannot get security from others.

Luvbeins, however, are often made to feel they are betraying a community that needs so much to feel secure and loved and valuable. We must bring that value with us. We must assume that value. Polyamory is a way of making loving and sexual contacts with others and is a valid way of spreading value and connection in any direction one chooses. This is nothing new. The new part is having a dialogue that is supportive and loving. The challenge is bringing up what we learned about this from the 1970s and continuing to bring fresh ideas and actions to the mix.

Luvbeins are making a change, feeling their feelings and choosing many ways to do that, whether that is being alone, with one or many others. Showing up, telling our truth as we see fit, and loving ourselves. What a gift; what a concept.

Patriarchal Monogamy

Judith P. Stelboum

SUMMARY. The equating of sex, sin and death in Patriarchal Judeo-Christian religions continues to affect the social and moral consciousness of Western societies. The concepts of the impure body, the inferiority of women, importance of monogamy and marriage, and the negative ideas of sexuality have been so absorbed into all cultures that their origins as mainstays of patriarchal religions have been obscured, and these ideas have become accepted as the natural phenomenon of human relationships. Lesbians, already out of the mainstream of heterosexual life, still structure their own lives around these archaic and restrictive codes. *[Article copies available for a fee from The Haworth Document Delivery Service: 1-800-342-9678. E-mail address: getinfo@haworthpressinc.com]*

Judith P. Stelboum, PhD, is Associate Professor of English and teaches literature, Lesbian Studies, and Women's Studies at the College of Staten Island, City University of New York. Her essays, fiction and poetry have appeared in *Common Lives/Lesbian Lives*, in *Sinister Wisdom*, and in the anthologies *Sister and Brother*, *Dyke Life*, *Resist: Essays Against a Homophobic Culture*, *Not the Only One*, *Heat Wave*, *Tangled Sheets* and *Hot Ticket*. She is a reviewer for the *Lesbian Review of Books*. She has written on two American Lesbian poets, Olga Broumas and Marilyn Hacker, for the *Oxford Companion to Twentieth Century Literature in English*, and her essay on monogamy-non-monogamy is included in *The History of Homosexuality: Vol. 1: Lesbian Histories and Cultures*.

Address correspondence to Judith P. Stelboum, English Department, 2S224, College of Staten Island, 2800 Victory Boulevard, Staten Island, NY 10314.

[Haworth co-indexing entry note]: "Patriarchal Monogamy." Stelboum, Judith P. Co-published simultaneously in *Journal of Lesbian Studies* (The Haworth Press, Inc.) Vol. 3, No. 1/2, 1999, pp. 39-46; and: *The Lesbian Polyamory Reader: Open Relationships, Non-Monogamy, and Casual Sex* (ed: Marcia Munson and Judith P. Stelboum) The Haworth Press, Inc., 1999, pp. 39-46. Single or multiple copies of this article are available for a fee from The Haworth Document Delivery Service [1-800-342-9678, 9:00 a.m. - 5:00 p.m. (EST). E-mail address: getinfo@haworthpressinc.com].

and from your name Eve we shall take
the word evil.
and from God's the word good.
now you understand patriarchal morality.

–Judy Grahn, *The Work of a Common Woman*

The classical Greek philosophers distinguished between two kinds of love, Agape and Eros; the beginnings of the sacred vs. the profane, the spiritual vs. the physical. Early Christian writings make clear distinctions between the pure soul versus the unclean body. The connections between sin, sex and death in the Judeo-Christian tradition have had a profound effect on many of our present day attitudes. The current fundamentalist attitude towards people with AIDS supports the Christian idea of just punishment for the sin of sex. The associations of sex with evil and evil with women are basic tenets of the church, and the corruption of man through woman is established in the earliest sections of the Bible with the story of Adam and Eve. Adam relinquishes his place in the patriarchal hierarchy because he is responsible for Eve. Early Christian writings as written in the King James version of the New Testament reinforce the biblical Hebrew text. "For the husband is the head of the wife, even as Christ is the head of the church : and he is the savior of the body. Therefore as the church is subject unto Christ, so let the wives be to their own husbands in everything" [Eph. 5:23-24]. Man was created in god's image. "For the man is not of the woman; but the woman of the man. Neither was the man created for the woman; but the woman for the man" [I Cor. 11: 7-10]. Monogamy, marriage and the inferiority of women are linked under a universal patriarchal system which is built on the concept of male superiority.

This essay focuses on some basic ideas of the Judeo-Christian religions, but we can speak of the universal religion of Patriarchy which pre-dates the Judeo-Christian world and has been in effect for over 3,000 years. All of the present major religions of the world are based on similar patriarchal concepts. Biblical scholars state that Abraham lived between 1800 and 1500 B.C.E. Prior to the patriarchal social and religious systems under which we now exist, there was, in the Neolithic period (about 7000 B.C.E.) and in the Upper Paleolithic period (from 30,000 B.C.E. to 10,000 B.C.E.), a different way in which women were viewed. Most of human history did not exist under a patriarchal structure. Just as patriarchal religious beliefs and social structures are now in place in the contemporary world, so too, for most of Neolithic Europe and the Far East there existed a homogeneous system based on the Great Goddess. She was immortal and had many names depending on her location and on her function in the world. The Goddess was the Mother and the Giver of All. She was the source of all nature and life. While patriarchal religions are a fairly recent phenomenon in human history, the erasure of all of previous forms of religion has been so complete that it has taken us thousands of years to re-discover that for most of human history we lived in matriarchal, matrilocal or matrilineal societies.

The pace at which patriarchy replaced matriarchy varied in differing parts of the world. It took thousands of years for the patriarchal beliefs in male superiority and female subordination, control of women's sexuality and inheritance based on male lineage to replace the earlier matrilineal, matriarchal and Goddess cultures. Genesis was composed between 1200 and 500 B.C.E., and the system of patriarchy was already in place. Centuries later, the Christian religion and the values of Christian culture were disseminated throughout the world through missionaries and military conquests, forcing other societies through coercion or subversion to abandon their "pagan" beliefs. White men's misogynistic creed now became the standard for religions in Africa, Asia and Europe. Polygyny and polygamy, alternatives to monogamy, still exist in some areas of Africa. Polyandry, even rarer, can be found in some tribes in the Himalayas and in India. Mormon polygamy was declared illegal by the U.S. Supreme Court in 1870, and the practice was officially discontinued by the Mormons in 1890.

Anthropologists and archeologists are discovering that early societies held to a belief in the natural order, which respected the powers of the Goddess and the interconnectedness of all living things on the planet. The linear and hierarchical view of the world is a patriarchal one which places one group of people over another based in a descending order of importance resulting in sexism, slavery and racism. The hierarchical, dominator-dominated model has ordered corporate organizations, affected governmental decisions in social policy and education, and has determined military policies. The patriarchal pattern of hierarchies also mandates that humans are superior to, and should control, all other living creatures. The patriarchal Bible states that Adam named all the other creatures and had "dominion over the fish of the sea, and over the fowl of the air, and over every living thing that moveth upon the earth" [Gen: 2:28]. This belief has led to the ongoing destruction of animals and natural environments.

Even the manner by which we record time is a patriarchal phenomenon of the Christian church marking the years before Christ and after Christ. The patriarchal Christian calendar gives a slanted version of life on earth and also discounts the cultures and societies which existed for most of human life on this earth, which are now lumped together under the heading of "pre-history."

The matrilineal societies of the Paleolithic and Neolithic periods, where people lived in tribes and clans, were times of great advances in agriculture, art and architecture. The remarkable cultures of ancient, Minoan Crete (2200-1500 B.C.E.) and Catal Huyuk in Anatolia (7,000 B.C.E.) reveal that for thousands and thousands of years matrilineal and matrilocal worlds existed and lived peaceably.

Feminist scholars state that the origins of monogamy have their source in patriarchal thinking. Viewed as the possessions of the male, women were used for barter and/or procreation. Patrilineal descent decreed that males inherited from their fathers. Legitimacy of a child relates to acknowledgment of the child's father, not to the child's mother. This definition of legitimacy is still a legal reality in many cultures and children born to unmarried females are classified as illegitimate. Women who have children, but who do not have a husband, are negatively viewed as "unwed mothers." In Paleolithic and Neolithic periods, lineage could be traced through the mother. People recognized kinship through consanguinity as well as through social ties to clans and tribes, and fathering children was insignificant. Patriarchal societies create their own versions of birth, negating the importance of the female, even in the act of creating life. Athena springs from the head of Zeus. Eve is created from one of Adam's ribs, and childbirth becomes a punishment. Patriarchy invented the concept of the father as an important social entity. The Bible speaks only about inheritance through the father. This emphasis on the male line is emphasized in the Bible by the many references to, and importance of, sperm. The seed of the man is planted in the woman. The woman is passive, the man active. His seed and his offspring are essential. The woman becomes the empty vessel into which is poured the seed of life. She is no longer the creator and sustainer of life.

To maintain a line of inheritance and to assure a father of the legitimacy of the male heir, the female must be confined in her sexual activities. Monogamy is, therefore, a necessity in marriage and patriarchy in terms of the bequeathing of familial inheritances of material goods and properties to heirs. In a patriarchal society, marriage and female fidelity are requirements for heterosexual relationships.

The concept of the virgin as pure, untainted and unspoiled is given a new meaning in Christianity. Since sex is associated with sin, Mary, the mother of Jesus cannot be a sinner; therefore, she cannot have had sex when conceiving her son. Mary was officially declared virgin as early as the seventh century. Though the image of Mary can be traced back to some recognition of the early Goddess worship, the emphasis is now on Mary's divine son and not on the power of the Goddess. Mary is non-threatening, passive and obedient. She becomes the model for all women.

Marriage and female confinement are essential in most all patriarchal cultures. Monogamy and non-monogamy are terms which societies have employed to differentiate between people who have sexual and/or emotional relationships with just one person and those who have relationships with more than one person simultaneously. Generally, the designations refer to sexual relations confined to one person or sexual relations outside of marriage. These distinctions and restrictions grew out of the formalizing of the institution of marriage. Marriage can be interpreted as the joining together of two people (generally male and female) in a special kind of social and legal dependence for the purpose of founding and maintaining a family. Monogamous is defined as "mono" "gamos," one marriage only during a life, or marriage with one person at a time.

In the nineteenth century, the Marxist philosopher Frederick Engels considered both marriage and monogamy restrictive states reflective of the theories of capitalism, ownership of goods and of people. "The overthrow of mother right marked the world wide defeat of the female sex. The man took command in the home; the woman was degraded and reduced to servitude; she became the slave of his lust and a mere instrument for the production of children" (Engels, p. 16). Engels further observed that the monogamous marriage established the wife as head servant of the household and that prostitution was a necessity for monogamous marriage.

By the twentieth century, marriage and the belief in the natural state of monogamy have been so integrated into our present day thinking that they are both sanctioned as the normal mode of behavior in human relations. In present psychological texts, practicing monogamy has been viewed as a sign of stability and maturity, while non-monogamy, especially for females, has been labeled as immature, or worse, transgressive behavior, punishable in some cultures by death.

For many centuries, scientists attempted to reinforce the supposition that humans were naturally monogamous by citing examples of monogamous coupling in other animal species. This has since been disproved by social scientists who attribute linking of human behavior to behavior of other animals as anthropomorphic (human-centered) thinking. In terms of sexuality, human beings cannot be compared to other animal species as they mate whenever they desire, not only when the female comes into heat. Further, very few animals mate for life, and those animals that do, remain together only long enough to protect the young of the species.

In those cultures that regard monogamy as ideal, non-monogamy is widely practiced, secretly. Frederick Engels speculated that "the only reason the Catholic church abandoned divorce was because it had convinced itself that there is no more a cure for adultery than there is for death" (Engels, p. 62). Serial monogamy, facilitating the rejection of one person for another, has resulted in the abandoning of children.

The socialized patterns of patriarchal monogamy and its historical and theological derivations go largely unquestioned by many lesbians. The implications of the historical prerogative of male inheritance have little relevance for the lesbian community, but the social values and behavioral modes of the dominant heterosexual community have been firmly implanted within most of the lesbian population.

In the late 1960s through the 1970s, the second wave of feminism in the U.S. attacked all forms of heterosexual sexual practices, and monogamy was seen as a restrictive tool used by the patriarchy to thwart women's sexual energies. Soon though, in the 1980s, the general backlash against women's equality began. The Barnard Women's Conference on Sexuality in 1982 created a major furor among feminists when the conference organizers attempted to include representative speakers expressing the diversity of women's sexual experiences. Non-monogamy was viewed by many as promiscuous behavior and no longer politically correct.

Non-monogamy is practiced by only a minority of the lesbian population, and lesbian non-monogamy can be differentiated from heterosexual non-monogamy as its purposes are intrinsically related to the structures that characterize the wide variety of lesbian lives. Lesbian non-monogamy can be a political statement that rejects the confining heterosexual models of monogamy as not applicable to the diverse nature of lesbians. Non-monogamy may be a response to personal situations where individual lesbians do not feel the need for constraint in a relationship that has not been legally sanctioned. Non-monogamy can be a way for two women to define autonomy within a coupled situation and avoid the intense bonding typical of some lesbian partners. It can be a method of extending friendship or a manifestation of friendship. Often, as in the heterosexual model, non-monogamy is a way to make a transition from one monogamous relationship into another monogamous relationship.

Lesbian non-monogamy can be an active force reflecting the openness and willingness of the participants to view non-monogamy as a positive and not as a negative aspect to their lives. The boundaries of lesbian non-monogamy are continually being reset and invented depending on personal arrangements and agreements. It is important to understand the historical context in which the concepts of monogamy, marriage and sexuality have been linked in order to reassess our own choices. Nicole Brossard wrote in *The Aerial Letter*, "A Lesbian who does not re-invent the world is a lesbian in the process of disappearing" (Brossard, p. 136).

REFERENCES

Brossard, N. (1988). *The Aerial Letter.* Toronto: Women's Press.
Engels, F. (1951). *Bourgeois Marriage, The Woman Question.* p. 36. New York: International Publishers.

FOR FURTHER READING

Brooten, B. (1966). *Love Between Women: Early Christian Responses to Female Homoeroticism.* Chicago: University of Chicago Press.
Daly, M. (1973). *Beyond God the Father: Toward a Philosophy of Women's Liberation.* Boston: Beacon Press.
Gimbutas, M. (1982). *Goddesses and Gods of Old Europe, 7000-3500 B.C.* Berkeley: University of California Press.
_____ (1987). *The Language of the Goddess: Images and Symbols of Old Europe.* New York: Van der Marck.
Lerner, G. (1986). *The Creation of Patriarchy.* New York: Oxford University Press.

Pomeroy, S. (1975). *Goddesses, Whores, Wives and Slaves: Women in Classical Antiquity.* New York: Shocken Books.

Spretnak, C. (1982). *The Politics of Women's Spirituality.* NY: Doubleday.

Stone, M. (1976). *When God Was a Woman.* NY: Harcourt, Brace, Jovanovich.

Vance, C. (1992). *Pleasure and Danger: Exploring Female Sexuality.* London: Pandora, Harper Collins.

Warner, M. (1976). *Alone of All Her Sex: The Myth and the Cult of the Virgin Mary.* New York: Knopf.

Turning Down the Jezebel Decibels

Marny Hall

SUMMARY. According to conventional wisdom, many breakups are due to "the other woman"–the home wrecker who comes between perfectly contented lesbian partners. In this excerpt from *The Lesbian Love Companion: How to Survive Everything from Heartthrob to Heartbreak*, author Hall explores the fresh ways we might retell the traditional "other woman" tale. Also included in this excerpt are the benefits that accrue to monogamous and polyamorous lesbians who learn to tell such alternative stories.

INTRODUCTORY NOTE

Turning Down the Jezebel Decibels is the seventh chapter of Marny Hall's newly released book *The Lesbian Love Companion: How to Survive Everything from Heartthrob to Heartbreak*. In the previous chapter, Hall identifies jealousy as one of life's unavoidable emotions and presents a specific method for taming the green-eyed monster.

Marny Hall, PhD, is a San Francisco Bay Area psychotherapist with twenty years experience specializing in lesbian relationships. She is author of *The Lavender Couch: A Consumer's Guide to Psychotherapy for Lesbians and Gay Men*, editor of the anthology *Sexualities*, and contributor to a number of lesbian anthologies. She lives in Oakland, California with Killer, her philodendron. This is a chapter from the book *The Lesbian Love Companion: How to Survive Everything from Heartthrob to Heartbreak* (©1998 by Marny Hall, HarperCollins Publishers). Reprinted by permission.

Address correspondence to Marny Hall, 4112 24th Street, San Francisco, CA 94114.

[Haworth co-indexing entry note]: "Turning Down the Jezebel Decibels." Hall, Marny. Co-published simultaneously in *Journal of Lesbian Studies* (The Haworth Press, Inc.) Vol. 3, No. 1/2, 1999, pp. 47-62; and: *The Lesbian Polyamory Reader: Open Relationships, Non-Monogamy, and Casual Sex* (ed: Marcia Munson and Judith P. Stelboum) The Haworth Press, Inc., 1999, pp. 47-62.

There is another tale or two that we might want to add to our small but growing anti-jealousy kit. Instead of featuring our own modest triumphs, these other stories showcase an even more improbable heroine: the other woman.

One of the main imports from the het culture is a folk myth about mate-stealers: those designing and unscrupulous females who break up happy couples. According to the myth, these sorcerers work their wiles on unsuspecting partners, luring them away from the hearths and hearts that hold them dear. We might call these tales "jealousy-feeder myths." Big-J jealousy depends on them. If we hadn't been thoroughly steeped in such tall tales, that green-eyed monster might lose its clout–might even become a diminutive creature cute enough to cuddle.

The best way to get rid of the feeder stories that nourish jealousy is to replace them with different sorts of other-woman fables. Instead of cautionary tales that feature scheming couple-busters, these rehabilitated other women can be harmless diversions or valuable fantasies. In some cases, they can even enhance our relationships.

POSITIVE OTHER-WOMAN STORIES

The following tales are only the beginning of myriad possibilities. Positive other-women stories are all around us. As soon as we turn down the Jezebel decibels, we will begin to hear them.

The Other Woman as Occasional Lark

Rand, Victoria, and Victoria's Secret

The workshop was such a groaner that even though they had never met, the two of them were immediately joined in a communion of horrified eye-rolling. Without any prearranged signal, they both escaped before the question-and-answer period. Once in the hallway, they decided to draft a protest letter to the conference chair about the ineptness of the presenter. But instead, they just had coffee and talked. After an hour together, spending the night together was a foregone conclusion.

The next day, when Victoria caught her flight home, she decided not to tell her partner what had happened. But, somehow Rand knew. When she insisted that Victoria smelled different, Victoria blurted out, "But, I took a shower."

"A shower after what?" Rand asked acidly. And Victoria confessed. It was nothing, she assured Rand. She had no intention of seeing her again.

The never-to-be-repeated slip at a conference or a weekend away may be a story that we've heard and dismissed with a shrug. But instead of forgetting the story, or filing it away under "Ho hum," we might want to retrieve it, consider it carefully–even give it a more reputable role in our stock of other-women stories. Why? In the first place, the partner who has been dallying may be wrestling with another mega-myth. Because she had a great time, she may be telling herself such a chance encounter was a one-in-a-million longshot. How can she ignore such an obvious subpoena from Cupid? She would be a fool not to follow up–not to seize such an opportunity. And an encore would be so easy to arrange. A few keystrokes, and thousands of miles dissolve instantly.

For most of us, the line between meaningful and casual is a fine one. Just how fine is evident in the account of lesbians who have sex outside of the contexts of dating or long-term relationships. Robin, a friend and frequenter of Bay Area lesbian sex clubs, recalls a recent encounter at the Ecstasy Lounge: "We had a wonderful time . . . tender, caring, exciting. Afterward, we talked for awhile and showered. I made sure to get her address and phone number. For the next couple of weeks, I played with the idea of calling or writing. Then I got a note from her: she had been wondering whether to call me. She wasn't sure if she would, but she told me she had a wonderful time and gave me her address and phone number again. I sent a similar note back to her. Neither of us ever called."

As both women contemplated making something more of their encounter, their future hung in the air. But perhaps because both were experienced one-timers, they decided not to pursue it. Robin's summary: "It was a delightful memory . . . one of the most pure, definable relationships I ever had."

While such brief encounters foreclose one kind of future, they open a door on another one–that is, the permanent possibility of such miniaturized relationships. Part art-form, part serendipity, one-time meetings offer us a gift. But in order to accept it, we have to have a readily available story that tells us that these experiences can be both exquisite and complete. Being able to tell such a meaningful mini-story is vital for the partner who has had a fling. And it is equally important for her primary partner. Why?

Because, contrary to popular opinion, the glue that holds couples together is not sex or good communication. It is mutual storytelling. The more couples can improvise together as they go along–weave events into collaborative stories–the sturdier their relationships will be. Take the example of the conference fling. Say the partner of the one-timer knows only two-timing stories. What if, as soon as she hears what happened at the conference, she starts invoking the standard other-woman doomsday scenario? All hopes of any collaboration are dashed. In reaction, her wavering partner is likely to become defensive and guilty. Eager to find some credibility for *her* story, she is much more likely to look for confirmation from the only other person who knows the encounter was casual. She calls her conference buddy, only to find out that she also got a hostile reception at home. Now the two have much more reason for bonding than their brief fling provided: they can commiserate about their intolerant lovers. It is this collaboration rather than anything erotic that forms the basis of their new relationship.

On the other hand, if the stay-at-home partner has her own well-developed fund of girlz-will-be-boyz capers (and has done her jealousy practice), she may even embellish her partner's fling story with a few lewd observations or recollections of her own indiscretions. The result: by converting a potentially divisive tale into a whimsical fable, the couple has proven that their partnership is strong enough to withstand outside sex.

Perhaps next time they go out with friends, they may even jointly relate the story to the rapt group: "As soon as she came off the plane, I knew. I could smell it." "Yeah," her partner retorts with a mock scowl, "she always told me about the summer her mother bred bloodhounds. Before this, I always thought she just meant her mother *raised* them." Their friends' amused reactions to the story further certify the sturdiness of the couple.

The Modular Other Woman

Impetuous-moment stories are important additions to every couple's jealousy prevention kit. Another kind of story installs the other woman more permanently in the life of the couple. Harder to tell, these stories are nevertheless an equally important addition to anti-J repertoires.

Siri and Rusty

When Siri, a starry-eyed twenty-five-year-old, first arrived in San Francisco, she made a beeline for gay bars and found herself in the middle of Carnival. Ms. and Mr. Leather were in the process of being crowned at a popular hot spot. In the ensuing revelry, Siri went home with a runner-up. By the next morning, she and Rusty were an item.

From the beginning, part of the Rusty package was a Saturday night play party once or twice a month. The rest of the time, the two of them were indistinguishable–except perhaps for an occasional private scene– from the vanilla couple next-door. A year later, Siri and Rusty broke up. When Siri started seeing someone new, she was surprised to find out that Saturday night parties were not automatically part of dating. And even more amazed to realize that her new girlfriend expected a sexually exclusive relationship.

In 1951, anthropologists Clellan Ford and Frank Beach published the first exhaustive study of sexual practices around the globe. The two researchers found 17 out of 139 societies in which extra-marital relations were extremely common. Probably they were not even counting a unique cluster of lesbians. Along with the Chukchee of Siberia, the Ammassalik of Greenland, and the Banaro of New Guinea, a small band of lesbians has learned to tell their own unique other-woman stories. Under certain circumstances, both partners assume the other woman exists. From time to time, one or both partners will have sex with her.

How is it possible for couples to tell tales that run so counter to most other-woman stories? These gifted storytellers start with an entirely different premise: instead of expecting lifelong fidelity, these partners believe it is only a matter of time until the potentially disruptive outsider shows up on their door-step. They don't wait for their hunch to materialize. Applying a strategy that sociologists call "anticipatory coping," they prepare for the inevitable knock on the door by putting up a series of greeting signs: Yo, stranger! Welcome! We've been expecting you. No, don't enter here. Go around the corner. Take the second door to the left, and follow the green arrow. You'll find a small but well-appointed room at the end of the corridor. Make yourself comfortable.

In other words, certain partners define the separate quarters of the newcomer in terms of a series of do's and don'ts. For example, one couple may agree that playing at sex parties or clubs is okay, but private dates are off-limits. Other lesbian couples establish different ways to encapsulate the other woman. Outside dates, for example, are permitted, but they can occur only, say, on Wednesday nights. As long as she is securely contained, the other woman can become a staple, even a relationship enhancer–as predictable and indispensable as a regular yearly vacation. A few mutually agreed-upon rules can turn potentially menacing intruders into insignificant others.

The Invisible Other Woman

Another way to neutralize the other-woman threat is to enlarge each partner's personal sphere. After a slight adjustment in what each partner accepts as a "normal" amount of privacy, cheating is no longer possible. The tired old tale of the secret affair becomes a story of healthy boundary maintenance.

Margot and Rish

Margot and Rish refer to themselves as space queens. But they didn't start out that way. Five years ago, just when they were about to move in together, an old girlfriend of Rish's resurfaced. According to Margot and Rish, if they had been under the same roof at the time, they wouldn't have weathered the affair. As it was, they barely spoke for a year after it was over. But Rish persevered in making amends, and, eventually Margot relented. Or rather she adopted a wait-and-see policy.

During the probation period, both came to realize that there would be other problems if they lived together. Margot requires a certain amount of squalor to function, whereas Rish is a neat-freak. Rish uses Mozart for background noise, and Margot never turns off the sports channel. So they decided to make their temporary living-apart status permanent. Now, each suits herself when she is alone.

Having learned the hard way that they can't survive outside affairs, they have decided to limit information about them. They spend most nights together, at one apartment or the other; but for one day and

*night, each week, they have agreed to log off each other's gaydar
screens. As far as each is concerned, the other could be watching
football, picking lint off the carpet, or having orgies. Mostly, they
confide confidentially, they spend the time wishing they could be together.*

When partners first get together, they may have different ideas
about what is mine, yours, and ours. Time, money, even how many
daydreams to share are up for discussion. And no two relationships are
alike. For some couples, the "us" pile is so huge it dwarfs both the
"me" and "her" stacks. In less mutually-oriented partnerships, the
opposite may be true. And, of course, the stacks aren't static. Renegotiations are always underway. In a given week, for example, one
partner may want more together-time, the other more alone-time. Or,
if they move in together, they may decide to pool resources to pay for
household expenses. As a result, the togetherness pile may surge.

Acknowledged or not, many couples also have three sex stacks.
There is ours, yours, and my sex. Private sex may consist of a favorite
fantasy or a vibrator quickie after a girlfriend has gone to work. The
erotic activities in one's private domain are not exactly secret. But just
as we don't divulge the amount we paid for a pair of birthday earrings,
we don't announce every time we plug in Magic Wanda.

In other words, the ongoing collaborative story that most partners
tell about their relationships includes a chapter or two about privacy.
In most cases, this privacy does not extend to other sexual partners.
Yet, what if it did? What if, right between the chapters entitled "Time
Apart" and "Separate Friendships," there were a section called "Pri-
vate Part(ner)s?"

Because there is a cultural consensus about certain kinds of priva-
cies, most couples don't even have to agree about rules. We take it for
granted, for example, that we won't listen in on our partner's phone
conversations or open her mail. The fact that there is a great hullaba-
loo when such violations *do* occur only proves that a partner has,
indeed, stepped over the line.

When it comes to other women, however, an opposite set of un-
stated cultural rules immediately goes into effect. As mates, we *know*
we must be vigilant–head off any Jezebel headed our way. Therefore,
previously taboo behavior–spying, prying, or even hiring private de-
tectives–is suddenly culturally mandated. If either partner suspects an

other-woman invasion, she is almost obligated to violate her partner's privacy in ways she would never consider under any other circumstances.

In order to tell new stories, therefore, we needn't find ways to domesticate or diminish the other woman. We need only consciously extend the usual cultural rules about privacy–the ones that already apply to our fantasies and our vibrator–to other sexual partners. How? There are plenty of ways to tell the Private Part(ner)s story.

For example, some partners agree to being unaccountable to each other during certain specified periods of time. During the blackouts, each is free to do what she likes without reporting in. By mutual consent, all traces of other partners are meticulously removed from housing and conversation.

Still other partners may prefer the information filter to be partial. In other words, they prefer to know about the existence of other sexual partners but want to be spared all the details.

For example, after much discussion about what each needed to know about her partner's extramarital encounters, one couple devised a postsex questionnaire that included the following multiple-choice queries:

1. If your fling had placed a personals ad, what would it say? (e.g., "married babe seeks chick on the side.")
2. How would you rate this experience?
   It sucked
   Not sure if it was worth it
   It was better than sitting at home
   It was as good as *Red Rock West*
   It blew my mind
   It changed my life
   Jury is not in yet
3. How would you rate this person overall?
   Serial killer
   Drip
   Unremarkable
   Nice
   Really cool
   Want this person in my life (sexual interest dead)

Can imagine long-term something (my interest isn't dead)
Can imagine falling in love (my interest isn't dead)
4. Should I worry about the state of our relationship?
No, you should join me in laughing at this pathetic person who tried to pursue me.
No, you should be happy that I'm having fun and learning new tricks.
You should know that this person is important to me and I plan to have her in my life in some way.
Yes. A letter follows.

Another couple consciously made information about outside sex optional. Each kept a brief log of her encounters with other women. Both partners' record books, which listed only names, places, and dates, were left on top of the bookcase–available for either to check if she so desired. One partner never checked the log. After a peek or two, the other stopped.

This kind of other-woman story can be told in many ways. Even so, it may not suit all storytellers. For example, the inadvertent clairvoyants among us may be at a distinct disadvantage. Intentional informational blackouts don't work for those of us who rely on ESP to track our partner's moods and maneuverings. In fact, for the very sensitive, maintaining the psychological space required for private part(ner)s may not be possible under the same roof. And living apart may not be a desirable option. For many couples, the delights of living together clearly outweigh the more uncertain pleasures of privacy.

One couple, however, seems to have devised an eat-your-cake-and-have-it-too solution. Eager to maintain a high level of privacy *and* intimacy–and avoid the schlep factor of crosstown apartments–the women live in separate flats in the same building. Together for ten years, they seem to have proved that forever-after is indeed a multistoreyed affair.

When they need privacy in small quarters, the Japanese use shoji screens to cordon off certain areas. These room dividers can be shifted according to the needs of the moment: a child's play area in the morning becomes a dining room in the evening and a bedroom at night. It doesn't take a heavyweight to move the light as-a-feather shoji screens. A subtle touch will do it. And even though the illusion is transparent, it gets the job done. If we figure out ways to devise our own shoji screens, we are relieved of the necessity of telling any stories at all about the other woman.

The Other Woman as Permanent Partner

Another set of lesbians, perhaps the wily coyotes of the dyke tribe, also balk at other-woman stories, negative or positive. Their solution to the problem? They simply turn the outsider into an insider. They marry the other woman.

PJ, Kelsen, and Dana

Longtime political activists and permanent partners, PJ and Kelsen were PFLAG darlings, the twosome who could be counted on to show-case their relationship whenever any lesbian or gay organization needed to display a lesbian poster couple. They got to know Dana when she joined the board of the AIDS hospice. Over the next year, all three had ample opportunity to work together on fund-raisers and staffing crises. It seemed only natural when Dana broke up with her girlfriend for Kelsen and PJ to offer her their spare bedroom. And even more natural, after about six months, to invite her into their bed. That was six years ago. Since then, they've bought a new king-sized bed, and a house big enough to accommodate it.

Mention threesomes, and most of us conjure up the relationship-from-hell story. In a desperate effort to ward off a me-or-her ultimatum–a forced choice between a new and an old lover–both members of the couple agree to an experiment. Somehow they will find a way to include the newcomer in their partnership. The ensuing folie-a-trois is foreshadowed in the first stanzas of "Field," a poem by lesbian poet Olga Broumas:

> I had a lover. Let us say we were married, owned
> a house, shared a car . . .
>
> . . . In time, my lover came to take
> another lover, of whom I also became enamored.
> There is a seagull floating backward in a rare
>
> snowstorm on an Atlantic Ocean bay as I remember this,
> its head at an angle that suggests amusement.

Had they been as detached as the bird, the poem makes clear, they might have avoided a tempestuous free-for-all. But, despite Broumas's bittersweet reflections, third parties are just what some couples need. In certain cases, the incorporation of the other woman into seasoned relationships can stabilize, and even enhance, partnerships.

When an old friend told me she had met a long-term threesome, I asked her to introduce me. Next time I visited her in Albuquerque, she arranged for me to meet them. Over the next six months, the Internet helped me find and interview two other long-term threesomes.

A dozen hours spent with three threesomes hardly constitutes an in-depth study of such relationships. But it does suggest that under certain circumstances, long-term partners can and do successfully re-configure their twosomes into permanent threesomes. How and why do such arrangements develop?

Actually, if we think about it for a minute, it becomes evident that threesomes are not exceptional. No matter how coupled we are, we rarely remain in actual twosomes for very long. Our intimacies are not hermetically sealed. Typically, pets or parents, children or friends are constantly joining and expanding our magic circle. In fact, most of us probably spend more time in threesomes and foursomes than we do in twosomes.

Sometimes the newcomer's presence is disruptive. Or sometimes the addition becomes a fulcrum, correcting a dangerous wobble between the two partners. Because these third parties aren't dreaded other women, however, we hardly notice the frequency of their comings and goings.

Each of the three threesomes I interviewed had evolved in a different fashion. One of the long-term arrangements was inaugurated when both members of a couple simultaneously became attracted to someone new and agreed to invite her aboard. In another situation, the already convinced–and smitten–half of the couple acted as Cupid between her dubious partner and the new recruit. In the third, one of the original partners was significantly older than her longtime partner. Because she was no longer interested in sex, she suggested that her partner find another sexual partner. Her partner obliged.

One of the threesomes had only three-way sex. Another alternated between two- and threesomes. In the third, where the sexually disinterested partner participated in the threesome in primarily nonsexual ways, only two of the partners were erotically linked.

Whether or not such relationships should be "open" to new members was just as much of a sticking point as it is for most twosomes. One threesome closed ranks quickly, declaring themselves sexually exclusive. Another, opting for a yeastier brew, continued to look for new family members. The third, like many twosomes, remains divided—and embattled—over the issue of open or closed boundaries.

The partners who made up these trios were very different from one another. In addition to ages that ranged, in one threesome, from thirty-one to seventy-two, partners had different backgrounds and occupations. The Albuquerque partnership, for example, consisted of a forty-year-old Hispanic pilot, a forty-two-year-old Jewish house painter, and a twenty-eight-year-old WASP who worked for minimum wage in a nonprofit agency (and who had changed her name in order not to embarrass her conservative Republican parents).

What struck me about all three partnerships was what I might call resource-intensiveness. When we think of threesomes, the metaphor of the third wheel—the unwanted extra—immediately comes to mind. After my exposure to these trios, however, the old metaphor never quite recovered its former potency. On the contrary, the extra wheel was usually an asset. Whenever a particular need arose, somebody was on hand to take care of it. For example, if someone was short of cash that week, someone else pitched in to cover household expenses. Ditto for emotional support, sexual energy, child care help, even companionship.

All this extra resourcefulness didn't come without a price. The profusion of people, pets—and in one household, two children plus a gang of their chums—probably made a quiet evening at home unlikely. And, besides being part of these abundant households, each of the women had her own outside life—friends, work, and recreational activities. Consequently, the appointment books of the partners resembled the radar screens in the traffic control tower at JFK. In fact, in order to manage the volume of incoming and outgoing messages, one of the three households boasted three phone lines, three computers, and two faxes.

In addition to the necessity for all the outside world links, the trios required more time for discussion about everything from hurt feelings to chores. Agreements about how to minimize friction among these menages had to be painstakingly hammered out. Item number nine in one of the threesomes' twenty-page contract, for example, reads as follows: "Household currently owns and maintains three cats and three dogs. Additional family pets or pets replacing existing animals which would impact family finances or shared spaces must be approved by all co-owners. If, however, an individual wishes to have a new pet which will reside exclusively in its mistress' office (e.g., fish or a caged pet), consensus is not required."

Diverse and lively as these arrangements were, there was one thing all the threesomes had in common. Though each woman was open about her lesbianism, all were very discreet about their current arrangements. Outside of a few trusted friends or close family members, no one knew about their three-way intimacies. It's not surprising. Lesbian couples are still on the fringes of reputability. What chance is there that a trio of loving women would be viewed with anything other than suspicion and hostility? Consequently, these trios have more than one reason for their extra-large closets. Unfortunately, their necessary protective secrecy shortchanges us all. As a result, most of us will never have a chance to be directly exposed to a truly unique otherwoman story.

The Other Woman as Forever-After Partner

Even without a face or a form, the other woman can be our ally. She can be a vital remembrance of things past, or a bridge to the future. She can be a foil for our living, breathing relationship or a crystal ball that reveals all sorts of otherwise inaccessible secrets.

Barb and Maggie

It was a funny thing. After a decade together, it became clear to Barb that Maggie wasn't going to leave her for someone else. The other woman whom Barb had always feared had never materialized. It was at that point that the sea change happened. Barb's fantasy tilted wildly and made a 180-degree turn. Instead of a marauder who would steal Maggie, the other woman she had been so afraid of turned into her own phantom lover. Vague, yet enticing, she was more a possibility than a person. She was an inviting envoy from the world beyond their relationship.

At first, the notion of intentionally dreaming up the other woman sounds as preposterous as having a piranha for a pet. But not if we think about it for a moment. Our lives teem with phantoms. These apparitions–typically in the form of abusive or simply absent parents–have a tendency to rattle their skeletons just when we thought we were safe at last. Or, instead of the ghosts of parents, they are ex-lovers we would just as soon forget. Just when we are getting ready to curl up with our girlfriends, they do a wild fandango across the bedroom.

Many of us spend small fortunes in time and energy and money ' trying to exorcise these phantoms. But instead of trying to dislodge our virtual visitors, why not add a positive spirit guide or two to our mental menageries? One who might exert a more positive influence?

Such additions to our spirit families are particularly important for those of us who specialize in the souls of others. Plenty of us work at jobs that require great amounts of handholding. Others of us, conscientious mothers and dutiful daughters and accommodating partners, simply nurture out of love or habit. Paid or unpaid, full-time caretakers rarely have time to reflect on the state of our own souls. Preoccupied with the needs of others, usually such mind readers extraordinaire have not cultivated the habit of probing their own psyches. Here's where the other woman comes in. When we conjure up our heart's desire, we create a delicate mirroring device. Other-women fantasies are crystal balls that reveal our souls.

Try for just a minute to summon her up. Perhaps she never quite comes into focus. Instead she is a vague longing for what might be–a nameless, faceless melancholy. About what? About everything and nothing. About life.

Or perhaps her contours are faintly familiar. Perhaps though not exactly a replica of someone who was once important to us, the new fantasy has the qualities of an ex. Perhaps, in our determination to put the past behind us, we have overlooked the fact that–along with all her disagreeable traits–there are qualities in an ex-partner that we miss and long for.

In other words, who we conjure up tells us something about what we are missing. If someone unfamiliar swims into view, be sure to examine her closely. Notice her hair, the way she walks, her breasts, her clothes. Is she older or younger? Bigger or smaller? Darker or lighter? All these details will tell us something about the state of our souls. If she turns out to be a Christiane Annapour clone who shuttles between Beirut and Sarajevo on assignments for CNN, chances are we are missing a certain on-the-edge-frisson. If she is a Jodie Foster look-alike, whom we sport on our arm, chances are we are limelight-deprived. If an earth mother smothers us in bosomy hugs, we might be feeling undernurtured.

You might want to develop your other-woman fantasy. Install her as your permanent muse. Pay attention to her. She'll tell you whether to sign up for a scuba class or just buy some new lingerie. And after you do what she suggests, check in with her from time to time. Has she changed? Is she suggesting another direction? You are entitled to keep her to yourself. She is, after all, purely your playmate, soul mate–combination projection, reflection, guide. And, Aphrodite forbid, if anything should ever happen to your partner, your fantasy lover will be there for you. She will share your memories and your tears. She will console and commiserate. And, one day, when the time is right, she will lead you back to the world.

WELCOME TO THE GLOBAL GAY VILLAGE

An ample supply of positive other-women anecdotes is not a magic pill. Such stories will not prevent suspicion or cure a breaking heart. They will never curb old familiar nightmares or incite a glorious revolution in intimacy. On the other hand, these stories may give our relationships the extra durability necessary to weather the ticklish situations that are likely to come up during the course of our relationships.

"We are everywhere" is a wonderfully affirming statement when it applies to all those institutions previously off-limits. The more lesbians and gays who manage to infiltrate the military, hold public office, or crack the lavender ceiling inside a Fortune 500 corporation, the better. But what about our private lives? Do we really want so many queers around after we have found our mate? When our lover has lunch with cruisy co-workers every day or has cozy electronic chats with intriguing strangers every night, we may feel like "we are everywhere" is just a keystroke away from "I am nowhere."

Hooked up and hypermobile, plenty of us now interface with dykes more often than we go to the bathroom. The sheer volume of queer contact almost guarantees that even after we have found our true love and settled down, we will probably experience flash-points–hot connections that, in the best of all possible worlds, would be reserved for lovers.

The stories we tell shape our lives. If we have only one story about forever-after, a tale about cloistered twosomes who always renounce the world's temptations, these inevitable flameups along the way are much more likely to turn our partnerships into flameouts. At the first knock on the cloister door, we will be convinced that our worst fears have come true. We know it. We can feel it in our bones: Our darling is in the process of leaving us. It is only a matter of time. Or, just as terrifying, we are the ones abandoning our mates. And the pain or guilt about such perceived betrayal may even hasten the end.

Paradoxically, the effect of the forever-after story can be even more damaging in situations where partnerships don't dissolve. Let's say, upon hearing news that an attractive stranger is lurking nearby, we beef up the border patrols. Nobody is going anywhere, we vow through gritted teeth. Even if our determination heads off a break-in or breakup, the price of forever-after may be high, too high. Ensconced in our newly-reinforced, us-against-them fortresses, we are likely to feel more besieged than beloved.

But what if we have other stories in our repertoire? Instead of limiting ourselves to fables about hermetically sealed relationships, we might have plenty of other tales about the periodic comings and goings of strangers. The visitors might be irresistible waifs who remind us of the blessings we have been taking for granted. Or envoys who bring enchanting news of faraway places we never even suspected existed. Perhaps our mi-casa-su-casa hospitality knows no bounds. Then again, it might be limited to a single night . . . at the crack of dawn, the guests must move on.

Stories about the myriad ways in which other women can make valuable contributions to our lives won't render our relationships intruder-proof. Nothing can do that. But, in today's meetmarket world, such tales will make our partnerships safer.

Poly Wants a Lover

Ellen Orleans

SUMMARY. Taking a humorous approach to the question of polyamory, this article recalls the author's first and only brush with the concept. After exploring several real-life complications that might arise when polyamory is put into practice, the essay then acknowledges some practical benefits of the multi-partnered lifestyle.

Well, we wouldn't be lesbians if we didn't explore a new sexual slant every few years, and more than that, have a catchy name for it.

Polyamory. It sounds friendly enough. Kind of like Pollyanna. "Oh, honey, it's okay, I see now that you weren't cheating on me. You were just engaging in a little polyamory."

Actually, that's not accurate. One of the givens of a polyamorous relationship is that there's no sneaking around. Extracurricular sex is discussed beforehand, everything out in the open. I only know this because I read it in a book somewhere. Truth is, I have no experience in polyamory land. Okay, once. Sort of.

The year is 1988. I'm 26 years old but have the sexual experience of a house plant. But that January night, I find myself watching videos at

Ellen Orleans is the author of four humor books including *The Butches of Madison County*, which won the 1996 Lambda Literary Award for best Gay and Lesbian Humor. She recently completed a two-act comedy, *God, Guilt and Gefilte Fish*, and is at work on a novel. This article first appeared in the May, 1997 issue of the newspaper *Weird Sisters* and is used here by permission of the author. Ellen is an adjunct faculty member at The Naropa Institute in Boulder, Colorado.

Address correspondence to Ellen Orleans, P.O. Box 1348, Boulder, CO 80306.

[Haworth co-indexing entry note]: "Poly Wants a Lover." Orleans, Ellen. Co-published simultaneously in *Journal of Lesbian Studies* (The Haworth Press, Inc.) Vol. 3, No. 1/2, 1999, pp. 63-65; and: *The Lesbian Polyamory Reader: Open Relationships, Non-Monogamy, and Casual Sex* (ed: Marcia Munson and Judith P. Stelboum) The Haworth Press, Inc., 1999, pp. 63-65.

a friend's house, a blanket draped over our laps. Her knee touches mine but I just figure that's because it's a small couch.

The last video ends, it's late, but we begin talking. She explains that she and her lover are trying an "open relationship" for the next few months.

For anyone else on the planet, this admission, coupled with the not-so-subtle knee contact, would be an obvious come-on. I, however, assume we are merely having another one of our fascinating interpersonal discussions. Finally, she spells it out for me. She's attracted to me. Am I interested?

I am. I am also nervous, flattered and curious. Not to mention inexperienced. *Really* inexperienced. I'm thinking: oh-my-god, can I do this? Will she guess how little I know? What if I'm awful at it? What if I'm not really a lesbian after all? What I am *not* thinking about is primary and secondary relationships, sexual theory, and especially not polyamory.

We kiss for a long time on the couch, then go upstairs. By this time it's two a.m. and to tell you the truth we don't do much more before falling asleep. We do, however, have a warm and cuddly conversation the next morning. We describe our fantasy houses. *This* I remember. (Mine had a wrap-around porch and a creek.)

The hard truth of polyamory arises the next day. It turns out that her lover isn't pleased about our encounter. Seems this lover (a prominent lesbian-about-town by whom I am greatly intimidated) had a different vision in mind. By an open relationship, she meant it was okay to have sex with someone passing through town. Someone you didn't know and probably would never see again. Certainly not someone you liked.

Which brings me to my problem with polyamory. On top of the jealousy, hurt and damaged egos, how do you work through all the nuanced interpretations, the immeasurable "*I* thought you meant"'s? Frankly, polyamory looks like processing hell.

And what about the little things, the small touches that only lovers know? How do you keep track of who takes milk in her coffee, who drinks it black, who won't touch caffeine? For that matter, stocking your refrigerator must be a nightmare. Sliced turkey for the meat eater, soy milk for the lactose intolerant, wine for the one not in AA.

And, to be blunt, how do you remember who likes what in bed? This is crucial. "But sweetheart, I thought you *liked* it when I slid my–oops, never mind."

And speaking of bed, what happens if you wake up with an early-to-rise lover but go to sleep with a late-to-bed lover? I'm sure sleep deprivation is really going to help you remember who likes what when.

Not that I have to worry about any of this. I mean even if I could perfect the art of negotiation and memorize countless intimate details, I'd still run up against the same basic problem. Finding lovers to be polyamorous with.

I mean, it's impossible enough to find *one* compatible woman, let alone two or three. Someone who can put up with my weird schedule, variable cash flow and easily-distracted mind. Someone who's stable yet flexible, discerning yet warm-hearted, knows her own mind but is not a control freak. Someone who is spiritual, intellectual, playful, outdoorsy, shares my sense of humor

Wait! I'm seeing the light here. With polyamory, nobody has to do it all! Lover #1 can be a stable and warm-hearted espresso drinker, while lover #2 can be an intellectual, outdoorsy vegetarian. And even if lover #3 is a meat-eating, control freak, well, if she's driving me nuts some weekend, I can always flee her place, and instead invite #1 or #2 over to mine.

As long as they aren't with each other.

And my refrigerator is properly stocked.

FRIENDS AND LOVERS

The Three of Cups

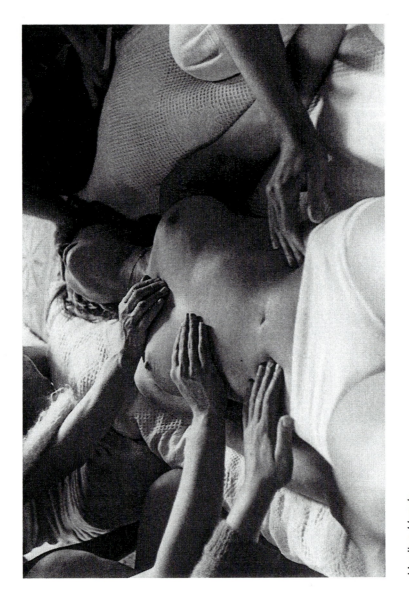

Healing Hands

Poly-Friendships

Esther (Polyester?) Rothblum

SUMMARY. In contrast to the monogamous model for sexual relationships (including those of lesbians) in western society, friendships are permitted to be polyamorous. However, friendships do not receive the level of salience and priority that sexual relationships do. This article focuses on three issues that keep lesbians from prioritizing friendships: (1) the culture of sex in the U.S. and western nations; (2) the way we define "sex"; and (3) the way we define friendships. *[Article copies available for a fee from The Haworth Document Delivery Service: 1-800-342-9678. E-mail address: getinfo@haworthpressinc.com]*

Picture the following scenario.

You live on a planet on which Friendship is the most important issue in people's lives. Whereas you are expected to have lots of lovers (and

---

Esther D. Rothblum, PhD, is Professor in the Department of Psychology at the University of Vermont, and editor of the *Journal of Lesbian Studies.* She has edited the books *Lesbian Friendships* (New York University Press, 1996) and *Boston Marriages: Romantic But Asexual Relationships Among Contemporary Lesbians* (University of Massachusetts Press, 1993). A portion of this paper appeared in *Out in the Mountains*, the gay/lesbian newspaper of Vermont, in September 1997, and is used here by permission.

Address correspondence to Esther Rothblum, Department of Psychology, John Dewey Hall, University of Vermont, Burlington, VT 05405.

The author would like to thank all her friends for serving as the inspiration of this article, especially Marny Hall for coming up with the idea of writing about friendships as polyamorous, and Connie Chan, Estelle Freedman, Nanette Gartrell, Marcia Hill, Joy Livingston, Naomi McCormick, Beth Mintz, and Diana Russell for their helpful comments.

[Haworth co-indexing entry note]: "Poly-Friendships." Rothblum, Esther (Polyester?). Co-published simultaneously in *Journal of Lesbian Studies* (The Haworth Press, Inc.) Vol. 3, No. 1/2, 1999, pp. 71-83; and: *The Lesbian Polyamory Reader: Open Relationships, Non-Monogamy, and Casual Sex* (ed: Marcia Munson and Judith P. Stelboum) The Haworth Press, Inc., 1999, pp. 71-83. Single or multiple copies of this article are available for a fee from The Haworth Document Delivery Service [1-800-342-9678, 9:00 a.m. - 5:00 p.m. (EST). E-mail address: getinfo@haworthpressinc.com].

also co-workers, acquaintances, neighbors, etc.), these represent weaker bonds on your planet. Every adult is expected to have one Friend, a person who is her soulmate, intimate partner, and life companion.

Furthermore, your planet is basically "mono-affilious" about Friendships. Though you can express "friendliness" in order to find your true Friend, once you have become part of a Friendship, you are expected to remain committed to this Friendship. You and your Friend will have an extravagant Friendship Commitment Ceremony that takes months to plan and to which you will invite all your lovers, co-workers, and other people you know. They will hear you exchange vows about remaining faithful to each other "in sickness and in health" for the rest of your lives.

There are strict rules on your planet about friendliness with anyone who is not your Friend. Friendliness is frowned upon in the workplace or other situations in which you are expected to maintain a professional identity. If you spend too much time with one particular lover, people may wonder whether you are more than "just lovers" and suspect that you are "cheating" on your Friend. You can have fantasies of being friendly with lovers, but you're not supposed to "act on" these feelings without endangering your Friendship.

Ever since you were a child, lots of toys and games focused on themes related to finding a Friend in adulthood. Your story books ended with Friends living "happily ever after." Friendships in adolescence are not expected to last long, because everyone knows that to enter into a serious Friendship you have to have a degree of maturity. Teens are encouraged to experiment in developing friendliness skills. However, adults have a lot of control over which people are appropriate Friends for young people, and in the past you rebelled when family members thought they knew who would make a good potential Friend for you.

Most official documents ask about your Friendship Status–single, in a Friendship, separated, or having ended a Friendship. There are some unkind words to describe people who don't have a Friend. Whether you have a current Friend and how things are going in your Friendship is the first thing that people around you, like lovers or family members, want to know when they see you.

There are other constant reminders about the importance of Friendships. Just about every popular song, television show, and magazine, as well as lots of books, focus on Friendship themes–people getting into and out of Friendships, finding the ideal Friend, losing a Friend through death or infidelity, or having Friendship difficulties. No matter what product you see advertised, it is somehow linked with your ability to get into and remain in your Friendship. In fact, it is hard to feel good about your Friendship because there are so many things you should be buying or doing to improve your friendliness. Scores of how-to books, many of them best-sellers, focus on ways to meet a Friend, to "work on" your Friendship, to keep your Friend from leaving you for another, or to keep a longterm Friendship from losing its spice. And everyone knows that the older you are when a Friendship ends, the harder it will be to enter into another Friendship because most people your age already have Friends and are thus "taken."

Of course, census data indicate that many people end their Friendships at some point, and others are "nonmono-affilious," often in secret. You know this because a sub-theme of most Friendship books, movies, or TV soap operas is about Friendships that are experiencing some difficulty. You are aware that spending too much time at work can interfere with your Friendship, and there were occasions when you told your lovers that you had less time to spend with them when you were entering a new Friendship.

Religious leaders on your planet are very concerned about the increasing rate of Friendships ending. Should you and your Friend decide to seek therapy for Friendship-related problems, you are likely to find a therapist who has been trained to view friendliness as one of the single most important themes underlying both healthy and maladaptive functioning. This is particularly true for followers of Dr. Freund (the German word for "friend"), although the general public finds his views controversial, particularly the idea that even young children *can have fantasies of friendliness.*

Recently, you were at a work-related conference and you met a woman whom you really liked and acted friendly with. Though you couldn't be certain, you were pretty sure that she was friendly to you, too. Since then, thoughts of her have consumed your day, and you have even confessed this to some of your lovers. But you also have some serious concerns. How would you find time to spend with more than one Friend? What if your current Friend found out and it affected your Friendship with her, which has been comfortable (though not perfect) for so many years? The two of you would need to discuss the ground rules of such a complicated Dual Friendship. Even if you decided to limit the new Friendship to out-of-town trips, wouldn't it affect your ability to be 100% committed to your current Friend?

If only Friendships weren't so complicated! Take your lover relationships, for example. Your lovers aren't jealous of each other and you're not jealous when they have sex with other people. Nobody cares about how many lovers you have. In fact, it's even hard to know who is and isn't a "lover" in your life right now because that term is used so loosely on your planet to describe anyone with whom you have sex. After all, sex is not well-defined and can describe all kinds of thoughts, behaviors, and relationships, so who could even begin to have criteria around lovers the way your planet does around Friendships? If only everyone weren't so obsessed with Friends, Friends, Friends! At times, it's enough to make you feel like an alien.

I have certainly felt like an alien in my own passion for my friends and friendships over my lifetime. Nothing quite matches the electricity of finding a friend who is a kindred spirit–someone with whom I can share my innermost thoughts. Going on a trip with a close friend–whether to the racquetball club or across the country–is better than eating chocolate. Getting letters, e-mail messages, or audiotapes from friends are delightful breaks from the routine of the day and I can't wait to respond. My favorite way of coping with stress or adversity is to phone up a friend for a sympathetic ear. Though I consider myself somewhat of a workaholic, most of my time is spent working around my friends; when they are free, I drop everything to spend time with them.

As a resident of Planet Earth, and in particular the United States, my passion about friendship coexists with the reality that most other women's passion focuses on sexual relationships. Surprisingly, this has some advantages. Unlike the women on the fictional planet described above, I have permission to be extremely "non-monogamous" in my friendships, and I do in fact relate intimately to a number of close friends. Many of my friends know one another; quite a few are friends with one another, too. Certainly I am "closer" to some friends than to others, though it is not so easy to define what closeness means in friendships–is it level of self-disclosure, hours spent together, number of years that we've known each other, being there for each other during hard times? I usually can't say definitively when friendships begin and end, and this feels comfortable to me, so different from the emotional summits of beginning and terminating relationships with lovers. The drifting in and out of friendships is not static, so that friendships may pick up at certain times when we need or want the togetherness. The major disadvantage in prioritizing friendships in a world that romanticizes sex is that friendships are not validated in the way that lover relationships are. So I rarely get the kind of attention for talking about friendships that others do when they talk about a new romantic/sexual relationship. In this article I will focus on three issues that I find keep lesbians from prioritizing friendships: (1) the culture of sex in the U.S. and western nations; (2) the way we define "sex"; and (3) the way we define friendships. I will also argue that friendships *are* polyamorous and this permission to love more than one friend is in contrast to the way we conceptualize romantic relationships.

THE CULTURE OF SEX

In the scenario that begins this article, the planet has developed into a culture of friendships–the friendship is the core method of relating. In contrast, women in the United States and other western nations live in a culture of sex. Being female in our society means being sexualized and objectified. Girls' toys and products for female adolescents focus heavily on their future roles as sexual beings. Susanna Rose (1996) has described how books and magazines intended for girls and women have a romance narrative, in contrast to the adventure narrative for boys and men. An enormous amount of attention is focused on women finding the ideal male romantic/sexual partner, celebrating this with a lavish ceremony (the wedding), and staying with that same partner for a long time, preferably "forever." (Of course, since women live longer than men and tend to marry men who are somewhat older, "forever" means that women will be alone in their old age anyway). Sex and romance are the themes of songs, movies and television programs, and how-to books and advice columns, especially those intended for women. There is never enough that women can do to feel secure in their sexual attractiveness, even after they are married. Even violence against women often takes a sexual form.

Women's sexuality is portrayed in the media as lighthearted and trivial, yet billions of dollars are at stake. The U.S. economy alone consists of an annual $33 billion diet industry, a $20 billion cosmetic industry, a $300 million cosmetic surgery industry, and a $7 billion pornography industry (Wolf, 1991). The culture of sexuality and its correlates, the cultures of fashion and pornography, portray women almost overwhelmingly as Caucasian, young, extremely thin, middle- or upper-class, able-bodied, and heterosexual. For the majority of women who do not fit this narrow demographic profile, privilege is attained by mimicking this image as closely as possible.

It is vital for the appearance-related economy that women feel responsible for our own sexual attractiveness, so that we will purchase products and engage in practices (e.g., dieting, cosmetic surgery, exercise) to enhance sexual appeal (see Rothblum, 1992; 1993; for reviews). The economy would have much to lose if women stopped being influenced by its messages. This culture of sex, not surprisingly, prioritizes sexual activity, sexual attractiveness, and sexual relationships to the exclusion of all other ways of relating.[1]

How does the culture of sex affect lesbians? Lesbians, too, are socialized as girls and women to value sexual attractiveness. Most lesbians work and socialize with heterosexual people, and are influenced by the sexual messages in the media. Lesbian books and magazines, like those for heterosexual women, focus on the romance narrative (Rose, 1996). For example, in the Naiad Press novel *Never Say Never,* two co-workers, Leslie who is a lesbian and Sara who is heterosexual, become close friends. Though it is obvious to the reader and to both women that they are sexually attracted to each other, the suspense builds as to whether or not Leslie and Sara will "consummate" their relationship–that is, become genitally sexual. Whether or not the women do "it" will affect the reader's perception as to whether the book had a happy ending (they became lovers) or an unhappy one (they remained "just friends").

WHAT IS LESBIAN SEXUAL ACTIVITY?

"Sex" is commonly defined as heterosexual intercourse. JoAnn Loulan (1993) has described how adolescents who have engaged in a number and variety of sexual activities but have not had intercourse will say that they haven't "gone all the way." Sexual activity, as defined by lesbians, is greatly affected by heterosexual definitions of sexual activity. Two women are considered to have engaged in sex if they performed mutual genital stimulation. A lesbian who has never engaged in this activity will probably not believe that she has "gone all the way." The first time women have genital sex has a powerful definitional value, because it distinguishes the relationship from other, non-sexual relationships (e.g., friend, colleague, acquaintance, neighbor) that symbolize weaker bonds in Western society. Women may recall their first experience of heterosexual intercourse as somewhat disappointing, but they knew that the experience "counted" (and in fact, most people can count the number of sexual relationships they have had in a way they don't count numbers of friends, relatives, and co-workers).

Often women tell me that I am using a very narrow definiton of "sex," and say that they define sex in broader terms. Surveys also indicate that lesbians, being women, placed more focus on love, affection, and romance, than on genital sexual activity (e.g., Klinkenberg & Rose, 1994). Nevertheless, ask any lesbian couple that is celebrating the anniversary of their relationship what in fact they are celebrating–that is, what happened on the day they are counting as the anniversary–and the majority (but not all) will say it was the day they first had genital sex (actually, they say sex, not genital sex, but we have a very specific social construction of what we "allow" to be included in the word "sex"). Furthermore, if I come back from a sabbatical year and rave about a new, close friend with whom I spent all my time there, friends are less interested than if I casually mention a one-night sexual encounter with a relative stranger. If I further describe the brief sexual encounter as consisting only of mutual kissing, for example, friends will feel betrayed–this is not "real" sex. If I add that the close friend is sexually attracted to me, this immediately changes the valence of the relationship, because now it includes sexual possibility. In fact, friendships may include a level of flirtatiousness and sexual energy, but if genital sexual activity is absent then the friendship is probably considered to be "nonsexual." What does this say about the narrow definition of sex? What does this say about the salience of sexual encounters–even brief anonymous ones–over friendships–even long-term close ones? If you ask your friends about the number of sexual relationships they have had, they will not count, for example, friends who have been sexually attracted to them unless this friendship became genitally sexual.

This sex-focused definition of a partnered relationship has a number of implications for lesbians in relationships. It focuses on an aspect that may not be what is most important to lesbians in a relationship. Lesbians may feel pressure to have genital sex in order to provide a definition for their romantic feelings for another woman. They may feel pressure to continue having sex in order to view themselves as still being partners. If genital sex ceases, and if one or both partners tells close friends about this, the lesbian community may view the couple as having ended their relationship, and the members of the couple may be considered sexually available by other women (this is different from legal marriages, in which the heterosexual couple is considered to be married even if they have stopped having sex or are having sex with other people). Lack of sexual activity may be interpreted (by the couple, their therapist and the lesbian community) as a sign that something is seriously wrong with the relationship, even if all other aspects of the relationship are satisfying.

Further, the genitally sexual definition of what constitutes a lesbian relationship ignores the reality of women's ways of relating. Certainly romantic love as it has traditionally been conceptualized is a way for women to relate closely to men. Yet for centuries, women have felt strong love, affection, and intimacy for other women, even when both women were married to men. When two unmarried women lived together as "spinsters," they were considered to be in a "Boston marriage," a term that reflected the presumed asexual nature of the relationship (the city of Boston was home of many colleges and universities, and thus some highly educated women). Lillian Faderman (1993) has described the passion and love between U.S. women in the nineteenth century. She stated (1981, pp. 17-18): "It became clear that women's love relationships have seldom been limited to that one area of expression, that love between women has been primarily a sexual phenomenon only in male fantasy literature. 'Lesbian' describes a relationship in which two women's strongest emotions and affections are directed toward each other. Sexual contact may be a part of the relationship to a greater or lesser degree, or it may be entirely absent."

One group that continues to have close, passionate, and nonsexual relationships today are female adolescents. Lisa Diamond (1997) has described what she terms "passionate friendships" among adolescent and young adult women. These friendships are portrayed as "love affairs without the sexual element" (p. 5), with elements of romantic love, idealization, obsession, exclusivity, possessiveness, and sexual desire. Nevertheless, such relationships may be viewed (by the young women and by those around them) as a prelude to a future partnership with a man.

Similarly, Janice Raymond's (1986) book *A Passion for Friends* includes descriptions of women's intimate friendships in non-western cultures in which women, even if married, spend most of their lives in close contact with other women. Oliva Espin (1993) has portrayed close, intimate but nonsexual relationships among unmarried women in Latin American cultures.

WHAT IS FRIENDSHIP?

What is a friend? Unfortunately, the term "friend," particularly in the U.S., has come to mean almost anyone we know who is not a lover. There are four categories of people: (1) lovers (usually one lover); (2) enemies (hopefully none or few); (3) people we haven't met; and (4) friends (that is, everyone else). The *American Heritage Dictionary* definition supports this claim; a friend is defined as: "(1) A person whom one knows, likes, and trusts. (2) An acquaintance. (3) A person with whom one is allied in a struggle or cause; comrade. (4) One who supports, sympathizes with, or patronizes, a group, cause, or movement. (5) A member of the Society of Friends; Quaker." Thus, friends include acquaintances, co-workers, fellow activists, and people who belong to the same groups that we do. Nowhere in this definition is a sense of the friend as soulmate, or the long-term friendships we have carried on for decades, or the best friend we had as young girls.

In contrast to a sexual relationship, a friendship is presumed to be independent of sexual behavior, and to a great extent, of sexual feelings and fantasies. Friendships are so secondary in importance to sexual relationships that many women (including lesbians) have had the experience of a friendship decreasing in intensity when one or both women became sexually involved with someone else. When friendships between women are especially close or intense, outsiders suspect the presence of sexual feelings or behavior.[2] One reason for the greater acceptance of non-monogamy in sexual relationships in the women's communities of the 1970s was the idea that feminists could be close to several other women in the spirit of "sisterhood."

These definitions of sexual relationships and of friendships, respectively, focus on genital activity as a definition (lovers do "it" whereas friends don't) and thus ignore other, nongenital, sexual experiences that women may have had (Loulan, 1993; Rothblum & Brehony, 1993). We have no terminology for the early sexual crushes that some girls develop on other people, usually a female friend. We have no language for the sexual feelings that arise between adult friends, even when both friends are in sexual relationships with other people. In contrast, if the friends engage in genital sexual activity with each other, we immediately have language; they are having an affair.

Furthermore, friendships and sexual relationships are not separate entities. Lesbians often feel that their lover is their friend, even their best friend. Similarly, friends may have sexual feelings for one another, though they may or may not acknowledge these feelings to each other (or even to themselves). Discussion of sexual feelings between friends may interfere with the friendship, given the high salience of sex over friendship in our society. Lesbian ex-lovers often remain friends (see Becker, 1988, for a review), and the passion of the friendship may have the eroticism of the prior genital sexual relationship.

Situations in which one woman has sexual feelings for another, but these feelings are not reciprocated, are not viewed as "real" sex; in fact, the term "unrequited love" reflects the lack of legitimacy of these feelings. The woman who is sexually attracted to her friend has less power than the one who is the object of the crush. In the Naiad Press novel I described earlier, Leslie and Sara gain power and lose power relative to each other as they deny and admit their sexual feelings for each other, respectively. Similarly, the person who initiates the break-up of a relationship has more power than the one who wants to remain in the relationship. Yet relationships where feelings of sexual attraction exist–requited or not–are no longer viewed as legitimate friendships.

Lesbians may become sexually attracted to heterosexual women who do not reciprocate the desire for a genital sexual relationship. As part of my interviews for a previous book on lesbians involved in romantic but nonsexual relationships, one of the interviewees, Laura, moved to San Francisco and became attracted to her heterosexual roommate Violet. Violet seemed to encourage the relationship in multiple ways, such as having heart-shaped tattoos made with each other's names and telling Laura it was okay that people mistook them for lovers. Laura refers to their relationship as: "When we were whatever we were: Whatever it was that we had." When Laura suggested they become lovers, Violet said she couldn't do it; Laura was devastated (from Rothblum & Brehony, 1994).

CONCLUSION

What would be some components of a women-focused not sexual revolution, but friendship revolution? First, I think we need to celebrate friendships in equivalent ways to the ways in which we celebrate sexual relationships. For example, for twenty years I have talked on the phone every Sunday with Nancy. We met in 1976 in graduate school; I was in love with Nancy but she was heterosexual and we never became lovers (though she married a man called Nestor which I think bears an interesting resemblance to my name, Esther). In 1986, to celebrate ten years of friendship, I flew to Denver where Nancy was doing her post-doc and we each pierced one ear (I guess our ears symbolizing the part of our bodies that was most connected by our ten-year weekly telephone conversations) and split a pair of ear studs.

When I was doing the interviews for my book *Boston Marriages: Romantic but Asexual Relationships Among Contemporary Lesbians,* I began to feel like an imposter because most of my friends told me that they and their partner had sex often, "all the time." Then, when a few of these friends broke up with their lovers, they told me it was because they had "never had sex." These were the same women; how could their stories have changed so much? Marny Hall has written about this phenomenon in her forthcoming book entitled *The Lesbian Love Companion: How to Survive Everything from Heartthrob to Heartbreak*–she argues that we create stories to make sense of our lives and then change these stories when our lives change. I think it's important to change the stories of our lives so that they don't revolve around our sexual relationships to the exclusion of all other ways of relating. Instead, we need to honor our friendships, and also those relationships in which it is not clear whether we were friends or lovers; "when we were whatever we were."

In a non-patriarchal way of relating, perhaps we can de-emphasize power, including the power of genital sex. What does it matter if one friend has sexual feelings for, or is in love with, another who does not view the friendship in this same way? In reality, no two women view any mutual relationship in the same way, whether they are friends, lovers, co-workers, acquaintances, etc. Think of all the ways our women's communities would be strengthened if there were fewer misunderstandings or even outright hostilities due to power imbalances.

What would it mean if friendships became the core of our relationships, and other forms of relating (including lovers) became secondary? Similarly, what if we had more socialization in friendship skills, so that sex and romance were not as important, or interesting, or we accepted erotic feelings in friendships but didn't view this as problematic? Given the polyamorous nature of most friendships, we can co-exist with several close friends and not have to choose among them. Could polyamorous friendships serve as a model for sexual relationships? We need to be aware, however, that this will cause a vicious backlash from the economy and the media if women do not need to focus on sex and sexual attractiveness to the overwhelming extent that we do currently.

In Audre Lorde's (1984) classic article "The Uses of the Erotic: The Erotic as Power," she discusses the need for women to recognize the erotic in all aspects of our lives. Sexual activity can be independent of genital activity, so that "sex" can truly encompass all aspects of women's bodies, spirituality, love, and passion. Sexual relationships are so influenced by patriarchal definitions that we cannot truly conceive of women relating in ways that feel authentic to us. This is an area of tremendous power, and one in which we do not even know what our questions are, let alone our solutions.

NOTES

1. One other permissible way for women to relate passionately to others is in the role of mothering children.

2. This suspicion is even more salient when heterosexual women become friends with heterosexual men.

REFERENCES

Becker, C.S. (1988). *Lesbian ex-lovers*. Boston: Alyson Publications.

Diamond, L. (March, 1997). Passionate friendships: Love and attachment among young lesbian, bisexual, and heterosexual women. Paper presented at the annual convention of the Association for Women in Psychology, Pittsburgh, PA.

Espin, O. (1993). So what is a "Boston marriage" anyway? In E.D. Rothblum, & K.A. Brehony, K.A. (Eds.). *Boston marriages: Romantic but asexual relationships among contemporary lesbians* (pp. 202-207). Amherst, MA: University of Massachusetts Press.

Faderman, L. (1993). Nineteenth-century Boston marriage as a possible lesson for today. In E.D. Rothblum & K.A. Brehony (Eds.) *Boston marriages: Romantic but asexual relationships among contemporary lesbians.* Amherst, MA: University of Massachusetts Press.

Hall, M. (1998). *The lesbian love companion: How to survive everything from heartthrob to heartbreak.* San Francisco, CA: Harper Collins.

Hill, L. (1996). *Never say never.* Tallahassee, FL: Naiad Press.

Klinkenberg, D., & Rose, S. (1994). Dating scripts of lesbians and gay men. *Journal of Homosexuality, 26,* 23-35.

Lorde, A. (1984). Uses of the erotic: The erotic as power. In *Sister outsider.* Freedom, CA: The Crossing Press.

Loulan, J. (1993). Celibacy. In E.D. Rothblum, & K.A. Brehony (Eds.) *Boston marriages: Romantic but asexual relationships among contemporary lesbians.* Amherst, MA: University of Massachusetts Press.

Raymond, J. (1986). *A passion for friends: Toward a philosophy of female affection.* Boston: Beacon Press.

Rose, S. (1996). Lesbian and gay love scripts. In E.D. Rothblum and L.A. Bond (Ed.) *Preventing heterosexism and homophobia* (pp. 151-173). Thousand Oaks, CA: Sage Publications.

Rothblum, E.D. (1992). The stigma of women's appearance: Social and economic realities. *Feminism and Psychology, 2,* 61-73.

Rothblum, E.D. (1993). I'll die for the revolution but don't ask me not to diet: Feminism and the continuing stigmatization of obesity. In S. Wooley, M. Katzman, & P. Fallon (Eds.) *Feminist perspectives on eating disorders* (pp. 53-76). NY: Guilford Press.

Rothblum, E.D., & Brehony, K.A. (Eds.) (1993). *Boston marriages: Romantic but asexual relationships among contemporary lesbians.* Amherst, MA: University of Massachusetts Press.

Wolf, N. (1991). *The beauty myth: How images of beauty are used against women.* NY: William Morrow & Company. Holland, D.C., & Eisenhart, M.A.

Seven Poems for Three

Amanda Kovattana

SUMMARY. These poems describe the evolution of a polyamorous relationship among three women over a period of a year and a half. The original couple had been together five years and was ready to explore a more complex family structure as a powerful alternative to the hetero-sexual nuclear family model.

INTRODUCTION

For five years I lived with a woman as her lover and partner in a largely monogamous relationship. The quality of our relationship was based on day-by-day appreciation and honesty rather than long-term promises. We entertained a great deal and made a home for our numerous friends, some of whom joined us in our bed. A woman came into our lives looking for escape from an unsatisfying relationship. My lover and I felt that we had an abundance of love in our own relationship that would only increase exponentially if we were to share it with a third. We were thrilled with the prospect of creating an alternative family structure that would ultimately link entire communities.

When we invited her to live with us, I did not know that she was

Amanda Kovattana is a freelance writer and professional organizer in the San Francisco Bay Area. Her essays have appeared in *Dyke Life* (Basic Books, 1995), *Encountering Cultures* (Blair Press, 1995) and *On My Honor: Lesbians Reflect on Their Scouting Experience* (Madwoman Press, 1997). Several of the poems in this paper first appeared in the author's chapbook *Nine Poems for Three* and are reprinted here by permission.

[Haworth co-indexing entry note]: "Seven Poems for Three." Kovattana, Amanda. Co-published simultaneously in *Journal of Lesbian Studies* (The Haworth Press, Inc.) Vol. 3, No. 1/2, 1999, pp. 85-95; and: *The Lesbian Polyamory Reader: Open Relationships, Non-Monogamy, and Casual Sex* (ed: Marcia Munson and Judith P. Stelboum) The Haworth Press, Inc., 1999, pp. 85-95.

already having an affair with my lover and thought that she was courting me. Eventually we all shared a bed together. This became a compromise for the new lover who just wanted an exclusive relationship with my partner. She turned away from me, soon forcing my partner to exclude me from their bed. I lived with them for a year longer before my partner felt she had to make a choice in order to have peace and she asked me to leave. These poems describe the transitions in this polyamorous phase of my life.

The Lover

My love, and I,
we sit on the couch and wait
for her new lover's return.
For the delivery of that in-love high,
now for us but a fond memory.

Just as we begin to question her power,
she is with us, the lover,
carrying over her shoulder, like Santa Claus,
that big bag of desire.

She sets it down; it opens up
and fills the room, enveloping us,
with that cloud of pungent feeling,
thick with want, full with ripe promise
of deep, wet, flesh.

She applies the magic with a kiss
feeding my love with her mouth,
waking the lotus bud of want,
and again we know we can come.

Changing Places

We changed places you and I,
like slow trains passing.
You impatient to meet the lover
who still held me in her arms
so sweetly every night.
Me, listening to your hunger
as you paced in your room.

I gave you what I could
of my life with my love.
I stood to let you pass
as she beckoned to you.
Your desire I honored,
for, in truth, I loved you, too.

The journey began for you and me;
we stopped at every station.
First it was a night with her,
you asked for once a week.
And though it was spent in passion,
intimacy you couldn't reach
in such brief moments,
while our lover lay with me
and knew she was safe.

You saw despair where I sought your gratitude.
What could we do for peace,
my love asked the Guides.
They said it would be wiser
to bow to your need.
They asked me to give all that I had left
and fear struck my heart
for what would I have for me?

The morning I left my place in her bed,
We shed quiet tears for our gentle love.
Remembering all that we had shared
those five short years.

Now you have reached your destination
and I lie in the other room,
listening to your happy laughter.

I was torn away, but my love and I,
we did not stop loving.
We are family, still, and that we fight to keep.
Intimacy we have on your nights away.
I hold her close and will it to be enough,
but still I wonder if you have the heart
to leave me what I have,
or will your hunger take it all.

Deception

Sweet deception like a drug
feeding the imagination,
with a temporary grace,
to buy time with a secret lover.

How easily you slipped into this
old habit from twenty years
of marriage. That aphrodisiac
of secrecy heightening desire with
the possibility of being caught
while your life was safely
steered by our commitment.

I had a secret lover, too,
after you had your open one.
Secret because you wouldn't stop
bugging me about the absurd
possibility of my running off with her.
Our lovemaking was a good-bye gift
and she was soon gone, to another state,
safely married to a man.

Your lover stayed, moved in,
wove a complex trail of fractured
memories for me to repair, later,
when you told me, for fear
your heart would turn black from the
casting of lies.

You watched with compassion for my struggle
as I pasted the missing pieces into
my muddled brain. And you looked
with fascination at your longtime belief
that you can't have what you want
unless you buy it with a lie.

Shadowlove

That summer afternoon
when I didn't know
you were my lover's love,
you sat across from her
at the museum cafe,
her comments enticing you
with erotic undercurrents
that made you smile
and I had this sudden, unexplainable
desire to kiss you.

Tall, prickly woman
espousing facts
I didn't care to know,
my lover took you riding
and discovered your soft core
inside that too-smart
lonely teenager
you thought you left behind.

She brought you home
−persuaded me to help
save your soul from
quickening into stone.
I forgave you, doctor,
your cocky arrogance
when she invited me
to touch you.

My love and I, we dreamed up
a vision of sisterhood,
empowered by the thought
of three women together.

One night you kissed me
in front of Louise
and I thought this flirtation
was for me alone.
I pursued this shadow love
drawn by its mercurial mystery.

I didn't know I was
caught in the crossfire;
the erotic energy of your affair
coursing through me
like a palpable current
lighting every open circuit.

Flattered by my attention
and thirsty for friendship
you let me love you.
What does it matter that
you say you didn't love me.
That Louise, your bright star
soon eclipsed me.
You held me and spoke to me
in intimate tones that
promised family like a
long awaited firstborn child.

Now I grow cold in the
dark shadow of this love affair,
yet I hold open the space
that grew love for you
for fear that hostility
will tear apart my soul.

Wild Life

I follow them upstairs and
patiently wait on my bed like
duck hunters in camouflage
holding guns erect behind blinds.

Sometimes I wait in vain
with ears tuned for any sound
from the room next door,
and get nothing but laughter
and conversation too muffled
to make out, then the quiet of sleep.

But more often silence breaks into
the squeak of the bedsprings
and a telling groan.
This is my cue to leap
quietly to the wood floor
and lie by my open door in the dark.
Sweeping up the sounds that
slip under the crack of their closed door,
my mind's eye imagines
the hands at work building
muscled sensation into orgasm.

First the eager partner,
her urgent groans demanding
immediate gratification
in anticipation of the work ahead.
I imagine her unguarded desire
and take her place with my own body.

I see the slam of the drawer
where the dildo lives
and picture her with it strapped on
when I hear footsteps on the floor
as she walks around the bed.
Her big body carrying that bulbous
lavender latex thing more

gracefully than I, as she fucks
my ex-lover with determined rhythm.

More often the chainsaw buzz
betrays the wielding
of the Hitachi vibrator,
the cord clunking on the floor.
Muffled speech tells a fantasy,
promising some titillating technique.
The tandem breathing, one encouraging
the other to take all.

Then my ex-lover's groans evoke
the remembered expression on her face
as she lets it all go in triumphant bellows.

The immediacy of their pleasure has me riveted
to the urgency of the moment
storing for later use
the narration of an orgasm
more vivid than any fantasy
I care to make up.

As silence falls with an imagined sigh,
I jump back into bed to replay
for my own body's ecstasy,
the erotic image of the lovers
who can't exclude me in their pleasure
as they do in their union.

Lost Thailand

You saw your lost Thailand
when you looked at me.
The girl you left behind
who had your heart but
didn't ask for your body.
The Thailand you never
intended to leave, where
you made a home in the tropics

far more whole than your
desert childhood had ever been.

You gave me the affection
that is second nature
among the people of my homeland.
That touch of reassurance
that we are part of the whole,
never alone without community.

You gave me back the Thailand
of my childhood so brusquely
torn away from me.
That loss forcing me
to construct the identity
of the lone cowboy
Westerners seem to prize.

You didn't see the American
lesbian I had become,
aroused by your touch,
by the flirtatious game
you were trying out
since your new lover
awakened your erotic soul.

You gave me more than Thailand.
You kissed me and asked me to
sleep with you in celibate intimacy
as you had done with your Thai friend.
And you are shocked that
I wanted more?
Did I betray you with my
sexuality?
Didn't your girlfriend in Thailand
want this too? when she
went alone with you on holiday.
Why else would she have been
so cool to you afterwards?

Now you tell me it is against
your nature to be affectionate.
That you touch no one but your lover.
You treat me the best you can
like a member of your desert family,
showing all the intimacy
of a cactus in the wind.

You've made it clear
I can no more go back
to that Thailand we shared
than I can go back to my
childhood homeland.
How dare you touch me
twenty-five years later
on that ten-year-old's
wound of abandonment.

Three

Pull down the power of three
and see the possibility of unity,
strength, community, world peace.
Beatific visions only
the divine could sustain.
Three is a number for the Gods.

I wanted three to be like
ancient priestesses initiating
a new lover into the sisterhood.
But one of us wasn't ready
saw us as two and one left out.

Living against the power of three
pitched yin against yang,
broke the circle; the energy
turned against itself, tearing
us apart.

We saw the roots of war
when two must fight over one and
harmony is traded for competition.

To love one and reject the other
meant seeing both our beginnings
and our endings simultaneously,
in a cruel zen exercise of the heart.

Loving both kept the heart open
to pain from the hurt one.
and hurt from the hostile one.
To keep the love, we had to stay
and tolerate the pain; it made us
stronger–able to risk greater joy.

As we struggled to embrace uncertainty,
we learned gratitude for what we had,
and made fast our commitments.

Runaway emotions took control
out of our hands, taught us
the power of fate.
What a teacher is three for
the fatalities of the heart.

Addressee Unknown

Karla Jay

SUMMARY. In addition to furthering our knowledge and filling out résumés, academic conferences play an important role in the social lives of gay men and lesbians, providing many with unique opportunity to meet fellow queers in our fields. In a satirical spoof of the presumed bed-swapping that transpires at such meetings, "Addressee Unknown" is the correspondence–letters both mailed and those, more wisely, never posted–of Estelle, a collector of lesbian academics. *[Article copies available for a fee from The Haworth Document Delivery Service: 1-800-342-9678. E-mail address: getinfo@haworthpressinc.com]*

July 1, 1996

Dear Zena:

It was great to finally meet you at the National Women's Studies Conference last month in Saratoga. The presentation you gave on women artists in sixteenth century Bulgaria was terrific. You must

Karla Jay, PhD, has written, edited, and translated ten books, the most recent of which is *Tales of the Lavender Menace: A Memoir of Liberation.* Her anthology *Dyke Life* won a 1996 Lambda Literary Award in the category of Lesbian Studies. She has written for many publications, including *Ms. Magazine, The New York Times Book Review,* the *Village Voice, Lambda Book Report,* and the *Harvard Gay and Lesbian Review.* She is Professor of English and Director of Women's and Gender Studies at Pace University in New York City. She is currently at work on *Ten Decades of Struggle: Gay and Lesbian Life in the United States* (Oxford UP).

Address correspondence to Karla Jay, P.O. Box 1235, New York, NY 10008-1235.

[Haworth co-indexing entry note]: "Addressee Unknown." Jay, Karla. Co-published simultaneously in *Journal of Lesbian Studies* (The Haworth Press, Inc.) Vol. 3, No. 1/2, 1999, pp. 97-103; and: *The Lesbian Polyamory Reader: Open Relationships, Non-Monogamy, and Casual Sex* (ed: Marcia Munson and Judith P. Stelboum) The Haworth Press, Inc., 1999, pp. 97-103. Single or multiple copies of this article are available for a fee from The Haworth Document Delivery Service [1-800-342-9678, 9:00 a.m. - 5:00 p.m. (EST). E-mail address: getinfo@haworthpressinc.com].

have done an incredible amount of research to put together such a tight presentation. Like everyone else, I was overwhelmed by the large turnout at the conference and by the general enthusiasm of the women. The entire weekend was a wonderful experience, don't you think?

Well, maybe we'll run into one another at another conference soon. Write me when you get the chance.

Best,
Estelle

What I didn't mail:

Dear Zena:

Why can't I just tell you that I fell madly in love with you? Because of your damn lover, that's why. Why, oh why, do I always have to fall in love with "married ladies"? Not fair.

The hell with that presentation, too. It really wasn't bad, but, honey, sixteenth century Bulgaria is BORING. Truly. It was only the flickering of your lips, the red flush that rose and fell in your cheeks, the beads of perspiration racing down your forehead (oh, how I wanted to lick them off, right there in front of everyone!). . . . And your hand gently pulsating on the water glass in between paragraphs! I could feel my breast in its place. Could you see me blushing in the first row? Could you feel my hot breath burning in your direction?

To think how things would have been so utterly different–so utterly awful!–had your fucking lover decided to come to NWSA with you. Thankfully, she was at some business meeting for the Dull Lead Pencil Company or whatever pencil-pushing crappy corporation she works for. How can you live with someone so utterly bourgeois? Me, I'm pure . . . pure what, I don't know. But I am a poor graduate student, and that is *politically correct,* isn't it? You couldn't possibly prefer an executive to me, who lives and suffers on the Lower East Side! And she's so old–in that photo you showed me of her she looks at least a hundred. Well, fifty maybe. I know ageism isn't cool, but, hey, I'm the future tense, and she's the past (and I don't mean the past perfect).

Despite the mistake you've made in living with HER, I forgive you. I do love you–Bulgarian art nonsense and all. Just think how different my life would have been had I not spotted you at the registration table! You were filling in one of those forms, and I was next to you pretending to fill in mine, but secretly reading yours. I was mesmerized by your beauty, but I was really thrown off when I saw your address. "The hick," I said to myself, "Who the hell could live in Iowa? Is there really such a ridiculous place? Yuk." You didn't look like you lived in the Midwest. I thought everyone there was blond and blue eyed–just like Garrison Keillor says. Or was that Minnesota? Whatever. You looked ethnic with that black, black hair cascading down your back, those dark eyes that flashed at me as if you had caught me reading the newspaper over your shoulder in the subway. I mean, really, you could have passed for a New Yorker– that's a compliment! You must think my mind is like that *New Yorker* poster: New York, Hoboken, and then the Pacific. Well, I have spent all of my life in New York, and from what I saw of life in the Midwest at one conference, I know I have been truly *blessed*. So I'm a chauvinist. . . . Tough shit.

Anyway, as soon as I got my program, I scrutinized every panel looking for your name, and there you were down for ten in the morning the very next day. But Bulgarian art? And from the University of Iowa? Excuse me, is this planet earth?

At the end of your paper I clapped like mad. But even though I didn't know what the hell you were talking about most of the time, I asked you a very clever question–at least, I hoped it was–about "the circulation of ideas and the performance of art." Hey, I got that post-Structuralist jargon down tight. You smiled at me for being so interested in your work. I beamed at you for noticing me. (Did the other women in the audience know we were flirting? Did *you* know?) I still don't know how I did it–after all, what the hell do I know about Bulgarian art? But then what the hell does ANYONE know about Bulgarian art? Does Bulgarian art truly exist outside your research? Where the hell is BULGARIA anyway?

I spent the afternoon sessions wandering from room to room hoping you'd be sitting in one of them–especially in one of those *lesbian* workshops. (Though at NWSA, they're all lesbian, believe you me.) Then I'd know. Then we'd *both* know. Your paper didn't mention anything about lesbian artists in Bulgaria, but maybe there were no lesbian artists in Bulgaria. Probably there were no lesbians at all in Bulgaria that far back. According to Lillian Faderman, there weren't any lesbians anywhere before 1900, and I doubt even she could locate a single one in Bulgaria today, and she's a real expert. They can't hide from her under some text or pretext. Ha.

The rooms were so crowded that I couldn't find you anywhere.

Finally I settled down to hear a panel about battered women. I could identify. Really, my heart felt assaulted. I started berating myself: "Why do I fall in love like this, all of a sudden? She's probably straight anyway." OK, so I have a tendency to whine. But how should I know whether there are any lesbians in Iowa City?

Finally, I found you that same night at the dance. I got up my courage and asked you to dance, fully expecting you to say, "How dare you presume there are lesbians in Iowa?" But you smiled and held me tighter than I had expected, and when the song ended we stayed glued in the middle of the dance floor. I was terrified that if we stopped moving, someone else would ask you to dance and I'd lose you. I felt abandoned when you went to the bathroom. Me, I would have allowed my bladder to burst rather than leave you so soon. Your need to pee seemed callous to me. Really, how could you?

When you came out of the john, you told me you're an Aries. My moon's in Aries. (I'm a Sagittarian. Double fire. Hot stuff.) You also said you were Italian. An Italian Aries! I almost swooned with delight. I could see we'd be compatible in every way. And then *you* asked *me* back to your room! No shit! I'm still surprised I could walk over there, I had such a pain between my legs. And as they say, the rest is history. . . .

And it's going to be *ancient* history if we don't find some way to get around your fucking lover and get together soon. Zena, you should spell your name XXenia, for all the female lust you inspire. I'm yours. Just find some way to take me.

Hot kisses,
Estelle

December 15, 1996

Dear Zena:

I got your note. Sorry the dog is sick, and that your car broke down again. Sounds like you have your hands full! At least, now that school is over you should have a nice vacation. I hope you and Maria enjoy Mexico.

Are you planning to go to the College Art Association Conference in New York in February? Let me know.

Best,
Estelle

What I didn't mail:

Dear Zena:

If you weren't so dumb and from Iowa, you'd fix that damn car and point it straight East! Drive it right into my fucking bedroom! (You'd have to–what with the parking situation here on the Lower East Side!)

I am really sorry the dog is sick: Wish it were Maria instead. Maybe she'll get sick and shit number two lead pencils all over Mexico. It will be the worst case of tourista in history. Truly.

Why am I so vindictive? I never even met Ms. Pencil. Really, maybe I'm not vindictive enough. She's probably the reason you haven't been to see me. You're such a hot number, I'm sure she's not going to let you slip through her claws.

Why can't you find some excuse to come to some convention, *any* convention, here in New York? We've got all kinds–book conventions, SM conventions, and we even let the Democrats come here from time to time. Are there any Democrats in Iowa?

If you only knew how much I love you! Why I'd even give up my apartment here on East 10th Street for you. Do you know what the words "rent controlled" mean? Hey, I'm talking about the greatest of all sacrifices here. I'd even move with you to the far off boonies of Brooklyn or Queens. But not Staten Island, Hoboken, or Iowa. Get real. I mean, where would I get the bagels and lox? Surely, I would die of withdrawal. Besides, I hear there's no good pizza outside of New York.

I know you love me too. That night you came *four* times. I mean, with a lover at home, you just couldn't be horny enough to come four times unless it was true love, right? And the next morning you wanted more! Really. Ha cha cha. And then that night. . . . and on and on until the end of the conference. Right! Admit it to yourself– you're in love with me for sure. Admit that we are a match made in dyke heaven and leave that possessive lover of yours. You must have SOME U-Haul sensibilities, even in Iowa! When you see her shitting all over Mexico, you'll realize it's me you love. Me, I'll never get sick. It's against my religion to waste food.

You don't know how much I miss you. I've even thought of moving to Iowa to be near you. I must be losing my mind, but at least I know where my U-Haul is parked, honey. If you find me in Bellevue Hospital in a very straight jacket, it's all your fault. (I hope Italians can feel guilt.) Good thing you're not a Leo. Leo's NEVER feel guilty, no matter what disgusting thing they've done. . . . Me, I would never be a Leo.

Now I'm crying, for Pete's sake. I'm going to dump a few tears onto my postcard to you. If I cry loud enough, maybe you'll hear me in Iowa. I can tell you all the neighbors can hear me cry in this dump. (They can even hear me *yawn*, what with these paper walls. I bet you wondered what they did with all those old *Daily News* and *Times*. They wind up as walls, that's what.)

No, it's you XXenia, who's gonna cry. When you remember those twenty orgasms, you'll come *crawling*. If you haven't come here yet, it's because you're paralyzed with grief, or because Iowans are so slow, or because the damn car is broken or Ms. Pencil is threatening suicide. Come to your senses. Admit you love me and can't live without little ole me. Take the risk. I'll forgive you for cheating on me with her. I'm nice like that, really. Just don't dare do it again.

I know you'll be here real soon . . . I'd better stop writing before the tears wash the ink off this page.

> Brokenheartedly yours,
> Estelle

> January 5, 1997

Dear Zena:

Glad to hear your trip to Mexico was a success. Thanks for the invitation, but I can't make it to the Midwest for the regional art conference. My cat is having surgery and she's going to need me when she gets out of the kitty hospital. I'm also having my apartment redecorated this month.

Sorry I won't see you. Catch you some other time. Enjoy yourself.

> Best,
> Estelle

What I didn't mail:

Dear Zena:

If my cat ever got sick, it would be from stuffing herself with mice and roaches, especially the ones whose freshness date has expired. Really, this place is a pit, but it is rent-controlled.

As for my redecoration, you should see the neat stuff I got on trash pickup day from the Upper East Side (where the rich nerds live). The stuff those jerks throw out! I got a great almost-new imitation Persian rug. Ha cha cha.

You really think I'd go to the Midwest for a conference? I mean, I'm not *that much* of a conference junkie. Have some respect.

If you had had any sense, you'd have gotten in that car and come here even if your muffler broke or even if the doors fell off. Better yet, get rid of the fucking car, I mean the parking in New York is lousy. But I guess if people in the Midwest had sense, they'd *all* move here—and then who would grow the cornflakes and spaghetti? My imagination fails me.

I must have been a total fool to think that I loved you. I couldn't love someone from Iowa (even an Italian Aries). I don't know what came over me. It must have been the moon or my period, or both. (I know it's not feminist to blame my period, but I didn't exactly see you worshipping my woman within.) Anyway, I blew months thinking about you (and forty cents in postage too, not to mention the time and effort of picking out just the right postcards).

Then last month at a mini-conference at the CUNY Graduate Center, I met this fabulous Gemini with her moon in Sagittarius. She lives up on the Upper West Side (that's part of Manhattan, hick). Well, it ain't the Village (East or West), but it's a damn sight closer than Iowa. Really now. This time I'm in love, and I finally know what true feeling is. With you, it must have been something else. I'm glad I realized my mistake before you came crawling here on your hands and knees in that broken down jalopy.

I guess I never loved you. You're lucky you have Ms. Pencil or anyone out there. Wonder what's wrong with *her* that she stays with you? If I hadn't met Patsy, I could have gone through life under the *delusion* that I loved you. How fucking dumb that would have been. Truly.

I mean, I'm so lucky. When I heard Patsy giving her talk on trans-cultural mud baths, it was true love. Anthropologists have class. Really, Bulgarian art is nowhere, sweetie. (Especially Bulgarian art in Iowa.) Patsy and I will go together to the Anthropology Association of America conference together later this year.

So toodaloo, honey. You'll never know what you missed.

Eat your heart out,
Estelle

Bad Friend Book

Katharine Matthaei Sprecher

SUMMARY. This piece was written for a one-woman performance in San Francisco. The theme of the show was "mean and nasty," and this piece focuses, with humor and without mercy, on the less enticing aspects of lesbian polyamorous relationships. *[Article copies available for a fee from The Haworth Document Delivery Service: 1-800-342-9678. E-mail address: getinfo@haworthpressinc.com]*

INTRODUCTION

Bad Friend Book refers to a series of my former and current friends and lovers in a haphazard style that does not recognize order according to time period in which the subject was known, length of our association, or importance or intensity of the personal connection. Nor, for that matter, does *Bad Friend Book* adhere entirely to fact: at times,

Katharine Matthaei Sprecher, MA, is a recent graduate of the Social and Cultural Anthropology MA program at the California Institute of Integral Studies in San Francisco. She is a writer, performer, and artist who wrote her anthropological thesis on conflict resolution in lesbian-separatist, rural, intentional communities in Southwestern Oregon. She currently works for a non-profit social service organization that promotes violence prevention through community outreach and education.

Address correspondence to Katharine Sprecher, 73 Potomac Street, San Francisco, CA 94117.

The author would like to thank all of her friends and lovers, without whom this piece could not have been written.

[Haworth co-indexing entry note]: "*Bad Friend Book*." Sprecher, Katharine Matthaei. Co-published simultaneously in *Journal of Lesbian Studies* (The Haworth Press, Inc.) Vol. 3, No. 1/2, 1999, pp. 105-110; and: *The Lesbian Polyamory Reader: Open Relationships, Non-Monogamy, and Casual Sex* (ed: Marcia Munson and Judith P. Stelboum) The Haworth Press, Inc., 1999, pp. 105-110. Single or multiple copies of this article are available for a fee from The Haworth Document Delivery Service [1-800-342-9678, 9:00 a.m. - 5:00 p.m. (EST). E-mail address: getinfo@haworthpressinc.com].

several characters are derived from one real person, and my reactions and "meanness" to my victims are often exaggerated. I must admit, however, that all of the unfortunates on my list fall under one (or more) of three categories: ex-lovers, friends who (at one time) had crushes on me, and friends who drove me crazy with the melodrama of their own amorous affairs.

Often, my frustrations in regards to such "friends" arose from my inability to extricate myself from the relationship, or an uncomfortable part of the relationship, such as being someone's endless drama-witness, lesbian-love support system, or the recipient of super-crush attentions I could not return. For me, this is a primary attribute of lesbian polyamory: not only are we often involved in our own number of romantic partnerships, sexual liaisons, and unreciprocated crushes, but we are usually deeply involved with those of our friends as well, as active witnesses and support systems. It has been my experience as a lesbian to balance precariously on that line between joyful relationships and overkill. We lesbians expect a lot from each other throughout our constantly evolving affinities; lovers become friends, friends become crushes, and crushes, at times, become nasty little obsessions which consume the judgment abilities of our otherwise great friends. Therefore, it is my opinion that a sense of humor regarding the rather unique family tree of the lesbian community is necessary to insure both our emotional survival and our continuing love and appreciation for one another.

The women who provided the material for *Bad Friend Book* may never forgive me if they ever read it and are able to identify themselves in the list, and, in fact, I originally created this list with no intent of sharing it beyond a boisterous car trip with a best friend. Nevertheless, here it is in print, and I shall have to accept the consequences of this publicity; however, the rawness of this piece is due entirely to the fact that I never intended for it to be read, and I can only hope that the reader recognizes the devilish, rather than malicious, humor with which it was written.

I wrote and performed *Bad Friend Book* for a show titled *Below the Belt* that was presented at Lunasea, a women's performance space in San Francisco, in May, 1997. The theme of the *Below the Belt* show was "mean," a chance for gals to unabashedly get in touch with their "inner nastiness." My piece, *Bad Friend Book*, turned out to be a personally therapeutic rant on the defects of my friends, past and present; not surprisingly, this list of unfortunates included quite a few ex-lovers and romantic flirtations. Though based in truth, the descriptions are greatly exaggerated in their meanness, and all of the names I used are fictitious. As a woman who was indoctrinated into, and entrapped by, the feminine social characteristic of perpetual "niceness," I found that being as nasty as I wanted to be, without actually hurting anybody, was extremely liberating. In addition, I wrote and performed *Bad Friend Book* just as I was commencing a year-long anthropological study for my master's thesis on conflict resolution in a lesbian separatist community. After that much serious process and structured "niceness" around lesbian interactions (which is a nice way to put it, I think), I really needed an outlet where I could be completely self-indulgent and outrageous, and express "mean" feelings without actually being mean *to* anyone. *Bad Friend Book* has been just that outlet, and has offered me the opportunity to look very honestly, and humorously, at some of the not-so-nice aspects of lesbian (or womyn-loving-womyn!) relationships.

BAD FRIEND BOOK

[An easel stands to slightly stage left of center. On it is a large list (18 by 24 inch pad of paper) of women's names–three in all–headed by the very large title BAD FRIEND BOOK. The stage is dark, except for a light that is focused on the easel and list. I emerge from behind center backstage and walk slowly and purposefully towards the audience while boldly surveying them with haughty, and somewhat malicious, amusement. My hands are behind my back hiding my small reference list and a retractable metal pointer. I am dressed in a tight, short black dress with black knee-high go-go boots.

When I have reached the easel, I stop, imperiously scan the audience from one end to the other, and pull my list and retracted pointer out from behind my back. My demeanor is condescending, stoic, and completely self-controlled. I quickly pull out the pointer to its full length and whip it over to the title of the large list, pointing harshly at each word as I read them aloud in staccato.]

BAD. FRIEND. BOOK.

[I bring the pointer down, and throughout the performance, use it to point at names, or at the audience, to punctuate what I'm saying.]

Not necessarily a list of bad friends, but rather,
a list of friends to whom I have been very BAD.

[I whip the pointer up to the first name.]

Doria. I never return your phone calls.
And I probably never will.

Sarah. Your incessant chatter makes me nasty.
I start to ignore you, then I snap at you with a viciousness you are
always unprepared for.
You deserve it.

Angel. You dubbed yourself fashion and cultural elite, when you
should have gotten fifteen years to life for your painstakingly chosen
apparel and superficial snobbery.
I'm sorry we had to stop having sex. I did like it.
It's just that when we weren't having sex,
I had to talk to you.

*[At this point, I step in front of the BAD FRIEND BOOK and pull
out the paper clips which are holding the rest of the scrolled-up list at
the bottom of the page. The rest of the list unrolls, revealing three more
page lengths taped together so that the list is about eight feet long. The
list is covered with women's names from top to bottom, with the written
names becoming smaller, closer together, and messier as they get
nearer to the end of the list. I bring the pointer up to the next name.]*

Charlotte. I moved in with you only to be traumatized by your war-like
romance with our other roommate, and the very NOT trained dog you
bought, without warning,
to try to save your relationship with her.
Thanks to you, all of my childhood dysfunctional family issues have
come blaring back into my life. I can't afford therapy, so I just speak
scathingly about you behind your back–because it's free, and it *does*
make me feel a *little* better.

Janet. You were Charlotte's girlfriend.
All of the above applies to you. *Plus*, you stole my curtains.
I hate you.

Carla. I have always found your perception of reality to be rather. . . .
interesting. Since I never know whether or not you are telling the truth,
I have decided simply to treat you like a romance novel:
oddly entertaining, purely fictitious, and low in content.

Anne. Oh Anne. I *tried* to escape you.
I moved three times. I put the phone in someone else's name.
And still, you found me by locating an acquaintance of mine over the
Internet
and calling her to request my whereabouts.
When you finally caught up with me,
because I forgot to screen my telephone calls that day,
I immediately found an emergency to attend to.
   I guess I just haven't forgiven you for the time when we were
roommates and you clogged the toilet–on TWO occasions–with tam-
pons and shit, and then pleasantly told me that I had to take care of it
because you had to go to work.

Theresa. I talk about you continuously behind your back,
because there is so much to say.

Marie. I talk about you too, and I should probably do it more.

Tonya. Stop obsessing, Tonya. Don't call me, *anymore*.
You're acting just like Rebecca.

Rebecca. You and Tonya might as well be the same woman.
Contrary to both of your unprovoked convictions,
you are NOT special. I am never going to have sex with you.
Stop giving me presents.

Chris. I do not CARE that you are in your one hundred and sixteenth
love crisis with the same woman, who for TWO YEARS you have
hated to love and loved to hate.
You see, I *had* cared, and listened, and offered advice;
but mostly just listened to your endless litanies for twenty-five months
while nothing changed.
I have decided that you are a drama-junkie, and if you want to tell me
about it,
you need to start paying me $60.00 an hour.

I, your simple-minded support system (simple-minded for listening to you simper about the same thing for seven hundred and sixty days) am going on STRIKE!

So shut-up.

And thus concludes this week's entries into my *Bad Friend Book*, proving once and for all that I am, indeed, a very Bad Friend.

Now *you*, my adoring audience, may be thinking–
But why, Katharine? Why a *Bad Friend Book?*
And–because I am known for my undying patience and compassion for others' ignorance–
I shall explain it to you.

After a year of intensive research for my thesis on conflict resolution and mediation in a lesbian separatist community, I have come to the scholastic conclusion that–sometimes–
it is better just to be bad.

Therefore, may my unrepentant Badness guide you in your own exploits in nastiness and provoked cruelties, thus leading *you* to greater personal satisfaction and endless amusements.

So, for now, Adieu. And if we meet again, *pray* that you do not annoy me. *[I push the pointer back to its short, retracted length in one swift motion and the stage lights go to black.]*

The Spontaneous Imaginative Life

Joanne Hetherington
K. Linda Kivi
Catherine Fisher
Lyn Merryfeather

SUMMARY. From an interweaving of the journal entries of four dykes involved in a polyamorous network, a picture of the day-to-day complexities of polyamory emerges. Relationship to family and community, jealousy, shame and acceptance of self are some of the issues dealt with in this narrative. The story unfolds in a rural community in British Columbia, Canada, where they all live. This piece is an excerpt from a longer, ongoing work. *[Article copies available for a fee from The Haworth Document Delivery Service: 1-800-342-9678. E-mail address: getinfo@haworthpressinc.com]*

Jo:

As I sit down to our papers, I feel light years out of our time, not always a very comfortable feeling. Now that Catherine & KL & I are settling into our rhythm, the question–how do we fit into a couple-

---

Joanne Hetherington is a 50-something, mostly white astrologer and former sports hero. K. Linda Kivi (aka KL) is a 35-year-old Estonian-Canadian, peasant, dyke and writer, author of *If Home is a Place* and numerous stories and articles. Catherine Fisher is in her early thirties, a prairie girl, painter and queer feminist who lives with her three cats. Lyn Merryfeather, now 50ish, came out as a dyke in her forties; she is a multi-tattooed nurse, a grandmother and of Anglo-Saxon origin. None of the above share a residence.
Address correspondence to K. L. Kivi, S-19, C-14, RR#2, Nelson, BC, V1L5P5, Canada.

[Haworth co-indexing entry note]: "The Spontaneous Imaginative Life." Hetherington, Joanne et al. Co-published simultaneously in *Journal of Lesbian Studies* (The Haworth Press, Inc.) Vol. 3, No. 1/2, 1999, pp. 111-120; and: *The Lesbian Polyamory Reader: Open Relationships, Non-Monogamy, and Casual Sex* (ed: Marcia Munson and Judith P. Stelboum) The Haworth Press, Inc., 1999, pp. 111-120. Single or multiple copies of this article are available for a fee from The Haworth Document Delivery Service [1-800-342-9678, 9:00 a.m. - 5:00 p.m. (EST). E-mail address: getinfo@haworthpressinc.com].

111

socialized world?–is very stark. As KL puts it, who does she signify to the world as her partner, Catherine or Jo? This partner issue is not a new one for KL and me. It has always been a question mark in our relationship because of KL's need to be "single."

I've been in relationships with various women since 1962, with maybe one year of accumulated time when I called myself single. Through the process of KL and I developing a non-monogamous frame of relationship and dealing with KL's singleship issues, I am evolving as a single person, too. Since I've been in a couple for most of my adult life, this has been difficult at times. My emotional pattern has been to merge with the other, lose myself to the relationship, then blame the other for suffocating me. Then, I break up and move on, immediately, to another. I have "done" relationships. I haven't done single much. I've chosen non-monogamy in order to develop a sense of myself.

At the same time, I've had to deal with all the issues non-monogamy brings up in my other relationships. The question of whether to come out to my biological family as a non-monogamous alien becomes more relevant as I find myself on the threshold of developing a lovership with Lyn. My Mum has gone through a lot with me. First, I came out as a dyke, then I became an alternative insemination parent, then becoming a back-to-the-lander and an astrologer. Is it necessary, I wonder, for her to know about my non-monogamous lifestyle? How do I explain that I have Lyn's car when I go to visit them in Vancouver and that I'm going to spend a night with her in a local hotel. It seemed easier not to say anything when KL was the one with the other lover. And now, I don't know.

When I find myself weary like KL or stretched like Catherine, it signals a time for me to be with myself at home. Last Sunday, when I had an opportunity to stay over at Lyn's, I chose to come home because I felt overwhelmed and confused–our impending lovership as well as the process of balancing all the energies between us seems complex. I told myself, "Jo, go home and do wood!"

As I wrote at the beginning, I come from a place of merging. Choosing now not to go into the sexual energy of a couple gives me a sense of self-control. I have a primary relationship that is with myself and when I feel strong and stable with myself, everything is possible.

As we gain strength in our inner matrix, we are going to be more visible. And it will take strength to meet the monogamous, coupled world and create space for us to be.

One of our ongoing problems is that if people see Catherine and KL at a dance, they assume that KL and I have finally seen the light and broken up. The same goes for me going to Vancouver with Lyn. The question seems to be on people's lips quite often. We've put a lot of energy into communicating with one another so that the monogamous energy around us doesn't overwhelm us completely.

Catherine and I went to Kokanee Creek park the other day and it felt good to continue getting to know her on a one-to-one basis. I'm relieved that we like each other and want to develop a friendship because this will help our triad as well. It will help relieve the pressure KL feels in maintaining her lover relationships with both of us. The very act of the three of us writing these papers distributes the energy more evenly in the triad.

K. Linda:

My fingers are cold from sitting here typing but I feel compelled to continue. These non-monogamy papers have become a compulsion for the three of us. We eagerly await our turn to do an installment and prod whoever has the latest wad of papers to pass them on. I hadn't realized what a need we all feel to express ourselves and communicate to our community (and the world at large?) what this experience signifies in our lives.

Just went out for a pee and put on a new tape; Cassandra Wilson begins to croon about what love is. Appropriate, eh?

I realize, as I read Jo's last installment, that family, in the broad sense of the word, is much more important to both her and Catherine than it has been to me. Catherine has already written to her parents and come out to her sisters about being in a non-monogamous relationship. Jo contemplates it. I react with horror: come out to my parents as non-monogamous! No way! They still haven't accepted my lesbian-ism and I've been out to them for over ten years. My mother's big step towards acceptance has been sending greetings to "Joan"; six years and she still hasn't got Jo's name right. Frankly, my biological family isn't that important to me. I feel no need, no desire, to keep them posted on aspects of my life they have no hope in hell of understanding.

At the same time, my parents are one of my few links to my culture of origin. The only time I speak my mother tongue (Estonian) is when

I talk to them on the phone or visit. This alone should be enough to guarantee the importance of our link. But it isn't. We have yet to bridge the gully of immigrant parent and New World child. Non-monogamy just makes the crevasse wider.

Since I left home 17 years ago, I've made some attempts at creating family but none of them have quite fit. Individual connections are much more important to me than the tight web of relations we call family. I don't tend to make friends with my lovers' friends. I don't necessarily embrace my friends' lovers. I choose the people I want in my life based on what I feel for them as individuals.

Jo and Catherine seem to enjoy webs; they create them and thrive on that sense of connectedness. The are both far more emotionally connected to their families of origin than I am. They want to develop a friendship between the two of them. I don't really care, one way or the other. In fact, the idea that they may be working on a friendship in order to "help our triad" (Jo) or "relieve the pressure KL feels" (Jo again), is a little frightening. I would hope that they are building a friendship because they genuinely enjoy each other.

When Jo came home from her time with a distraught Catherine at Kokanee Creek Park, Jo was all concerned about Catherine. "She's such a dear," she said to me. When Catherine said she was in too bad a space to be good company, Jo dragged her off to the park. Back at home, Jo suggested we invite Catherine to a dinner party we were giving. "That girl needs to be in the woods."

So, there we have Jo and Catherine doing their thing. But what about me? How am I going to deal with Lyn? Our interactions up until now have been pleasant but superficial. We have things in common–a love of gardening, birds, Scrabble–but I don't feel drawn to her. I wonder how keeping my distance will affect the flow of energy among us. Is the "let's all be pals" model the best one? I don't know. I know that everyone has to be respectful and civil, but more? I know there needs to be a willingness to communicate should troubles or issues arise, but more?

At this point, I feel like I need to help Jo communicate better about "Lyn stuff." This bit about the hotel in her last installment came as a surprise to me. "Jo, I don't want to read about what's happening between you and Lyn in the papers. Okay?" She agreed. If anything, a clear flow of communication seems to be the most vital ingredient in successful non-monogamy.

K. Linda:

So, Jo and Lyn are "on." I heard it last night at the dance. It was not news. What was difficult was hearing it through the grapevine, in the grapevine. People are talking. What should it matter? Regardless of what people say, what their speculations are, Jo and I have our agreements, our relationship, our love, the way we do things.

But it does matter. And it bothers me that it matters. I am in the public eye in a difficult moment. I can't pretend it's not difficult, because it is. I wonder what I feel. What does the word jealousy signify? Is it this sinking feeling in my belly, this irrational worry that I will be compared and found wanting? Is it what I feel when I look at Lyn, in her white pants and tank top, black vest and dragon tattoo, and see how beautiful she is?

To me, the word jealousy evokes a fierce image: someone in a rage of demands, face contorted like a child who's been pulled away from an electrical outlet for the fourth time. I don't feel fierce at all. The contrary. I feel small and wimpy and full of shame. I want to hide.

What is this shame? A bizarre thing to feel, I think, looking hard at myself for its origins. For one, there is the reality of knowing that I put Jo through similar times, perhaps, when I got involved with Catherine. Ow! Funny how something that is about love has so much power to hurt. Then, there is the shame of feeling what I feel at all. After all, who am I to gripe and feel sad? Don't I have another lover? Shouldn't I, of all people, be able to take this fully in stride, synchronize philosophy with action?

It is Catherine who reminds me gently of something Jo says: "The point is not to not be jealous. The point is to feel your jealousy and move through it." I suppose Jo knows what she's talking about. And shame, does it function in the same way? If I look my insecurities about my desirability straight in the face, will they move over, eventually, and leave room again for my self-confidence? At this point, all I can say is perhaps.

But when you're weak in the knees, stomach churning, heart half way up your throat, what good do perhapses do? My rational self tries to reassure the freaked out one that there is a way through this emotional morass. But I dramatize. Or perhaps I rationalize. It's hard to say. Part of me is very calm, accepting. The theory, however, is to feel joyful for the new love that Jo has attracted into her life, for the passion that enriches her. For the moment, that's a stretch. Instead, I accept. I can understand, on some level, that I continue to be an attractive, passionate, desirable woman and that Jo wants me.

What I wish for more than anything else is that I had other people to talk to whom I could trust not to think, "Well, you've got yours, haven't you?" I want to converse with well-journeyed polyamorists. I want to sit and lay my head in the lap of someone who understands all the contradictions I feel, make snarky remarks about the irony of it all while they stroke my hair and laugh with me. Where are the women who are in the prime of their passionate freedoms?

Lyn came and found me at the dance, wanting "to talk." We leaned against the hall wall outside, among the smokers and other conversationalists and "talked." She said she was a little uneasy, that she didn't quite know how to be around me, what should be said and not said. I talked about not knowing either. That we have to make it all up as we go along. The basics–respect and acceptance–exist between us already. What else do we need to do, to feel? Does anyone know?

I ask her if she'd like to join the non-monogamy papers discussion. This dialogue, in the secure realm of words, feels so vital to my process. I want her to join in so that I can understand and trust that we are speaking in similar terms, understanding what we mean when we use words like honesty. She agrees, is eager. Before me, I see a lovely woman, the same age as Jo, on the verge of 50, trying to be new in a world that wants us all to conform. I see her open, unsure and willing. In the midst of all the turbulence I feel, there is also a sense of elation; someone else has joined us in this crazy struggle to create space in the world. Someone else has taken a leap into "the spontaneous imaginative life of us all" (Adrienne Rich).

Jo:

"The spontaneous imaginative life of us all": I like this statement that describes our relationship lifestyle. I just received a letter from my astrological tutor and he commented on my cooperative, home lifestyle by saying, "Those kinds of social experiments are extremely difficult to pull off in a society that places so much value on private land ownership and material security." I wonder what he'd say about my relational social experiment.

Dealing with life as an environment of experiments provides me with innovative energy to show me the way through the consequences of non-monogamy in a monogamous culture. The consequence of jealousy and shame, I feel, is a reaction from a society that places value on emotional and sexual ownership in lover partnerships. Our emotional work is doubly difficult because before we even deal with our issues of individual ownership, we need to shed our societal patterns of ownership. There is no set way, there is no rule book, in developing new relationship patterns based on passionate freedoms. My experience of going through jealousy and shame and not getting stuck in them is that it continues to open up doors of possibility.

Today, KL, Catherine and I are helping friends move to a new house. Then I meet Lyn in town and K. Linda continues spending time with Catherine. The lover relationship of KL and Catherine is nearly a year old; my lover relationship with Lyn is in its infancy. I feel my lover relationship with KL is as strong and as solid as ever. I don't own KL's sexual feelings, Lyn and KL don't own mine. I think that sexual self-ownership is one of the fundaments of non-monogamy.

I'm glad that KL has asked Lyn to join in on the non-monogamy papers because it would feel scattered otherwise. It's now my turn to travel the road of two lovers and I need all the support I can get. My firm belief that I own my body and my sexual feelings is my emotional base. Instead of saying, "You make me feel sexual, jealous, happy, sad, etc.," I say I am open to feeling sexual while being with you.

Treating life as an experiment blows societal control apart. My individual self emerges, vulnerable and raw, ready to find out who she is in relationship to the others. There is a trust building between us, of being traveling friends, a sense of joint venture in the spontaneous imaginative life of us all.

Catherine:

Upon reading KL's installment on "passionate freedoms and shame" and Jo's comments on self-ownership of sexuality and self, I am once again surprised by how differently we experience a moment or an occurrence. I am pleased that KL's asked Lyn to write with us. I feel I could use as many points of view as possible. Something in each person's communication catches me and makes me think, or feel, or clarify something in my own experience. And, sometimes, part of the sharing between us is what we don't say and sometimes it's saying something and having the other person ask you not to talk about that particular subject.

An example: I was completely aghast at my response to K. Linda's reaction to Jo's involvement with Lyn. When K. Linda expressed some of her fears and feelings, I was decked by a huge wave of jealousy. I kept thinking that I must be wrong, it mustn't be jealousy; it was completely unreasonable. But it was.

I feel jealous that K. Linda was broken up about Jo being in a relationship with someone else. I kept thinking: I bet she wouldn't have such a hard time if it was me seeing someone else. She has such a depth of love for Jo and I find it hard to believe she could love me as much so I felt quite fucked up. Also, I often look to K. Linda to be the woman in this whole "spontaneous imaginative life" who is experienced, will stay even and reasonable and strong through it all. I sometimes forget that she has feelings just like I do. Not that I'm callous with her, generally, it's just that I presume that since she seems so together generally that I can bank on it.

I've been feeling very self-critical about this and I've noticed that while I no longer feel jealous, I still feel bad. That's the shame part: that I couldn't be supportive of my friend when she felt upset.

I told K. Linda the brief version of this. She said that she didn't need to tell me the details of what upset her about the situation if it would be hard for me to take in. "No way," I said. "I can take it!" Of course, I can't see how I could be much help for her if it involved suppressing my strong jealousy. It's ironic. I haven't felt particularly jealous when K. Linda sleeps with other women; this situation pressed other buttons for me.

And now that everything has settled down, I don't feel jealous any more. I feel as though I'm okay with talking about the situation. I want to work on letting my shame about not being helpful, about being jealous and possessive, trickle away into the fertile soil of experience and experiment.

I, too, wish that I could talk to other people who are living in polyfidelity–other queer people–but not necessarily close friends.

K. Linda:
I now have proof positive that jealousy
is utterly irrational, makes no sense
at all. She tells me that she is
jealous over my jealousy
of my other lover's other lover
are you following me?

that she wonders, when she has another
lover will I be as jealous
of her as I am of my other lover's
other lover. Who can say, I answer
I have proof positive that
jealousy is
not a rational thing.

Lyn:

One of the things I crave is the approval of other people. Even people I don't like. It's a learned thing of long standing, one that I'm trying to unlearn but it's a very slow process. Reading the papers on passionate freedoms and shame, I am struck by the honesty, the willingness to be vulnerable and the amount of work these women put into this way of living and loving. And I don't know if I can do this. I'm afraid that if I hang out my doubts and fears, show the real me, I'll be found wanting. I'll get an "A" in honesty but an "F" in substance. The essence of shame.

I told only a carefully selected few about my relationship with Jo. The ones I was pretty sure would be supportive, if not approving. Now everybody knows and are no doubt making judgements and having their own opinions. Why do I care so much what people think? Isn't it good enough to approve of what I'm doing myself? I am so glad I took the plunge and found out what was on the other side of the wall I'd put up. No amount of speculating, intellectualizing (which I love to do) could have prepared me for the exhilarating feeling of stepping through my fear and finding the freedom on the other side.

One of the women at the dance who talked with me about my lover relationship with Jo was very happy for me until she discovered that Jo and KL are still lovers. She was at a loss for words and just stared at me. Finally, she shook her head and pronounced "the whole thing" very "hedonistic" and I felt a big wall drop into place between us. End of discussion. I know it's about her fear and yet I still feel cut off, not heard, judged. Somehow, I felt as if I had betrayed her, in her mind. I'm no different than I was before. What difference could it possibly make to her that I choose to build a lover relationship that does not demand an abandoning of other lovers, both current and future ones?

I want to be able to share with people how incredibly real and wonderful this relationship feels. It dawns on me as I write this that the good feelings are because of non-monogamy, not in spite of it. I feel as though I didn't choose non-monogamy, it chose me. And yet, after a year or so of thinking and talking about it, it was I who finally opened the door. I feel as if I've stepped into freedom. To have that freedom dismissed as hedonistic is painful, but I've done the same sort of thing myself. Take something that is 3-D and make it flat because that's the only way it's manageable.

When KL and I "talked" at the dance, I was humbled by how vulnerable she made herself to me. And I feel welcomed as an equal by KL, Catherine and Jo, which is scary because I don't really know what I'm doing. I have intentions and desires about my own behavior, but I also know that I can be caught up in my feelings. I'm going to need help here and it's good to know that this "spontaneous imaginative life" (I love that!) is considered a joint venture.

LIVING THE DREAM

May Day Celebration

Festival Showers

Matriarchal Village

Thyme S. Siegel

SUMMARY. This story of a gypsy-dyke first experiencing polyamory is set in the 1970s in an Oregon college town, where radical feminists considered non-monogamy an important way to strengthen lesbian tribal bonds. Personal struggles with jealousy and community support for rejecting coupleism are captured in this piece. *[Article copies available for a fee from The Haworth Document Delivery Service: 1-800-342-9678. E-mail address: getinfo@haworthpressinc.com]*

INTRODUCTION

In the 1970s, a new kind of mingling occurred among lesbians of various classes, races, ethnicities, and ages who met on the road, at music festivals, on women's land, and in campgrounds. They formed

---

Thyme S. Siegel, MA, is an instructor of Women's Studies and a writer of numerous autobiographical stories, journal and newspaper articles. Her story "My Mother Was a Lighthouse Keeper" was published in two anthologies. Her story of growing up in backwoods New Jersey, "The Lost Tribe," appeared in the *Bridges* issue of *Jewish Women on Land*, January 1996.

The following matriarchal village description is true, but the story which follows comes from a different channel. It is at least as much fiction as autobiography.

Address correspondence to Thyme S. Siegel, 147-44 69th Road, Flushing, NY 11367.

The author would like to acknowledge her mischief in trying to steal the essences of the real-life characters who inspired the fictional part of Matriarchal Village.

[Haworth co-indexing entry note]: "Matriarchal Village." Siegel, Thyme S. Co-published simultaneously in *Journal of Lesbian Studies* (The Haworth Press, Inc.) Vol. 3, No. 1/2, 1999, pp. 125-133; and: *The Lesbian Polyamory Reader: Open Relationships, Non-Monogamy, and Casual Sex* (ed: Marcia Munson and Judith P. Stelboum) The Haworth Press, Inc., 1999, pp. 125-133. Single or multiple copies of this article are available for a fee from The Haworth Document Delivery Service [1-800-342-9678, 9:00 a.m. - 5:00 p.m. (EST). E-mail address: getinfo@haworthpressinc.com].

traveling bands and caravans. They were visible in beads, feathers, and bare feet. They held workshops on non-monogamy, masturbation, class, and race, while encouraging each other to share money as if they were part of the same tribe. They began to share bodies, money, vehicles, and homes. They envisioned a "matriarchal village" where they could belong and be cared for. They viewed themselves as creatures of the earth, on a communal journey.

I met these Amazon women, the gypsy dykes and country women, at age 30 when I joined up with a caravan of women departing a mid-summer women's festival. From them I sought a basic source of inspiration I was lacking . . . love. They read my chart. They read my palm. They brought me into fire circles. I re-named myself with them.

A poster from 1975 shows four naked women dancing in a meadow. The caption underneath reads, "Remember The Future." The future was the future of wild women, free women. The new world being created would bring everyone together in harmony. The Matriarchal Village that I became part of was in "Emerald City," the college town of Eugene, Oregon.

Many counterculturalists had moved to Eugene in the late 1960s. Matriarchal Village was one place among many, on country land and in college towns of the 1970s, where a lesbian village emerged. The excitement of this historical moment produced an intensity which brought many women out, and many of them came to Oregon. Some came to Emerald City to work in Full Moon Rising, a women's crew that was part of a large forestry cooperative. Some came and stayed to be part of Gertrude's Cafe or Mother Kali's Books, two collective women's businesses that started in 1975. Our Matriarchal Village was an outgrowth of these projects which provided an open and cohesive women's community. It was easy to become involved then, to help run things. It was easy to find lovers then, too. The network was visible, a perpetually arriving party. Gertrude's and Mother Kali's were the channels through which waves of women filtered in. Upstairs at Gertrude's there was a massage room, a darkroom, a woman-school class space, and a pool table. Downstairs was an ample kitchen, and dining room with fireplace. Paintings by local women covered the walls; poetry readings and home-made music filled the evenings.

Collectively owned women's lands in Southern Oregon, such as OWL Farm and Cabbage Lane, were also part of our community. Workshops at Cabbage Lane were part of the exploration of communi-

ty, *privacy, and coupleism. There was an eagerness among the women
to sort out these issues, and there was heightened consciousness of
identity. Masturbation circles were meant to break down concepts of
what could be shared. Non-monogamy workshops were experiments in
group living, in creating a tribal feeling.*

*We considered ourselves radical feminists. Survival in the 1970s
was eased for many women by group living, shared bulk food, and the
food stamp office. These young and old lesbians did not work full-time
jobs. The counter-cultural, back-to the-land movement, the rural, hippie life, had taught many of the women how to share resources, children and living space. The opportunities to live and work together
came in many forms. Land trusts were started with the help of women
with money. Migratory work at women's festivals as well as fruit
picking and forestry were also available. There were all-women crews
who lived in a particular national forest for months at a time and
either worked directly for the Forest Service or with a re-forestation
co-op. There were house-sitting opportunities. Rural lesbians working
with urban lesbians were producing books and magazines.* Country
Woman *magazine from Northern California and* Woman Spirit *magazine from Oregon attracted great numbers of lesbians to the west
coast. The magazines told women that it was possible to live in the
country with other lesbians, and they were a unifying force for the
far-flung "tribe." The concept of "tribe" was an important organizing
feature at this time and for this population. The country communities
were intricately connected with the movements in the cities. Few of
those women would have believed that the main issues for lesbians of
the nineties would become gay marriage or gays in the military.*

*Emerald City's Matriarchal Village was one place among many, on
country land and in college towns of the 1970s, where lesbian villages
emerged. Most of these villages were characterized by various sorts of
"non-monogamy," harmonious and not. The energy of the times was
high, and considerations for jumping into bed with a new person were
few.*

This is the story of my first experience with polyamory.

In Matriarchal Village, Oregon, it was summer. Ah, what did this
mean in a land of rain? Lovely dry heat in a lush green environment.

Hot weather turns me on. I like to wear as little as possible and go
barefoot, skinny-dip in wild rivers and go naked in the sun.

My lover Sage was busy working on contracts for the Forest Service. She knew all about planting trees and picking cones. I loved the woods too, but as a wild creature, not burdened with heavy boots, a chain saw, a shovel, and 500 seedlings.

Sage's hair smelled of soft pine seedlings mixed with sage, and her skin was as velvety as hot moss. She looked like she tasted like vanilla cream cake with her tan skin, fine light blond hair and green-brown eyes. She was the ideal androgynous human being with her macho work ethic and female beauty.

We lived along the river, just inside Matriarchal Village, in a house with two little back bungalows and an orchard. We were part of a hippie lesbian Shangri-la. Our home had become a social center, since we had built the wood stove sauna in the back yard. We only invited women, although we worked cooperatively with men in some high-powered businesses in Emerald City, on the other side of the river.

One morning when Sage and I were waking up, I told her about my dream. It was about Mugs. My hands and legs were tingling, thinking about the dream. Sage knew Mugs, because we were all part of the Village.

"You have a headache? Want me to rub your neck?" she asked.

"No, I'm turned on. I dreamed Mugs was penetrating me with her big, rough hand."

This did not upset Sage. She was in fact looking for someone for me because she wanted to have other women lovers. She wanted freedom from my jealousy so I was not surprised when she said, "That can be arranged."

"Really?"

"Yeah, in fact I'm supposed to see Mugs today to arrange a deal with a food delivery." Mugs was a trucker for a food co-op. "I can tell her you're interested."

"Really?" I was amazed at her broad-mindedness.

Sage was everything to me. The cornerstone of my existence. I wanted to be with her above all. But if she was going to have other lovers, I had to do something. Emerald City was so provincial, and the Matriarchal Village was so inter-connected that it was hard for me to find a dynamic attraction anymore. Actually, I felt ready to move on to a world of quirkier, more lively lesbians than I was finding in Matriarchal Village. I spent my days up in a radio station trying to entertain the masses of woods-working dykes who called this burg home with a weekly program called "As the Women Turn." I was almost ready to call it the home-town-I-grew-up-in-and-had-to-leave for the glittering skylines to the south. But since I loved Sage I was doing my best to stay.

The next evening, Mugs appeared in our narrow kitchen. Her real name was Polly, but she had decided that it was too feminine. "Mugs" was a nick-name from childhood, and she was a lifelong dyke. She was very chunky and plain looking, a look that attracted me since I seemed to interpret it as "butch." A funny whimsical intelligence played on her face. She grew up in an old neighborhood in L. A. and came north to Emerald City in the early 1970s because there was woods work for women's crews. She fell in love with a succession of women and was known as a diesel dyke who was into meditation and could also have an intelligent conversation. I looked over at her. Her breasts were large and muscular . . . dense. But her mind, I knew, was light and airy.

It was midnight and still quite hot. The three of us had been talking in the living room but then decided to go out and look at the plum trees. The air smelled clean and sensuous. Mugs and I decided to ride bikes to the canal and take a dip. Sage didn't want to go, because the canal was in a filbert orchard where she had spent the day working on a project spraying enzymes to kill the filbert worms. After her day's work, she didn't want to go back there now. For Mugs and me the moonlit canal was magical, and a dip in the river was perfect bliss.

A few evenings later Mugs came over to take a sauna with us. The three of us could easily fit with room to spare on the wide top shelf. I was longing to caress Mugs's dense breasts when Sage had to leave the sauna to take a phone call. When she left, Mugs said, "I don't want to be called Mugs anymore. Some people still think I'm just a butch truck driver."

"OK Polly."

She took my hand and we moved closer together. We kissed, a kiss that tasted like hot sake, long and fulfilling. Our sweat mingled and our bodies merged. We arose finally and emerged into the cooling mild night wind. An apple fell from the huge tree into the grass by the sauna. Then another apple fell. We settled on the foam rubber on the deck after dipping into the cold pool which was really a white porcelain bath tub. We listened to the night. There was the periodic whine of distant train brakes from a switching yard, a mournful high-pitched whine. There were crackles from leftover firecrackers from the Fourth of July mingled with thunderstorms in the distance.

"Sage's dog's been gone since July 4th."

"The crackers?"

"Yeah, she freaked out and wandered off." I remembered the dream I'd had about Mugs. I wanted to fly with the cool wind caressing my airborne skin.

"I can produce invisible airborne particles that catalyze people into action. I can do this naturally, just as I can fly."

"Elves can do that," Mugs said.

I was excited suddenly–she recognized me. "The particles cause a mental sparkle to blaze up and override the tedium of ordinary life."

"I need some of that."

"Said Polly," I said. I felt safe because she understood me.

We decided to make a little sleeping spot by the fire pit. We spread the foam rubber bed on the far side of the pit, away from the falling apples. I wanted to taste her kiss again. I caressed her dense, huge breasts and felt her large callused hands. She held me and lifted me slowly as if I were a ballerina. As if I could just fly off from here.

"What else do you like?" she asked.

"I like . . . what we're doing . . . and then, sucking, rubbing, being pinned down, penetration. . . ."

"Pinned down, not being able to move?"

"Yeah, hands, hands only, and being spanked, hands only."

"And penetration, hands only?"

I laughed. "Yes, and also a good big thick . . ."

"Power tool?" Polly showed me she understood all of what I was saying that night in the tall grasses.

In the morning Sage came into the back yard and looked at us awkwardly. She was trying to encourage us to be together, but it was still hard for her to take, liberal though she was. I didn't realize the extent of her discomfort. Did she think when she connected us that this really would not happen? She was my life and my light. I totally needed her approval. I felt guilty and withdrew a little. I didn't know what Mugs could be for me. Sage set the chocolate chip ice cream out for us. It was soft, cold, sweet, and crunchy in the hot breeze.

It's a shame to have to choose between vanilla and chocolate," I said. "At least with vanilla chocolate chip you get them both at the

same time. That's why it's my favorite." Could that explain my polyamory? Was it linked to my favorite ice cream?

Sage and Mugs were discussing the Idaho cone bid, a lucrative
forestry project they were both going on. Mugs was a cone picker
when she wasn't driving trucks. It was the most daredevil of the
contracts, but both Sage and Mugs were heavies in the world of
forestry work. I did not consider myself a femme exactly, but no way
was I going to climb up eighty feet of some Douglas Fir. I felt left out.
I was tired of entertaining the troops when they came back to town but
I was too scared to pick cones with them. Sage was the crew leader
and Mugs was the high roller and this was a most lucrative season
coming up. I realized suddenly what was going to happen. They would
both be leaving. Irritated, I got up and left them to go on talking about
their work.

I needed to go to my radio program anyway. Later when I returned
to the Village, Crazy White Elk was sitting on the back steps of the
front house polishing her work boots. Sage and Mugs were gone.

"Where are Sage and Mugs, and are you . . . going with them?" I
asked.

"I heard your radio program."

"You didn't like it?"

"You don't really believe in that 'monogamy' stuff, do you?"

"What do you mean?"

"I mean Polly. I mean are you with Polly now? Why did you speak
about her on your radio show?"

"Why do I entertain people with stories from my own life?"

"Bird, I want to tell you something, and I want you to listen very . . . "

"No, Crazy Elk, don't tell me." Crazy got up and went out toward
the road. I followed her to the river.

"Don't follow me Bird, because you don't want to hear what I have
to say."

It was true, so I tried to stop following her, but I could not stop
myself. Crazy White Elk had helped me once at a crucial moment
when I was insanely jealous of Sage because she had a new lover.
Sage expected me to be non-monogamous, because she had claimed
this for herself shortly after our live-in relationship began. I wanted to
marry her, so I would have agreed to anything. That day, I had interviewed a mutual friend of all of ours on this very subject on my radio
program, "Free Spirit."

Crazy Elk whirled and aimed her antlers at me. We were on a little beach clearing by the rushing water. "Your program today fed into this coupleism. We need to think more like a tribe."

"Ah yes, the exogamous extended family. You know what? I never got cured of jealousy. Never!"

"You are a major hypocrite, Bird. You who claim you can't handle your girlfriend having other lovers. But it's always OK if you have another lover."

"I'm going to split this burg, Crazy Elk. This whole woman-identified Village scene is too encircling. I'm gonna freak if Sage and Mugs . . . Did you know that open relationships is a silly expression? There's something essentially ridiculous about it."

"So you said on the air. Why are you trying to tear down this attempt to get beyond the 'couples' system?"

"I'm no good at it. I'm always grateful just to even have one lover."

"You stand forewarned with Sage."

"Yeah, but . . . "

"Stop whining." With that Crazy Elk bounded off down the river path, and I was left with the conventional thought that wherever you go, everything's the same.

I ran after her. "I'm going to get out of this Matriarchal Village," I shouted petulantly at her when I got back within hearing distance. "I'm sick of being only with women-identified women who are only with other women-identified women!"

Crazy Elk looked at me pityingly. I was so hot I decided to strip and jump into the river.

Elk was looking at me intently as I emerged in a different mood. "C'mere" she motioned to me and drew me close. Softly, she spoke. "I can't imagine . . . I can't envision the future here if you are not in it. The Matriarchal Village . . . what about our visions for the future?"

"Ah, the Village, what is it exactly? It's funny, these dreams I have of flying. I want to fly away."

"Why?" asked Elk.

"Because Sage and Mugs belong together. I saw that suddenly, and I feel like a 'wannabe' around them. It's always like that for me here anymore, that I am not fitting in–and I'm not gonna find what I need here anymore. I have to let go of Sage because I will always be jealous of her. I have to find my own life and it may not be in a matriarchal village."

I continued, "I mean, I love women. I only wanted a wild dykey free spirited woman as a life partner, but ah, these women I want, they are always so free . . . too free for me."

I felt angry at Sage. Why couldn't she just be with me? When she would go off to Idaho, I knew she always had a fling with someone on the crew.

Elk looked at me gravely. "Bird, you are not going to have a life partner. You will have many partners in life and you will weave a thick lush tapestry of relationships which will take care of you."

This time when she bounded off I did not follow her. But later her antlers were lying in the sand of that very spot.

A Boomer's View of Non-Monogamy

Molly Martin

SUMMARY. Recent generations of lesbians have been freer than ever to invent our own culture, including relationship models. My own experiments with relationships have prompted a new definition of polyamory which has more associations with community than with sex. *[Article copies available for a fee from The Haworth Document Delivery Service: 1-800-342-9678. E-mail address: getinfo@haworthpressinc.com]*

Like many of my generation of radical feminists who came of age during the 60s, I railed against the institution of marriage and practiced non-monogamy zealously. In that era of free love, opportunities for sex were plentiful. My subset of radical iconoclasts in college hosted organized and not-so-organized orgies, sex parties and porn viewings. Gay sex was acceptable and even avante garde. In the 60s and early 70s, when I was straight, non-monogamy was easy. I never fell in love with men.

Twenty-some years in the San Francisco lesbian subculture served as an excellent apprenticeship in the world of open relationships. Experience has tempered my early enthusiasm. Today lesbian polyamory–the loving of many women at one time–has for me more associations with community than with lust.

Molly Martin works as a building inspector for the city of San Francisco. She is the editor of the quarterly magazine *Tradeswomen*, and *Hard-Hatted Women, Life on the Job* (Seal Press, 1988, 1996).

Address correspondence to Molly Martin, 386 B Richland Avenue, San Francisco, CA 94110 (e-mail: tradeswomn@aol.com).

[Haworth co-indexing entry note]: "A Boomer's View of Non-Monogamy." Martin, Molly. Co-published simultaneously in *Journal of Lesbian Studies* (The Haworth Press, Inc.) Vol. 3, No. 1/2, 1999, pp. 135-142; and: *The Lesbian Polyamory Reader: Open Relationships, Non-Monogamy, and Casual Sex* (ed: Marcia Munson and Judith P. Stelboum) The Haworth Press, Inc., 1999, pp. 135-142. Single or multiple copies of this article are available for a fee from The Haworth Document Delivery Service [1-800-342-9678, 9:00 a.m. - 5:00 p.m. (EST). E-mail address: getinfo@haworthpressinc.com].

In the mid-70s, after a decade as a practicing heterosexual, the prospect of becoming a lesbian appealed to me for all sorts of reasons besides great sex. Without the constraints of het sex roles and family expectations, I reasoned, we lesbians were free to invent our own culture. Well, theoretically. With parents as our main role models, we tend to draw from the dominant culture. Then there was all that guilt about sex that females of my generation were stuck with. Still, we had more freedom than any previous generation of women to experiment with love and lifestyle. And we did.

Open relationships and casual sex were not unusual among San Francisco dykes I knew in the 1970s. Contrary to currently fashionable revisionist lesbian history which paints 70s lesbian-feminists as self-righteous Puritans, much sex was had by many. Perhaps the dykes partial to penetration were not the same ones who were writing theoretical diatribes, but I can testify we were not lonesome. As with many liberation movements, a whole subset of the lesbian community was committed to experimenting with nontraditional models of loving. Non-monogamy was politically correct.

I was a staunch believer in open relationships in 1977 when I got involved with a lesbian who already had a primary lover and a job that required waking at 4 AM. It took a year of crying jags and bedside bottles of bourbon to shatter my idealism, then two more years of break-ups, hot secret rendezvous, and renegotiations with the other woman to get free:

> *She*: OK, you can have her Friday, but I get her Saturday night.
> *Me*: What a rip! She's always asleep by nine on Friday.
> *She*: Yeah, well, she can't stay awake on Saturday either.

At one point, the other woman and I even resorted to sleeping together to get our lover's attention.

Non-monogamy might work, I decided, if sections of the triangle were exactly equivalent or if relationships were all we had to devote our lives to. But for wage slaves like me, with more to do than process relationships, having one lover at a time was the only practical option. Besides, I'd fallen madly in love with a new woman.

Many years of serial monogamy followed. A five-year relationship with a perfectly wonderful woman ended when my commitment to monogamy failed. My lover had made it clear that the relationship would end as soon as I slept with another. She defined the boundaries, but I agreed that the intimacy we felt would not survive non-monogamy. She was the supersensitive type who knew what I was feeling even before I felt it:

> *She*: Something's going on and I want you to tell me what it is.
> *Me*: Going on? What do you mean by going on? If it stays in my head is it going on then?

The contradiction: I wanted to stay in the relationship, and I didn't want to hurt my lover. But I developed obsessive attractions to other women and worried constantly about my ability to stay faithful. By then I knew better than to end our relationship by running off with another or lying, and I never had an actual affair while we were together. Finally, though, I found the monogamous vow to be one I wasn't able to live with any longer. Our parting was not without trauma, and healing took time, but my ex is now a dear friend.

Early on I observed that lesbians in my generation talked a lot about long-term monogamy, but few really practiced it. We acknowledged the two-and-a-half-year itch and the five-year itch, at which time it seemed natural to move on to a new love interest. The therapeutic community, watchdogs of lesbian culture and creators of relationship lexicon, did not disapprove as long as you were honest and made sure your lover understood your feelings. (Don't run off without telling her in couples therapy. That'll be $40.) Sometime in the mid-80s, in the wake of AIDS hysteria, therapists decided that we were not working hard enough at our relationships and that divorce was pretty uniformly a bad thing. No doubt lesbians broke up just as frequently thereafter, but our level of guilt rose dramatically.

While our subculture reflected the changes going on in popular culture at large, lesbians knew we were unique. That had become more apparent as we watched the gay men's and women's subcultures develop so divergently in the decades following Stonewall. In general, women shunned casual sex and valued emotional intimacy. Picking up a one-night stand was a tougher assignment than finding a gal who wanted to get married. Our interest in the intricacies of personal interaction made us highly evolved players in the realm of relationships. We talked endlessly about sex and love and all of our new discoveries, and we spent thousands on therapy.

In 1982, my lover of two and a half years dumped me, and then my mother died. My intense grief led to an existential epiphany. Suddenly

I was hiking down the other side of that mountain of life, where the air is fresh and where the continuity of all our human connections creates a clear vision. Friends, girlfriends, ex-lovers and lovers–my established family–all assumed a much greater level of importance for me. Once they came into my life, I decided, they were permanent lifetime fixtures. Keeping them, maintaining relationships in whatever their changing forms, became my central focus. Instead of putting all my emotional eggs in one primary lover basket, I vowed to distribute them widely.

That web of constructed and nurtured relationships is, for me, polyamory. I love many women, and the boundaries of our relationships are not always clearly defined. Perhaps one problem is the dearth of available descriptive terms. To adequately represent the depth and breadth of our relationships in lesbianland requires many more categories than the two basics: lovers and friends.

Just as I began to feel a tinge of wisdom, an unexpected new pattern emerged in my forties. At the end of 1993, I wrote to my first woman lover:

> *Age has humbled me, especially in the realm of personal relationships. Remember when we broke up, I vowed I had done with non-monogamy forever? To my great surprise, I've spent the first half of my forties practicing something very like it, though not exactly. Now six years out of a relationship, I've always had lovers, but not in succession as lesbians usually do. These non-relationships seem to take place simultaneously and overlap each other. We move apart, then we might come back years or months later. The transitions tend not to be traumatic as they were years ago. We might break up as lovers, but it is always with the expectation of continuing a friendship or reconnecting as casual lovers in the future.*
>
> *I've lived alone for the better part of the last decade rather arbitrarily, for it was never what I would have chosen for myself. I would prefer to live with people, though I've never aspired to live in a couple with a lover, which, to my dismay, remains our dominant model. Still the experimenter, I seek to invent new models, but there's little support for that, at least among dykes in our age group. I do get lonesome for a daily presence in my life, but I don't miss the "work" of relationships. Actually, I've come to believe that if it takes very much work, I'd rather not be in it.*

Still, I'm halfheartedly seeking Ms. Right, answering personal ads, and asking my friends to fix me up with single women. . . . I find that I take affairs of the heart much less seriously than ever before. I'm seldom driven by the sexual obsessions that continually threatened to break up my 5-year relationship (is that a function of age or marriage?), and I'm much better at casual sex than ever, which I mostly think is good but sometimes makes me feel terribly jaded. Mostly I stand back and watch my own life with wonder and sometimes surprise (sometimes boredom), anticipating the next chapter.

My specialty became distance. Not emotional distance, though some have argued this point. Rather, loving women who lived great distances away. The first lived in rural New Hampshire. We had been lovers briefly years before when she had lived in California. Our paths crossed again as tradeswomen organizers, and we kept meeting at the same conferences. The flame spontaneously rekindled when we began to work on organizing a national conference in 1988.

Fortunately, our affair coincided with a planned year's leave from my work. I could stay with her for a month or two, then return home again before domestic strain or lesbian bed death began to set in. We had no expectation that our lover relationship would last forever, and in fact, my returning to work in San Francisco was the beginning of the end. We couldn't see each other often and the physical distance translated into emotional distance. It took another year for us to call it quits as lovers, with the full expectation that we might again become lovers in the future, since that had been our established pattern. Now solid friends, we've seen each other through many subsequent relationships. She has acknowledged her own pattern of serial monogamy and now tells lovers up front not to expect long-term commitment.

In the meantime, my sex partners included ex-lovers, old friends and new interests. All my relationships, even fuck buddies, required an emotional component, and I found I became disinterested in sex when the romance died. I allowed myself to be strung along for several years by a babe who maintained another primary relationship (hadn't I learned this lesson?). I kept my head above water by telling myself I knew how to leave when it got too painful. She was one of those non-verbal types whose distaste for process eclipsed even my own:

Me: I've wrestled in my own mind with the other woman thing, the age difference thing, those awful shirts you insist on wearing. I think I'd like to continue seeing you. If we have a relationship, what would it look like for you?

She: Wow, look at the time! I think I have a tennis match. Gotta go.

Relationship discourse was futile, but I felt compelled to try periodically to explain my feelings. For two un-drama queens, we generated our share of lesbian drama. Today, as I watch her dramas continue with others, I'm relieved we're no longer lovers, and glad to call her family.

Overlapping love interests presented unique challenges. I found I needed some time to decompress after one before going on to another, although I didn't always heed my own advice. At least once I was compelled to see three in one day and more than once I was caught in flagrante delicto with one lover by another. A familiar scenario from my youth was repeated–of waking up in the morning to a head of short dark hair on the pillow next to me whose face might be one of several. Fortunately, I'm a morning person who usually wakes before my lovers, so I had the advantage of a few private moments to get my bearings before murmuring the wrong name. I soon learned to avoid the emotional yo-yo effect of moving too swiftly from one to another by taking some time to myself in between.

When I began an affair with a New Yorker I'd met river rafting, my friends and even casual acquaintances pointed out that long distance love affairs had become my pattern, and what did that mean about my inability to commit? The therapist suggested this "avoidance of intimacy" meant I'd suffered abuse as a child by my father. Repressed memories failed to reveal an explanation, so I decided to relax and enjoy the present.

My dalliance with Ms. New York continued for four years, and while it often left me longing for the kind of daily connection that a local lover provides, I still swoon with fond memories. Our cross-continental meetings every month or two were adventures in a luscious sea of sexual abandon. Always on vacation, we could strip off all our mundane work-a-day worries and have fun. Issues did arise, and were discussed by phone, but didn't become the focus of our time together.

Our relationship did not fit into any common lesbian-accepted categories. We debated how long an affair can last before it must turn into something else. I contended that, under the right circumstances, it could go on indefinitely, although without living examples, the case was a hard one to argue. Everybody I knew who'd engaged in long-distance affairs had broken up before too long. My lover imagined a different scenario: the relationship just continues to mature, toward greater commitment, toward greater closeness, the goal being a kind of lesbian nirvana–moving in together. I was having trouble visualizing the ultimate emotional goal. My hunch was that the hot sex and passion were directly related to that distance. Could we sustain them if we lived in the same city?

> *She*: The sex will just get better as we get closer.
> *Me:* Do we just get closer and closer until we implode?

The ending? More like an explosion. Our relationship was open, we both dated others, and we'd acknowledged that one of us might get involved with someone else closer to home eventually. It happened to be me. Polyamory, it turned out, wasn't a model Ms. New York could live with. Now that we're no longer lovers, we're trying to figure out how to build and sustain a long-distance friendship without our most compelling element–sex.

For three years now, I've remained happily monogamous with a lover who's newly out. Again, it was she who set the parameters. Our continuing discussion:

> *She*: Sleeping with anyone else is a divorceable offense.
> *Me*: How about only once? How about having sex with some-one else at a sex club when your lover is present? How about in a three-way with your lover and someone else?
> *She*: How about getting over it?

Remaining monogamous has been easier for me in my later-forties. Perhaps peri-menopause reduces the quantity of sexual energy, or perhaps there are just fewer temptations. Since my lover and I maintain separate homes and separate busy lives, the time that we do spend with each other is highly valued, as is the time we are each alone.

In retrospect, I'm glad I haven't lived by a strict definition of the parameters of relationships. The rules have changed according to my life's circumstances, the preferences of my partner at the time, and the compromises we've made to keep us both happy.

We boomers came of age in the 60s, that heady era of principled experimentation, with an ardent belief in our ability to construct a new world. Because the feminist movement–with our enthusiastic participation–did fundamentally change our own lives, many of us retain that idealism. I'm still committed to building relationships based on our own desires and needs rather than traditional patriarchal models. The next generation of dykes will have a fresh perspective and vision.

The lesbian culture we're building continues to offer a critique of the dominant heterosexual culture, even as our own relationships are influenced by it. As we blur boundaries and redefine relationships, we're sensitive to the connections we make with each other on all levels. Our freedom and willingness to experiment will result in lots of new models that hets can copy.

I don't regret any of my relationship experiments–even the painful ones. My only regret is losing contact with friends and former lovers, because I expect them to stay in my life forever in some form–maybe one we have yet to invent.

Impossible Body

Lisa Lusero

SUMMARY. This play tells the story of one woman coming to terms with her "poly" identity through a journey into the multiple layers of love, race, sex, appearance and Otherness. The one-woman show *Impossible Body* was first performed for a reading series sponsored by "Onstage" at the University of Colorado, Boulder, in February 1997. A revised version was developed and staged at the University of Puget Sound in Tacoma, Washington in April 1997. The current script, from which these excerpts are taken, was first presented at the Queer Studies Conference in Boulder, Colorado. *[Article copies available for a fee from The Haworth Document Delivery Service: 1-800-342-9678. E-mail address: getinfo@haworthpressinc.com]*

Space 2

I just kept falling in love with women; it wouldn't stop. So I realized I was a lesbian. Now, I'm a lesbian trying to be in a monogamous

Lisa Lusero is a playwright, activist, and graduate student working on her MA in theatre at the University of Colorado. She has written and produced several plays including *I Envision a Room,* which was developed through a grant from the University of Puget Sound and was recently staged at the Colorado Shakespeare Festival. Her work seeks to unite, challenge, and transform an audience of diverse people.

Address correspondence and performance inquiries to Lisa Lusero, P.O. Box 482103, Denver, CO 80248 (e-mail: lusero@ucsu.colorado.edu).

The author would like to thank everyone who has provided encouragement and support, specifically her partner Allison Hoffman for the honesty, endurance and ongoing trust, and Gretchen Haley who acted as a dramaturg and an inspiration for this piece.

[Haworth co-indexing entry note]: "Impossible Body." Lusero, Lisa. Co-published simultaneously in *Journal of Lesbian Studies* (The Haworth Press, Inc.) Vol. 3, No. 1/2, 1999, pp. 143-150; and: *The Lesbian Polyamory Reader: Open Relationships, Non-Monogamy, and Casual Sex* (ed: Marcia Munson and Judith P. Stelboum) The Haworth Press, Inc., 1999, pp. 143-150. Single or multiple copies of this article are available for a fee from The Haworth Document Delivery Service [1-800-342-9678, 9:00 a.m. - 5:00 p.m. (EST). E-mail address: getinfo@haworthpressinc.com].

143

relationship. But–I still keep falling in love with women. Finally, I have had to realize that I'm a polyamorous lesbian.

Unfortunately, my partner wasn't thrilled.

Yes it's a word. Polyamorous. Loving many all at one time.

Space 7

Allison and I met freshmen year of college. We lived in the same dorm and each had three roommates. One of my roommates knew one of her roommates and one day I overheard them talking about her. How she cried all the time, and seemed so lonely–all she did was talk to her best friend from Colorado. So I wrote her a card–saying: Hi, Lisa here. Y'know the Coloradan who writes poetry and lives in 106. I sat next you during that first hall meeting and I *specifically* remember you had good vibes. When I heard that "the girl with good vibes" was feeling really homesick I wanted to let you know that you're not alone, I've been really homesick too. And I just want you to know that I'm totally here if you need to talk. Basically, I'd just like to get to know you better.

She loved the card and ran up to my room to give me a big hug. From that point on we spent hours and hours just talking and laughing and eating pizza after pizza! Little did I know I was already desperately in love. Little did *she* know until–well, I kissed her. I was out of my mind. I said something like–the lips of my soul touch your face, the lips of my soul soft upon your face, I see, I understand–do you?

And she said, "no" just as a single tear trickled down her cheek and fell onto my lip.

Space 9

We've been together now going on five years. And she puts up with my affairs because mostly they're in my head.

Space 12

When I was sixteen–I was so scared that I might be gay and I didn't know how to tell. So I went to the library. And I typed in: G-A-Y. I was hoping to find some manual on how to know if you're gay, like a book of symptoms or something. All I found was a scientific study on homosexuality in cows.

Which I read.
Apparently, cows are gay too.
But that wasn't very comforting at the time.

Space 24

Okay–I'll admit it. I cut my hair because I wanted people to know I was a dyke. I may be breaking some lesbian code of silence by admitting this–I think we're supposed to pretend that our haircuts happen independent of our sexuality, and for some this may be true. But for me–there is a direct connection. I am conscious of my sexuality all of the time and I don't want it hiding under a conventional do. Passing for straight makes me feel invisible. And I hate that. I want to be seen clearly and explicitly for who I am. This haircut is a way of saying–don't expect me to speak the same language as you–don't expect that I have the same story to tell. Don't expect that I will understand how hard it is to decide on what color the bridesmaids should wear, or how boys will be boys, or how difficult it is raising children in a dual-income home.

Don't assume that your world is mine.
Then again. Don't assume that it isn't.

Space 25

Sometimes I imagine myself with long black hair, dark skin to match the Chicana in me, and long nails painted red. I wear a tight leather skirt to tempt you with, and I am full of power and controlled desire. I stand back, watching you watch me; weaving fantasies before your eyes. *[She walks in front of the audience temptingly, knowing that she is being watched, and loving it. She taunts them with her eyebrows, lips, hips.]* Habla Espanol? Necessito una persona con la lengua, con las palabras.

If I had words, I could speak. If I just had the words I could weave fantasies before your eyes. But this woman doesn't know how to speak. I'm caught. Trapped in a confused body. I *am* the Chicana woman. Soy Lusero! Entiendes? Soy Lusero. I feel sexy; full of power and controlled desire. I feel like the spider woman weaving fantasies before your eyes.

But I don't match.

Last fall I was invited to a reception for graduate students of color. When I arrived, the woman at the door promptly told me:

"There's a reception here right now."

"I know."

"Did you receive an invitation?"

"Yes."

And that was just the beginning. Needless to say, the evening didn't have the warm air of camaraderie that I had hoped.

Something in my skin lied. See–they didn't know that hidden beneath this ivory white skin is a real Chicana woman, a real woman of color–right? They couldn't see Grandma Lusero marching under my skin to Spanish Mass. They couldn't hear in my ears the drunk-slurred "Hey wet-back, where's your fuckin' green card?" as my uncles almost launched a barroom brawl. They couldn't see my beautiful, brown-skinned cousin Sylvia whom I've been in love with all my life. And they couldn't see Gilberto sitting there behind my eyes, Dr. Lusero, relegated to the empty wing of a hotel when they realized Lusero was a dirty Mexican and not the doctor they expected to greet.

They couldn't see beneath my skin to this real Chicana lesbian woman who doesn't know how to be any more brown, who doesn't know how to be any less lesbian, y que no sabe como hablar mas Espanol. They couldn't see beneath my skin–and sometimes, neither can I. Only I'm left to ponder what's inside. So as a "student" of color I left that reception with only one solid lesson: race doesn't make any more sense than sex.

Space 35

Don't bother looking at me, it just doesn't make sense
I can't summon the goddess to take shape
I can't pull the moon from my fingertips or wrap a rainbow around your heart
I can't dance without legs or stand while flying
or battle without armor or sing without a face.
I've got no problem with my body, it's just always been surprising that I only have one.

Space 37

Maybe I should explain this polyamorous thing. Last year–I began a conversation with this girl and suddenly there were no more words. It happened by accident. Or maybe we planned it. It's hard to tell–because even as the conversation began the silence grew heavy and started flowing beneath every word until we were breathing each other's thoughts like air. I fell in love. Again. But I couldn't let this go like the angel in line or the woman in the grocery store. She spoke to me like a secret, in my own language. I couldn't help but listen.

And I was still in love with Allison but she didn't see how that was possible. And I didn't understand it myself–I just felt it to be true. And Allison felt scared. And I wanted to amputate this unfocused heart. Then I realized–my god!!–there I was again, tormented and scared of loving. And I remembered that I never, ever wanted to have that terror–that panic of loving wrong.

So instead of running from passion, instead of hiding in safety–we confronted the edges of feeling and possibility with honesty and love. If we didn't know how to communicate like we were fighting for our lives, then it might've killed us. But it didn't.

This was not just about submitting to one woman's sexual desires–it is about building powerful relationships based on unremitting honesty and agonizing trust. Mutual trust. Mutual freedom. Mutual love. This is about making up our own rules–together–rules that fit our loving better. Not every heart loves in a line.

And I think of that time I first kissed her–and I said I see, I understand–do you?

And she said, "no" just as that single tear betrayed her heart.

Our love is powerful and everlasting *because* it contains multitudes–the fabric of the world.

Space 40

We've been together going on five years now. She puts up with my affairs, and I put up with hers, because we don't want each other to hide.

Space 41

the problem is not
that i am in love with too many people
though i am
the problem is that i only have one body
to do the loving in

which certainly brings a new importance to the day planner
i mean
i always expected
that i would have to be a superwoman
i grew up in the eighties after all
i thought maybe, i'd have trouble
balancing work, family and career
but i never imagined that my loving
would come down to a matter of scheduling–
see the problem is not
that i am in love with too many people
my heart is a multiplicity
but my body
is only one.

Space 42

K-Sig's kick butt! I love to suck dick. Jesus died for our sins. God hates fags. There I was again–reading library desk graffiti. *[Now to the audience.]* Pot is my god. Praise god and fuck me. Why are you reading this? Erica gives good head. Lesbians lick pussy and go to hell. Help–I think this might be me. *[Pause.]* Lesbians suck pussy–Help. *[Pause.]* I think this might be me.

Suddenly this scared lesbian voice struck me–Help. Scrawled there in our most public forum for the honest exchange of opinions. I think this might be me.

So I left my name and number. I know, stupid, crazy. I'm asking for trouble. But if not me–who? Is this woman going to find wisdom and guidance from a K-sig pothead, or Erica the amazing cock-sucker? So I took a chance. I can help. Lisa–761-9074, call me. That night Allison answered the phone. And when I got there–nothing but that painfully empty dial tone. Allison said it was a girl. She sounded scared. And I knew it was her. From the desk. I just hoped she'd get the courage up to try again.

I visited the desk again the next day. She wrote: Sorry about the phone call. I'm chickenshit. Maybe I'll try again. Thanks.

Yes! Try again! I wrote. Or just write here. I want to help you. You'll be okay.

The next time I came to the desk she drew an arrow–down. Okay? I looked all over for another clue. And finally, crumpled up in a corner underneath the desk I found a note.

I felt bad about defacing the desk anymore–she wrote. So our conversations moved to paper–I left her the call number to an obscure book I felt confident would be left alone. And we stashed our correspondence in there. It was Gertrude Stein's *Geography and Plays,* by the way. I didn't think Gertrude would mind.

My first letter was desperate. I didn't know where this woman was at–whether she was near suicide–or just looking for a friend. So I rattled off hotline numbers, book suggestions, support groups, and encouragement–You're okay. You're not alone. You're courageous for just reaching out. You're gonna make it–it gets better from here.

She was beyond the initial–my god I might be gay. And was more in need of a friend, a voice. She asked me about myself. And apologized for not leaving her name.

My parents did not bless me with a name that would allow me to hide in the masses–she said.

And I tried to imagine what that name might be, as I began to tell her my story, to tell her anything and everything about me just to give her a real live lesbian being to hold on to–if only in her mind. I drew her a stick-figure picture of myself. In case we should pass someday in the library, I wanted her to be able to watch me, see me exist in body. Even if she never approached.

And her trust grew through the letters. And I suggested that we meet. And in her next letter she said–yeah–I think I'd like to meet you too. She described the rasta backpack she always carried, and the black cap she always wore. She left me her number and for the first time, signed her name. Ebony. I shook my head as her race bled through the letters of her name and I understood the nature of her multiple invisibilities. Race and sexuality colliding again.

We met. And talked and shared more stories with each other. I introduced her to my partner, my friends. She reminded me of the importance of visibility, the complexities of race and sexuality. I gave her a copy of my lesbian magazine with a beautiful black dyke on the cover. She gave me another story to tell.

Now, I never underestimate the writing on the walls. Behind every anonymous–"I love to suck dick," or "God hates fags"–is a real live body with a real live story to tell. When we finally talked the anonymous "Help" turned into a black lesbian rasta woman and that terrifying phone number transformed into me.

If it takes the anonymity of library desk graffiti to finally meet, then I am willing to wait. Because these bodies are proof of a beautiful and hard-won existence. And our stories are something powerful to share.

Space 43

I can feel the rush of everything moving in and stretching across my body.

It feels so good to touch
my warmth to your warmth
living breathing dancing alive

It feels so good to move–to run and jump and laugh and cry and pray and try and wish and scream and sew the stars into the sky.

It isn't about sex, really, it's about finding joy.

i welcome the moment
i welcome the light the air the growing trees
i welcome a silence a peace a slowness
i welcome my own power my own poet my own time
i welcome the limits and depths and possibilities

and I give thanks

for in this impossible body

I feel
    joy.

Paradigms of Polyamory

Margarita Zambrano

SUMMARY. The *paradigm theory* of Thomas Kuhn is used as a framework to discuss alternative ways of intimacy. The author discusses the implications of structuring actual lesbian relationships by a paradigm of monogamy among Latin-American women. The author proposes that creating alternative paradigms of multiple relationships would be useful for many lesbians as models for alternative life patterns. *[Article copies available for a fee from The Haworth Document Delivery Service: 1-800-342-9678. E-mail address: getinfo@haworthpressinc.com]*

I met Christina a year and a half ago. Since then, I have been struggling to create a safe space for her and for me, as well as for my long-term companion, who is also struggling to cope with the experience of *another* woman in our lives. In this essay, I would like to use the *paradigm theory* of Thomas Kuhn (1970) as a framework to discuss the way monogamy acts as a *paradigm* to structure lesbian relationships. In my discussion, I will refer to some examples of lived

Margarita Zambrano is a graduate student of the National Autonomous University of Mexico. She is currently completing her dissertation on the Women's Movement in Belize.

Address correspondence to Margarita Zambrano, 50 Lexington Avenue, Apartment 23H, New York, New York 10010 (e-mail: mzvalan@msn.com).

The author would like to thank Judith Stelboum for her encouragement to write this article, and the two women who have endured the author's contradictions and certainties in the world of intimacy.

[Haworth co-indexing entry note]: "Paradigms of Polyamory." Zambrano, Margarita. Co-published simultaneously in *Journal of Lesbian Studies* (The Haworth Press, Inc.) Vol. 3, No. 1/2, 1999, pp. 151-155; and: *The Lesbian Polyamory Reader: Open Relationships, Non-Monogamy, and Casual Sex* (ed: Marcia Munson and Judith P. Stelboum) The Haworth Press, Inc., 1999, pp. 151-155. Single or multiple copies of this article are available for a fee from The Haworth Document Delivery Service [1-800-342-9678, 9:00 a.m. - 5:00 p.m. (EST). E-mail address: getinfo@haworthpressinc.com].

151

experience and to the implications of such a paradigm when the reality of our lives urges us to change relationship practices and attitudes. I will focus specifically on the experience of women from a Latin culture.

Kuhn explains the history of the development of theories and methods by using the concept of *paradigm shifts*. A paradigm refers to a belief system by which the scientific community performs their tasks on a continuous basis, i.e., a shared set of norms or criteria for choosing problems and a set of rules to solve those problems. This is a period of *normal science*. At times when some facts cannot be explained or solved by the recommended procedures, revolutionary scientists are willing to take the risk of thinking in entirely new ways. In so doing it becomes apparent that the accepted paradigm of any historical period *often suppresses fundamental novelties because they are necessarily subversive of its basic commitments* (p. 5). As scientists grapple with unexplained phenomena, I find myself in transition between the monogamous paradigm and an emerging one that accounts for my reality.

In a period of seventeen years together, my partner and I have had experiences with affairs which we eventually resolved–not without agony and turmoil. When Christina entered into my life, I found myself in an entirely new situation. Under the rule of monogamy, the existence of another woman was a total threat for the life I had built. The potential of choice created tremendous internal conflicts. Because I refused to give up either the relationship with my partner or Christina, this new problem questioned our basic commitment to the tenets of monogamy. Only recently have I been able to tell my partner that I have been deeply involved with Christina for more than a year while assuring her that I did not want to end our relationship.

For a long time, a dictate from the paradigm was to break up with Christina. It was unbearable to remain silent. It was a time of many acrobatic moves: to conceal and to lie, and to pretend that I was not in love with Christina. The nature–and structure–of my love for her compelled me to think by *paradigmatic default* that it was the most appropriate decision to make. The love I have for my long-term companion did not diminish in any way. But my life with her lacked the honesty I wanted. The logical choice at the time seemed to be to end my *extramarital* relationship in order to recover the honesty and continue acting "love as usual" just as scientists do in the period of *normal science.*

My long-term companion had struggled with similar issues. She also had been involved with other women over the past years. However, she ended these affairs and since then, she has underscored her commitment to a monogamous life with me. In my own prior experiences with outside relationships, the internal and external pressure to submit to the rule of monogamy was so strong that I had to leave women whom I truly cared for. My relationship with Christina has taken a different path.

Christina's life had undergone various changes in the past. She had recently separated from her partner of ten years and knew about the pleasures and pains of long-term monogamous relationships. When we met, Christina had entered into a different state of being, involving complex constellations of affairs and multiple relationships. The state of dating and having sexual relationships with other women "defied" the monogamous structure. I had to learn to cope with the existence of *other(s).* Surprisingly, emotionally, and sexually, our relationship was not affected by Christina's other love affairs. We increasingly felt closer and desire was intense. We realized that our love was built on different grounds: respect, openness, compassion, and friendship. I was less willing to demand monogamy from her and in so doing, I also began to take my interior life seriously. Christina and I had moved to a paradigm of multiple relationships.

The first step toward a paradigmatic shift came when we created a fictitious character called "Laura" who vaguely resembled me. Christina had kept our relationship a secret because she respected my decision *not to tell.* However, she needed to create a safe space for her own emotions as we became closer. She wanted to share her feelings with friends, and most important, with women she was attracted to. The importance of being open about her feelings for me and her commitment to non-monogamy was apparent.

This move was significant for both of us. For the longest time I insisted in the invisibility of our love, but her story helped me to see that I had a concrete existence. She asserted her right to declare her sentiments toward me because she wanted to live her life honestly. By making me visible, she eased the burden of carrying a "secret" and she invested her energies in creative undertakings that did not deprive her from loving me. New, previously unseen phenomena became visible. With urgency, I took the "anomaly" seriously, and contemplated new ways to see our actual relationship. Instead of viewing our relationship as a temporary break from monogamy which had to end soon, I shifted paradigms. This was the beginning of a series of experiments to test the new paradigm with Christina: the paradigm of multiple relationships.

In the meantime, in my life with my partner, silence was consuming my inner world. Similarly, I could not say "I love you" to Christina, because it was such a complicated truth to cope with. The fear of betrayal to my long-term companion was overwhelming. I could openly talk and share my life with Christina while I missed not being able to do the same with my long-term companion. The idea of breaking up with my partner was painfully unthinkable. I was brought up in a Latin-American culture where monogamy as a social institution is applauded. I came out to my family very early on because of the strength derived from having established a stable relationship with only one woman for the rest of my life.

I relate to Joan Nestle's disenchantment of lesbians who

> *dissociate themselves from public sexual activity, multiple partners, and inter-generational sex. Lesbian purity, a public image that drapes us in the cloak of monogamous long-term relationships, discreet at-home gatherings, and a basic urge to re-create the family helps no one. By allowing ourselves to be portrayed as the good deviant, the respectable deviant, we lose more than we will ever gain.* (1987, p. 123)

I tried to be a ***clean sex deviant***. This is most probably the case of many lesbians whose honor and integrity depend on the ability to mirror the standard of marriage for women in our culture. Anything that falls outside makes it even harder for women to come out.

Within the heterosexual model of monogamy, sexual relationships with partners other than a spouse are generally frowned upon. However, men may have numerous affairs but women themselves are socially rejected if they dare to do so. Society accepts the existence of the *querida* as long as it does not challenge the nuclear unity. I remember a Latin friend's reaction to my story: *you are acting like a macho; you just have a concubine and leave your wife behind.* Her reaction came from the very dictates of this kind of paradigm. Moreover, she resorted to paradigmatic solutions: *either you just don't tell, or you just have to break up.* As lesbians, we share this paradigm because we internalized this way of experiencing relationships.

As a Latin woman and as a Lesbian, my sexual freedom has been constrained by the boundaries imposed on heterosexual women. Needless to say, I was reluctant to embrace the patriarchal model of monogamy once again.

When I began to acknowledge that I was actually in love with two women, the reality of my situation forced me to think about change in my relationship with my partner of seventeen years. I felt a sense of challenge, and even more, the desire to bring about change. I cannot sufficiently stress how empowering it has been for both of us to engage in creating new rules in the face of ready-made available solutions. Her love for me has encouraged her in exploring ways to accommodate my individual needs. Yet, I am aware that some natures are contested by paradigmatic prescriptions.

It's hard to imagine how the world of multiple relationships would be. My long-term companion is willing to undertake with faith a paradigmatic revolution. But it is not easy to let go of some symbolic deterrents: the politics of time and space, interacting with friends, and deciding on how to share resources. We find ourselves engaged in continuous negotiations and occasional emotional outbursts.

The most difficult part for me is to feel the continuing power of monogamy over my life while I experience the liberating potential of the multiple relationships' paradigm. Because change sometimes is painful and frightening, I sometimes find myself wanting to go back but then, I remember, it is the beginning; solutions are still imperfect. Even though I have not yet found a perfect model, the promise that a paradigm of multiple relationships can resolve many problems is keeping me alert and hopeful.

REFERENCES

Nestle, J. (1987). *A restricted country.* Ithaca, NY: Firebrand Press.
Kuhn, T. S. (1970). *The structure of scientific revolutions.* Second Edition, Enlarged. Chicago: The University of Chicago Press, Ltd.

If Love Is So Wonderful,
What's So Scary About MORE?

Ellen L. Halpern

SUMMARY. Attaching oneself to a single lifelong partner in a sexually and emotionally exclusive, all-fulfilling relationship is *the* romantic goal for many women in our culture. However, monogamous relationships of this sort provide no guarantee for either permanence or bliss. As many women are beginning to explore polyamorous relating, fears arise about loss of love if a primary partner wishes to love others. When lesbians and bisexual women open their relationships, fears that a bisexual women will abandon her lesbian lover for a man may evoke old fears of a competition that cannot be won. *[Article copies available for a fee from The Haworth Document Delivery Service: 1-800-342-9678. E-mail address: getinfo@haworthpressinc.com]*

Claude Steiner (1974) tells a fairy tale about a time when everyone gave and received warm fuzzies. Each person, young and old, had a bag of them. Anyone could ask for them when needed and give them to others, too. The warm fuzzies never ran out. Everyone was pretty happy most of the time. One day, a witch became angry, because people were so happy that they weren't coming to the witch for potions. The witch devised a clever and wicked plan. One morning the

Ellen L. Halpern is a bisexual woman, currently a postdoctoral fellow at New York University. Address correspondence to Ellen L. Halpern, PhD, Statistics for Mental Health Research Training Program, Dept. of Psychology, New York University, 6 Washington Place, New York, NY 10003 (e-mail: elh@psych.nyu.edu).

[Haworth co-indexing entry note]: "If Love Is So Wonderful, What's So Scary About MORE?" Halpern, Ellen L. Co-published simultaneously in *Journal of Lesbian Studies* (The Haworth Press, Inc.) Vol. 3, No. 1/2, 1999, pp. 157-164; and: *The Lesbian Polyamory Reader: Open Relationships, Non-Monogamy, and Casual Sex* (ed: Marcia Munson and Judith P. Stelboum) The Haworth Press, Inc., 1999, pp. 157-164. Single or multiple copies of this article are available for a fee from The Haworth Document Delivery Service [1-800-342-9678, 9:00 a.m. - 5:00 p.m. (EST). E-mail address: getinfo@haworthpressinc.com].

157

witch whispered to Tina,[1] who was watching Maggie play with the neighborhood children, "See all the fuzzies Maggie is giving to Lucy. If she keeps this up, soon she will run out and there will be nothing left for you." Tina was surprised; she had thought that there were unlimited warm fuzzies. The witch told her "No, once you run out, that's it." Tina began to get worried every time she saw Maggie give a warm fuzzy to someone else and she started to complain. Maggie liked Tina very much and didn't want to see her upset, so she started to save her fuzzies for Tina and gave fewer to others. To make a long story short, soon the children saw what was happening, and the other people, too, and fewer and fewer warm fuzzies were given out. The story continues, but the point is made. Where once there were warm fuzzies for everyone, now people began pairing up and reserving their fuzzies so they wouldn't run out.

Why is it that we are so stingy with our own and each other's love? Why do we call it cheating when someone we love loves someone else, too? Fear of polyamory–I'll call it polyphobia–strikes us all. Attaching oneself to a single lifelong partner in a sexually and emotionally exclusive, all-fulfilling relationship is *the* romantic goal for many women in our culture. We may reconcile ourselves intellectually to something less than this totality by saying that having all these things in one single relationship is just an unreasonable, unattainable desire. However, there is often a small voice inside saying that a failure to achieve this "perfect" union is just that, a failure. Why do we cling to this relatively recent, and heterosexual, fantasy? And what are the alternatives? In fact, over the course of a life each of us constructs a continuously developing and changing web or network of important attachments, which may include family of origin, friends, acquaintances, colleagues, and others. How is it that only one of these relationships merits being described as Love or Significant?

What makes the idea of non-monogamy scary to many lesbian and bisexual women? Fear of non-monogamy is a complex issue; when we break down the illusion of a "perfect" union, we must recognize our own limits to fulfill our role in relationships as well as the role of our partners. In doing so, we see the inherent fragility in maintaining a committed primary relationship: how little it takes to disrupt the twoness of partnership. It probably goes without saying that sexual nonexclusivity symbolizes emotional infidelity for a great many people, probably most. If my partner has sex with someone else, what does that say about our relationship? For many of us, sexual nonexclusivity is a BAD thing, and is often the catalyst for separation, break-ups, or at least a lot of rage at one's partner. Although we may be jealous when a partner spends time with a friend in a non-sexual way, we tend to manage these feelings, but if even a little casual sex enters the picture, the whole relationship comes into question. For lesbians and bisexual women whose social circles often include former lovers, the distinction between friendship and more romantic emotional involvement is often fuzzy and open to interpretation.

Fears about polyamory can be internalized in ways similar to homophobia. It is easy to internalize the social approbation toward having multiple relationships which include sex. There can be an inescapable suspicion that there is something wrong with oneself. If other people are able to be successfully and blissfully monogamous with a single partner forever and ever, then there must be something wrong with me if I can't do it. On the other hand, one can also begin to see oneself as more highly evolved and special for wanting and being able to do this really wonderful thing–love more than one.

On the surface it would seem that anyone who had fears or doubts about the possibility of achieving more than one intimate relationship would just not bother. While this is quite reasonable for many women, for others, rejecting poly outright is not an option. One's partner may request an open relationship or wish to explore adding additional members to the primary relationship. In some cases, a woman may have already had an affair and has decided to tell her partner about it. Perhaps many women would leave a relationship if this request were raised. For others, this request could provide an opportunity to explore each other's views on sexual fidelity, jealousy, what the addition of other partners might bring to their relationship, and what each person fantasizes about if multiple intimate relationships were possible.

Sometimes, the process begins, as described above, with the introduction of the idea by one's significant other. This process could also begin with the awareness within oneself, whether currently within a committed relationship or not, that the social expectation that a person can be committed to only one other feels like an artificial prison. It's not that she wants to rush right out and have a circle of lovers or create multi-adult family, but that she feels that the demands placed upon exclusive monogamous, forever, liaisons are too great.

It is an interesting phenomenon: one of the most common fears about poly is that the addition of sexual, loving relationships to a pair will increase the risk that the primary bond will be diluted or broken. We are so used to the classic "cheating" paradigm–that when one person has an affair, the relationship is in trouble–that we assume that this paradigm would apply to poly as well. In reality, the very assumption that the desire, intent, or act of having more than one sexual relationship should somehow lead to the demise of the primary bond may be creating a climate where that is the most likely outcome. When finding oneself in a new sexual, loving relationship is interpreted as morally wrong or symptomatic of serious problems with one's primary partner, the new liaison is often hidden from the partner. As this leads to more and more lies and secrets about time and money spent and unaccountable moodiness, a genuine rift is created where there may have been none before.

It is necessary first to define polyamory in a way that doesn't evoke images of "cheating": one promiscuous partner and the other feeling that she must accept it. The more reluctant partner may feel that her partner is just looking for permission to have affairs without having to hide it or feel guilty. Some forms of polyamorous relating are more likely to evoke these kinds of fears than others. For many polyamorists, open relationships, where each partner in a couple is free to have other emotional or sexual attachments while remaining in a committed primary relationship with each other, are not considered polyamory. Their view of polyamory rests on the idea that the relationship is a unit which is closed to outside emotional and/or sexual relationships, much like a traditional heterosexual marriage, but with more people. In this type of relationship, partners are motivated to keep the group together. This type of arrangement may lessen fears that one partner will become more loved than another, since decisions about who will be part of the marriage are made together.

There is also a more inclusive definition of poly, or what Anapol (1997) calls new paradigm relating. New paradigm poly would include any and all forms of loving relationships where the individuals involved are committed to honesty and authenticity in their relationships. It explicitly allows for and encourages the change and growth that a more flexible view of commitment permits. For example, a primary bond may exist among two or more women who live together, but each of them may have intimate relationships with one or more others which may or may not be shared with other members of the primary unit. New paradigm poly appears to assume a basic respect for all forms of expression of sexual-loving feelings in ways that facilitate individual growth, with the assumption that there can be no a priori limitation placed upon the number or nature of intimate relationships among consenting individuals.

Despite the fact that a multi-adult unit is likely to be no less stable than the traditional two-parent model, fears regarding the welfare of the children are very common. It is readily apparent that raising children can fit quite well into a multi-adult poly family. In favor of more adults is the possibility that the child will form a variety of stable attachments and that the greater availability of a known adult for support, supervision, and play will enrich the child's emotional and intellectual development. Creating a poly family where there are or will be children often evokes negative reactions from family, friends, and community, even if the concept of lesbian parenting is already tolerated. The perception that children will be exposed to sexuality in an unhealthy way is a typical way people express their fear and distrust of poly relating.

Individuals and couples interested in exploring poly relating for the first time benefit from making the effort and time to examine their beliefs about non-monogamy and discussing what kinds of relationships they wish to permit or discourage beyond the primary relationship with each other. Nearing (1992) gives some excellent advice on the kinds of topics potentially poly people should consider. She encourages individuals to share sexual and relational histories with each other and to become accustomed to discussing difficult feelings, such as jealousy, which will continue to arise even when having multiple partners is everyone's preference.

An additional problem posed by poly relationships among lesbian and bisexual women is that each person might be at a different stage in their degree of outness regarding both their sexual orientation and their poly lifestyles. When one member is out in all areas of her life regarding sexual orientation and poly, she is potentially outing the other members of the poly unit. While this may also be a problem for any lesbian couple, the potential avenues for leaks multiply quickly. And despite the challenge that lesbian and bisexual orientations represent to heterosexual relating, the opposition to poly relating among lesbians can be even more relentless.

LESBIANS AND BISEXUAL WOMEN AND MORE LOVE

Polyamory in lesbian relationships where at least one partner identifies as bisexual raises a whole set of myths about what it means to be bisexual in the first place. Bisexual women have labored long and hard (and not particularly successfully) to demonstrate to their lesbian sisters that being bisexual doesn't mean that one has to have lovers of both genders and that she can have a committed, monogamous relationship with a woman. While it is certainly true that many bisexual women will be happy with a monogamous relationship, many bisexual women prefer poly relating for the same reasons that lesbians do, and not just as a way to have both a man and a woman.

The fear that some lesbians have that a bisexual woman may leave them for a man has been greatly enhanced by the political connotations of such a transfer of love. While in principle it is natural for some individuals to change lovers over time, when a bisexual woman leaves a relationship with a woman and begins a relationship with a man, it is commonly viewed as a capitulation to heterosexual privilege. While this may be the case sometimes, the belief, by lesbians, in this myth as fact is a problem for bisexual women wishing to nurture the relationships which work best at a particular moment in time. Poly relating potentially provides a context for lesbian and bisexual women to explore the fears of loss and abandonment that, in my opinion, underlie most of the apprehension with which many lesbians view intimate relationships with bisexuals.

Unfortunately there are several problems standing in the way of real dialogue between self-identified lesbians and bisexual women. A large proportion of lesbians continue to insist that (1) there is no such thing as bisexuality, (2) a bisexual is just a woman who can't decide, (3) a bisexual is just a woman who wants to have it both ways, (4) bisexuals are lesbians who don't want to give up heterosexual privilege, (5) bisexuals are not real feminists because they sleep with the enemy, or (6) some combination of the above. Interestingly enough, there are a lot of self-identified lesbians having sex with men, having relationships with men, having committed relationships with men, and even marrying them. What's wrong with this picture? Given our (lesbian and bisexual) wide range of interest or desire to include males in our intimate relationship circle, why does the idea of negotiating poly relationships that may include a guy or two cause so much trouble?

When a woman tells her woman partner that she wants to add another partner, the gender of the other partner can be a very important issue. The possibility of it being a man can call up all one's concerns about the emotional safety of the household. It goes without saying that concern about sexually transmitted disease can be of major concern for women who have been monogamous or involved only with other uninfected women. For a lesbian, it must be very difficult to face the dismay or outright shunning of lesbian friends. Being involved with a bisexual woman who wants also to be involved with men is viewed almost as (or more) negatively among some lesbians as being involved with a man himself.

Biphobia is the dirty linen of the lesbian community. Lesbians, with their (sometimes closeted) bisexual sisters alongside them, have fought long and hard to have their sexual orientation respected. That many lesbians cannot just take bisexual women at their word that bisexuality is real keeps us apart when we both need and desire each other. For me, biphobia is the fear that someone you love will leave you because you are not the right gender, that a woman can never be as good as a man. For a lesbian to be in a poly relationship with a bisexual woman means that not only must she confront fears evoked by sharing love with others, but also her biphobia. As a bisexual woman who does understand that there are political reasons why some women might not feel strong enough to buck the heterosexual and monogamous status quo, I truly believe that being left is inordinately painful whether one is left for another woman or for a man. When the loss is unexpected, one always feels that one has failed. The feeling of betrayal is real, but it can also serve to hide the deeper feelings of sadness and loss.

In truth, our fears of loss and abandonment by loved ones can be almost unbearable. This fear is perhaps the greatest obstacle to acceptance of poly relating. Fear of being displaced by another doesn't begin at adulthood. Sibling rivalry is only one of many early experiences we have where we feel we must compete for love and often lose. It can be hard to admit that there is no guarantee that our life partner will stay with us forever. Given the divorce statistics and the evidence that lesbian monogamous relationships are not overall more enduring than heterosexual ones, polyamorous groupings are probably not any less stable. In fact, couples with open relationships often note that liaisons with others often enhance and improve the couple's relationship with each other. If we re-assess the belief that we must stop loving one partner before we love another, we find that there is plenty to go around.

NOTE

1. I've taken some liberties with gender and relationships here, but have preserved the overall sense of the warm fuzzies part of Steiner's tale.

REFERENCES

Anapol, D. (1997). Polyamory: The new love without limits. San Rafael, CA: IntiNet Resource Center.

Nearing, R. (1992). *Loving more: The polyfidelity primer* (3rd. edition). Captain Cook, Hawaii: PEP Publishing.

Rust, P. (1995). *Bisexuality and the challenge to lesbian politics: Sex, loyalty, and revolution.* New York: New York University Press.

Steiner, C. (1974). *Scripts people live: Transactional analysis of life scripts.* New York: Grove Press, Inc..

West, C. (1996). *Lesbian polyfidelity.* San Francisco: Booklegger Publishing.

A Long Journey
Towards Polyamorous Bliss

Cynthia Deer

SUMMARY. The author describes how her life has evolved over two decades from lesbian coupling which mirrored a traditional heterosexual marriage, to increasingly unconventional styles of relating. An open primary relationship was the first step away from monogamy, followed by stages of casual sex with multiple partners, a long-distance bi-coastal romance, being the "other woman" to someone with a primary partner, and finally, seeking multiple committed relationships. The question of how to maintain privacy while sharing honest communication is a theme throughout these different involvements. *[Article copies available for a fee from The Haworth Document Delivery Service: 1-800-342-9678. E-mail address: getinfo@haworthpressinc.com]*

Falling in love with a woman felt like a revolutionary act twenty-five years ago. But as I look back, I see that switching my romantic focus from men to women was just the first small step towards creating radical relationship styles in my life.

My first lesbian love affair was a very traditional monogamous coupling. Barbara and I lived together, traveled together, ate together, and made plans together. When we outgrew each other, we went our separate ways: she marrying a man and having kids; I exploring new lesbian involvements.

Cynthia Deer is a native Californian who currently lives in the San Francisco Bay Area and works as a software reliteration analyst. This is her first published work since she wrote for her junior high school newspaper, *Cougar Prints.*

[Haworth co-indexing entry note]: "A Long Journey Towards Polyamorous Bliss." Deer, Cynthia. Co-published simultaneously in *Journal of Lesbian Studies* (The Haworth Press, Inc.) Vol. 3, No. 1/2, 1999, pp. 165-174; and: *The Lesbian Polyamory Reader: Open Relationships, Non-Monogamy, and Casual Sex* (ed: Marcia Munson and Judith P. Stelboum) The Haworth Press, Inc., 1999, pp. 165-174. Single or multiple copies of this article are available for a fee from The Haworth Document Delivery Service [1-800-342-9678, 9:00 a.m. - 5:00 p.m. (EST). E-mail address: getinfo@haworthpressinc.com].

AN OPEN RELATIONSHIP

After a few years of adolescent-style frantic "dating," I met Lee, who became my second long-term lesbian lover. It was the late 70s, and open relationships were the community norm in Oregon. I was living at WHO Farm, a lesbian separatist rural community, sleeping with one farm dyke and two Portland women, when I met Lee. We fell in love, and I quickly dropped my other three girlfriends, an act that felt politically incorrect at the time. For nearly a year my attention was devoted exclusively to Lee, and to the women's wilderness adventure program we were starting together. We defined our relationship as "open," we just didn't have time for anyone else at first.

Then Katy ignited my lust. My attraction to her pointed out that my partnership with Lee was not as sexual as I desired. After several months of working on spicing up our sex life, Lee and I agreed, with the support of our friends, that I should find other lovers. I had a series of affairs, which were exciting, but somehow it felt wrong to be having sex with someone I wasn't in love with.

When Lee got involved with Nan, I don't remember being jealous at all. (I did wonder at times if I was inadequate because I couldn't inspire Lee's libido in the way I wanted to. Lee assured me that there was nothing wrong with me, it was she who simply wasn't so passionate. I accepted the explanation, and mostly didn't worry.) The night Lee and I moved into the mountain cabin we had purchased, Nan was there to cook dinner for us all. It felt like a warm, loving family.

For a year or so after Lee and I stopped defining ourselves as "lovers," we remained close friends, occasionally sleeping together and snuggling, until I moved out of state. Today, I have a warm but distant connection to Lee, maintained by a card or phone call once or twice a year.

SERIAL MONOGAMY

When I moved from Portland to Colorado Springs in 1980, I immediately noticed the different expectations of this new lesbian community. Open relationships were out, monogamy was in. For three years I was single and dating, or more accurately, in a series of "relationships" that lasted from four hours to four months. It seemed strange having to choose between "being together" and "splitting up," but every time one of us figured out that we weren't going to move in together and live happily ever after, we became "ex-lovers." I longed for a warm, intimate network of women in my life, like I had left behind in Oregon. I didn't know exactly how I wanted love, sex, passion, intensity, friendship, and sensuality all to fit together. I just knew that serial monogamy was ripping my heart apart with every breakup. There had to be something better.

LONG-DISTANCE LOVERS

In between Colorado Springs girlfriends, I would often fly to San Francisco, or invite Andrea to visit Colorado. We had met in Portland through a newspaper ad in 1979, shortly before she had been transferred to the Bay Area and I had moved to Colorado. Though each erotic rendezvous was a satisfying thrill, we encouraged each other to date local lesbians. When she fell in love with a San Francisco woman, I was disappointed, but understanding, and glad that we could talk about it. Six years later, when they split up and I was also single, Andrea and I had another exciting affair. We considered the possibility of serious involvement. But Andrea seemed too much like the "marrying" type. I shied away from pairing up with her. We now live nearby, and are good friends. Andrea is monogamously coupled with her life partner, so I doubt that our friendship will ever include another sexual phase.

AN AGREEMENT TO SILENCE

I knew I wanted to get to know Karen the minute I read her questionnaire for the lesbian computer dating service I was managing. I talked a friend into inviting us both to dinner, and I was immediately drawn to Karen. During our first few weeks of dating, we each said that we valued open relationships, but Karen noted that she often got jealous, and said she'd rather not hear about it if I slept with anyone else. Recognizing that I had been compulsively honest for most of my life, I agreed to experiment with silence. I made the mistake of never discussing the issue again. Two years later, when an old friend of mine moved to a nearby city, I had an affair with her, and simply didn't talk about it. A year later, Karen felt incredibly betrayed when she found out about the liaison. After months of emotional turmoil, I promised to be monogamous, hoping not to lose Karen. But it was too late, and too many hard feelings could not be erased. When Karen and I split up, I felt like I had failed at the best relationship of my life. I had blown it with this woman I loved passionately, respected fully, and traveled with smoothly. At that point, I resolved to always be completely open and honest with partners, whether we chose monogamy or open relationships.

GOING WITH THE FLOW

Over the next few years, I sporadically dated women, usually letting them define whether or not we were in an exclusive relationship. After moving to San Francisco, and finding myself sorely lacking in city social skills, I felt lucky to find anyone who would go out with me more than once. I tried to keep a low profile on the non-monogamy issue. It was so hard to find dates that I didn't want to alienate any potential lovers. I didn't think much about what I ideally wanted: A long-term relationship seemed unattainable, so I accepted that my life would continue to be a series of short-term connections.

BI-COASTAL DATING

At the National Lesbian Conference in Atlanta in 1991, I met Ruth. She lived in Brooklyn, I lived in San Francisco. Despite our blossoming closeness, we agreed that an exclusive commitment to each other would be ridiculous, since we could only get together every four to six weeks for over a year. Then, two months before she relocated to San Francisco, a move she was making in part to be with me, she asked me to be monogamous until she arrived. I thought the request was reasonable, but it felt like an unnecessary restraint. She was satisfied with my answer when I said I'd try my best to honor her wishes. I discovered that my body could respect her desires, but my heart could not. The anger and resentment I felt in those two months masked the love I had felt for Ruth. I was knotted in confusion, and Ruth immediately felt my emotional distance. On a day that makes me choke with embarrassment and pain to remember, we split up as soon as she got to town.

The experience taught me that being non-monogamous is as much a part of my nature as being a lesbian, or being an outdoorswoman. I can love long and well and honestly, but I can't love exclusively. I can choose briefly to behave otherwise, but monogamy just doesn't work out for me.

And yes, I do get jealous, especially when someone's new flame takes attention away from me. Though I was dating someone else, and we were no longer calling ourselves lovers, I was heartbroken when Ruth found a new lover and stopped spending so much time with me.

It took a rocky and difficult year for Ruth and me to successfully make the transition from being lovers to being friends. Now I totally adore her as an adventuresome backpacking buddy, reliable friend, and fun-loving travel companion. I believe that at the core, she is monogamous and I am not. That difference will probably always prevent us from trying to be lovers again.

LONG-TERM EROTIC FRIENDSHIP

Marilyn is the first open lesbian I ever met; Marilyn is the affair that split up me and Karen; Marilyn is the woman who reminds me that non-monogamy is OK. We recognize that we share a passion for modeling alternative forms of intimacy. Besides hiking, canoeing, and skiing together, we urge each other to write and speak up about loving in an openhanded way. When we get a chance, once or twice a year, we go to bed–for some of the most surprising, comforting, moving, and exotic sex I have ever experienced.

This is a friendship that I hope lasts many more years. Marilyn is a sex partner I cherish, a friend that I love, and a snuggle buddy I crave. But what do I call her? We've never been a "couple," so "erotic friend" is the only label I can think of that makes sense.

A HALF-TIME LOVER

Dorothy has an old lover she sees a couple of times a week, and Dorothy has me. I have Dorothy, and I have affairs–sometimes with old friends, sometimes with new acquaintances. Dorothy is an over-worked saleswoman with a yen for being entertained, and a disdain for being alone. She loves hearing of my adventures. I am a vagabond with insatiable curiosity about new places and new people. Right now, having a half-time "main squeeze" is an excellent setup for me.

Sometimes the emotional differences in our relationship bother me. I see her as my primary lover, but her commitment is stronger to her longer-term partner. I have to remind myself that no two people ever have "equal" feelings for each other, and that balance does not require both sides to be identical. When I listen to my heart instead of my head, this current lover feels perfect–especially when I come home after a week or a month of travel, and she welcomes me with open arms, anxious to hear of what I've seen and whom I've loved.

Things work so well because we each live alone, and because Dorothy has a predictable schedule with her primary partner–I know there's no chance of getting together on certain nights. It also works well because seeing a lover one or two nights a week constitutes a serious involvement to me–I've never wanted to spend every night with anyone. Her spending half the week with her primary lover, and my spending that time alone, with friends, or with another lover works well for us both.

We tell each other of outside romance, to a limited extent. She's interested in hearing more about my love life than I want to know about hers. We're careful to treat each other as special dates, not as old familiar stand-bys. For example, one Saturday night when I was going out with a woman I was hoping to sleep with, it became clear early in the evening that she was not interested. I knew Dorothy was free that night, and I was tempted to invite myself over. I resisted the temptation, knowing the act might be good for the moment but bad in the long run. No one wants to feel like a "consolation prize."

I don't expect my involvement with Dorothy to continue in its present form forever. I imagine that some year we'll evolve into erotic friends, seeing each other only occasionally.

THE OTHER WOMAN

Barbie is the "other lover" in my life now, and a fine lover she is. I'm the "other woman" in her life, too–she currently lives with her girlfriend of 18 years. Since we met at jury duty several months ago, we've been on an up-and-down merry-go-round trying to figure out just how we fit into each other's lives. The passion is strong, the camping-compatibility is a joy, and I love it that she's so open with the rest of the world about her multiple involvements. My connection to her is more than an affair, less than a primary commitment, and a very significant part of my life.

WHAT'S NEXT?

I like having more than one girlfriend in my life. Three nights with a lover and four nights a week alone feels like the right balance for me. I'd rather not always have the same woman in my bed. That gets stale after awhile. I'd also rather not always be the "other woman" to someone who is in a primary relationship. The whole primary/secondary thing feels too much like the traditional couple set-up to me. Plus, I don't always want to be in second place. I long to love women who have multiple significant intimacies in their lives, who make plans, agreements, and commitments with a variety of friends and lovers.

I don't want to live in one big poly-family, but I'd like it if most of my friends and lovers knew each other, socialized together, and maybe even loved each other. Of course, life these days is so hectic and alienating that I feel lucky whenever I encounter even occasional snippets of real intimacy. Hoping for robust polyamory seems like wishing on a star. But I do know that I feel more alone in the world when I'm part of a monogamous couple than I ever feel when I'm single, so I'll probably always be exploring alternative love-styles.

OCCASIONAL AFFAIRS

On a recent month-long trip out of state, I had the good fortune of sleeping with three friends on different occasions. In the first case, remembering the luxurious lovemaking we had shared years before, I asked my friend's current girlfriend if I could sleep with her sweetie. "Be my guest" was her reaction. Asking the question brought me closer to both of them.

My next sleeping buddy, though not a sex partner, offered perhaps the most erotic encounter of all. The touching, talking, and laughing late into the night with this woman left me charged up in a way that only new intimacy can do. I wondered what might have happened if she were not monogamously coupled, until she assured me that the romantic interest was completely one-sided. I was reminded that affection need not be expressed sexually.

A week later I had a surprise affair with a friend I've known for years and often been attracted to. At the end of our time together, we were discussing the possibility of encountering each other at a hot springs party that her current girlfriend would also be attending. "Don't ask, don't tell" she winked at me as she drove away. I concluded that her lover might not approve of the affair, but they probably wouldn't discuss it.

TRUTH AND PRIVACY

A few years ago, I was dating a cowgirl who agreed that we were free to see others, as long as we told each other everything. However, I soon discovered that the level of detail about my sexual and emotional life that she expected was more explicit than I wanted to share with anyone. I remember one night lying in bed being grilled for details, and making up lies just to get her to back off. It was the first time I had ever blatantly, consciously lied to a lover. I was shocked. Up until then, I had seen privacy and honesty as being at different ends of a continuum, with varying degrees in between. As I lay there that night hearing myself lie to protect my privacy, I felt the ends of that line bend around and touch each other. Now I see a big circle that includes tact, honesty, intimacy, privacy, truth, fiction, kindness, and common sense. We try to balance some or all of these elements each time we communicate with a friend, lover, family member, partner or other person in our lives.

WE'RE NOT ALONE

Dorothy, my current #1 girlfriend, doesn't talk much about her relationships to others, because she thinks her sales will be better if clients see her as a "single lesbian." We know several other women in the Bay Area exploring various forms of open, alternative intimacy, though few will talk about it.

For example, Marian and Sunny agreed when they got together not to tell each other of their frequent outside affairs–and this formula has worked for them for over 10 years. Keisha and Annette, who have lived together for nearly 20 years, both welcome Annette's other lover into their home, but Keisha always visits her other lover elsewhere.

Donna and Kim have a two-decade partnership that allows bringing home secondary girlfriends, but only when the primary lover is out of town.

In 1986, when Karen and I were struggling to sort out guidelines for our troubled involvement, we offered a workshop at the Michigan Women's Music Festival titled "Open Relationships." We hoped to find a dozen or so women to talk with. Three hundred showed up to share stories. Clearly this was a popular topic a decade ago, as it is now. It's probably always been discussed among women who love women. I wonder what Natalie Barney could tell us about having multiple lovers, or Sappho, or Eleanor Roosevelt.

WHY AM I POLYAMOROUS?

I see four major factors that have affected my preference for multiple intimacies over a traditionally coupled lifestyle. First, as a Girl Scout, I learned to "make new friends, but keep the old" and to switch buddies regularly. I think the steady-buddy-phobia of our leaders may have been a reflection of their homophobia, but in me it planted the seeds of couple-phobia.

Second, growing up in a single-parent family meant that I never learned to idealize long-term coupling. Oh, I was indoctrinated with the typical television-style happy family fantasies, but I outgrew dreams of marrying and living happily ever after soon after I gave up the expectation of meeting the "right man."

Third, I came of age in the 1960s, and talked of "free love" long before I ever had adult sex. It seemed an unarguable truth that "if you can't be with the one you love, then love the one you're with." I share a feminist awareness that this free love culture imposed a burden on many female heterosexual flower children, who felt they had no right to say "no" to sex. But personally, I've observed that we lesbians find plenty of reasons to say "no" to sex. I think most of us could benefit from some sixties-style free love flower-power.

Fourth, when I came out into Portland dyke culture in the 1970s, open relationships were the norm. We questioned all patriarchal institutions, including monogamy, and actively tried to create alternatives. Monogamy was criticized as reflecting the acquisitive, dominating male culture. Sharing lovers, friends, sex, and affection was an integral part of creating an alternative community. I still believe that sex is part of the glue that holds communities together. (I like it when I know a friend once slept with my new lover.)

I now see the many variations of monogamy and polyamory as options that lovers need to discuss with each other. There is a time and place for monogamy, for polyamory, for celibacy, for sex without love, and for love without sex. I enjoy talking about different relationship styles, with everyone from lovers to casual acquaintances.

Sometimes when I mention my own open relationships, the listener will frown and insist, "non-monogamy just doesn't work–I've tried it." I nod sympathetically and say I understand, because monogamy just doesn't work for me.

Other times, when I talk of my multiple intimacies, the listener's eyes will light up like those of a third-grader who has just heard the word "recess." She's often hungry to get out and explore.

SO MANY WOMEN, SO LITTLE TIME

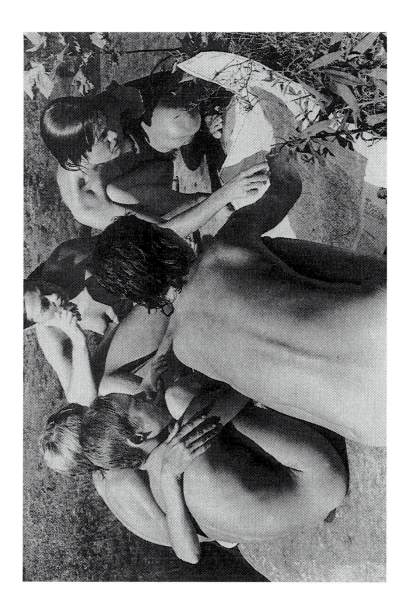

Traveling Amazons

The Henna Heads

Kitaka's Experiment
or
Why I Started the Ecstasy Lounge

Kitaka

SUMMARY. The owner of Ecstasy Lounge describes her lesbian sex club that operated in San Francisco in 1991 through 1996. She tells how her philosophy and desires led her to start the business, and how the sexual habits of lesbians and bisexual women were influenced by the existence of this club. *[Article copies available for a fee from The Haworth Document Delivery Service: 1-800-342-9678. E-mail address: getinfo@haworthpressinc.com]*

At 19 years old, I wanted sex from women–as much as I could get. I wanted to get large quantities of sex from many women, but couldn't

Kitaka is the founder and owner of the Ecstasy Lounge and Club Ecstasy Productions. She has been interviewed by several television talk shows and numerous magazines nation-wide on the subjects of safer sex, polyamory, and indulgence of sexual freedom.

Currently, she is concentrating on her first passion as a singer and musician, working on her first CD and starting her own record label. She wants to put Ecstasy Lounge in the annals of lesbian history by finding a publisher for a photo journal book and an autobiographical book, chronicling the club. She also has five years of club video footage and is seeking an editor to produce a documentary of Ecstasy Lounge for the International Lesbian/Gay Film Festival.

Address correspondence to Kitaka, Club Ecstasy Productions, 336 Arleta Avenue, San Francisco, CA 94134 (e-mail: ecstasy@kitaka.com).

The author wishes to thank Heather Cassell, Heather Gaddy, Jenny Strauss, Heidi Yoder, and Warrior Girl for their support and inspiration for this article; and Marcia Munson for her conviction to include the Ecstasy Lounge within this anthology.

[Haworth co-indexing entry note]: "Kitaka's Experiment; or, Why I Started the Ecstasy Lounge." Kitaka. Co-published simultaneously in *Journal of Lesbian Studies* (The Haworth Press, Inc.) Vol. 3, No. 1/2, 1999, pp. 179-184; and: *The Lesbian Polyamory Reader: Open Relationships, Non-Monogamy, and Casual Sex* (ed: Marcia Munson and Judith P. Stelboum) The Haworth Press, Inc., 1999, pp. 179-184. Single or multiple copies of this article are available for a fee from The Haworth Document Delivery Service [1-800-342-9678, 9:00 a.m. - 5:00 p.m. (EST). E-mail address: getinfo@haworthpressinc.com].

quite figure out how to get it without being in a relationship with a woman. When I did get sex, it usually meant that the particular woman I had sex with wanted to be my full-time lover. I was quite over that,[1] already having been in several relationships with women. I had always felt that non-monogamy was fun and a good thing, so I was always truthful to my girlfriends about sleeping with other women. But it seemed to become increasingly hard to find women who wanted to have sex without commitment. Perhaps I wasn't communicating my wants and needs correctly, or maybe I was too overt.

Whatever it was, I was not happy with how the lesbian community was handling their relationships, or the fact that I was not getting my needs met. I wanted to change that–somehow. I continued to go through jobs, therapists and relationships, trying to figure out what I wanted. I was still unhappy and horny.

By age 23, I had been working as a go-go dancer, cashier, and bouncer at several lesbian clubs for two years and found that also to be most unsatisfying. Dealing with drunk dykes, smoke, and bad attitudes was never my idea of fun. I felt that the bars were shallow meeting places of attitude and alcoholism where one could never meet the woman (or women, in my case) of her dreams, try as she might. I was also enraged at the fact that gay men had literally hundreds of bars and lesbians had maybe two. At all the women's bars, both gay and straight men would be there. It was either the fags taking over the dance floor and bumping into me, or the straight men trying to pick up on me, especially when I took my shirt off because I was hot from dancing. It was supposed to be a lesbian club. I wanted to take my shirt off, feel empowered among women and not worry about men tripping out on my tits! Even though I disliked the bar scene it was all we had. I knew women deserved more and I refused to settle.

In 1991, I started the Ecstasy Lounge, the world's only Lesbian Sex Club. I had never run any type of club before and never had a full-fledged business; my only experience had been working at lesbian bars. My drive and determination came from frustration and hope. I wanted to change the "Lesbian Nation," and I wasn't about to give up on my lesbian and bisexual sisters because of my prior community experiences. I knew it was the best that the lesbian community could do at that time, but I knew I could do better and instill a different attitude into the community without settling for less.

At first, my ideas were fueled by desiring a true woman-only environment, a safe space where women could have sex without the pressure of getting married and moving the U-Haul in after the first date. I began to develop a club where there were no men at all. I could hear women speak, have conversation with them and not compete with the loud thumping music of 140 beats-per-minute. Also, women were not so intoxicated that their judgment was off or the room was choked with smoke. I desired more of a sensual environment coupled with dancing, a cabaret show and spacious theme rooms for a woman's fantasies, if she chose to play them out. I wanted a private club where any woman could have sex without feeling bad about herself or her body.

This was what I wanted in my life and with my lovers. Over the five years that I developed Ecstasy Lounge, my concepts for myself became clearer as I realized what suited me best when meeting, dating, and sexing women. I learned new things as I watched women participate at the club in their socializing dramas and dating life.

I love sensuality paired with hot intensity and I wanted this in my life and at the club. I wanted a group of women in my life that I could depend on for support, love and with some of them, sex. I did not want a primary lover and still do not. I wanted closeness, compassion, friendship, trust, and passion; Ecstasy Lounge became my sexual science experiment. I had fun inventing "tests" and getting amazing results.

And results I got! Upon entering the club, members were warmly greeted by a hostess who toured them around the club, gave out free refreshments and introduced women to other women. Later, all hostesses would double as safer sex monitors, making sure women practiced safer sex in the sex areas. I provided latex gloves and oral sex barriers for all participants, for it was mandatory that members use a barrier if they were to engage in sex at the club.

If women had a hard time getting comfortable having public sex or couldn't find a partner, the hostess would introduce women to each other and if the hostess wanted to, she would engage in sex with the women to get things started. Of course, it took a bold woman to do that, but when it happened it worked very well. The hostesses were volunteers, as was everyone who worked at the club. They did not get paid to have sex with the club members, but found it an exciting way to be with women sexually and sensually. At the Ecstasy Lounge, they did not have the social barriers that usually kept them from pursuing women at bars or other public places. They had a reason to approach women for sex, it was their "job" as a hostess!

When things did get rolling at the club, it was truly amazing. It is a wonderful sight to see 50 or 100 women all having sex at the same time: couples, groups, partner swapping, laughing, moaning, and coming.

I was always inventing fun games for women to meet other women. I had kissing contests, where women were each handed a blue piece of string upon entering the club. If they were asked to be kissed, they would relinquish the string to the woman who asked. The winner was the woman with the most pieces of string. When the 11pm cabaret/strip show started, the winner got a year membership to the club, and got to kiss whoever she wanted in the club. Usually she picked one of the strippers.

Another game I had was called The Personals Game. I had a large corkboard with the numbers 1-100 corresponding to plastic necklaces with the same numbers on them that members were handed upon entering the club. If a woman with a particular number was interested in meeting another woman; she'd look for her number, write her a note, and pin it up on the cork board. I provided pen and paper, encouraged everyone to find their own number and look on the cork board throughout the night to see if they got any notes. It was a big success and fun. Women liked this game because it was like the newspaper personals and it was a way to meet women without being too direct, which is usually too uncomfortable for women. It provided a good reason for a woman to speak to another woman at the club.

I also had different theme rooms. The lap-dancing chamber was where strippers took you to a couch and gave you a lap-dance. The stripper would sit on your lap and "dance" around or give you a nice massage or hug. Some of the women did more, but it was a way for the members to get close to a woman, warm up, and be sensual. There was also the medieval king and queen's room, a D.J. and dance area, the catholic confessional, the SM dungeon, the school classroom, a tent in the forest, an erotic video lounge, the "Love Labyrinth," and many others that I experimented with. The best by far was always the cabaret show.

I was the M.C. I introduced the strippers and sex demonstrators, and made the customers come up on stage to get lap dances from the strippers, and generally made the women feel more comfortable. After the cabaret show, many of the women would be so excited that they would make a bee-line for the sex areas and look for someone to have sex with.

One of the main reasons I started the club was to try to teach the lesbian community how to be more open with sexuality. I wanted to deconstruct women's body shame and teach them male-like confidence in approaching others for sex. It always took so long for women to let each other know that they were attracted to one another, and I did not have any patience for that in my young, urgent life.

Now I can look at the lesbian/bisexual women's community and see a more confident attitude. One way to get a general cross-section of women's attitudes is in magazine personals. I can read them and see women's boldness coming out. Sometimes there will be a reference made about the Ecstasy Lounge and how they want to have an open relationship similar to the practices at the club.

There is also a sense of more freedom, that women can do whatever they want within their relationships. It's not bound to the monogamy-only model. I acknowledge there has been a lot of progress in the lesbian/bisexual women's community on many levels in the Bay Area and California especially. San Francisco is still known to be the most sexually ahead of the times, and this is made obvious in the community from confident lesbian attitudes that I have witnessed.

Women are more educated about sexually transmitted diseases but are unfortunately still in denial about using safe sex. This is an important area that still needs work, especially with polygamy and non-monogamy so much more in the open now.

In my life at age 29, after 5 years of doing the Ecstasy Lounge experiment, my ideal group relationship is becoming a reality. I now have a close group of women who support me. Some of these women I am sexual with, others I am not. I am flexible with my relations and I am still seeking women for my relationship circle.

As for the future, I would love to see women who have sex with other women support each other better around differences in our sexuality and come from a place of love, sisterhood, and complete respect.

I feel that in the lesbian/bisexual women's community there is a large influx of people fighting for marriage rights. While this may be a good thing to be happening right now, it is in a way a stance of "if you can't beat them (the heterosexuals), join them." I look to the day when we can define our relationships in any way we choose instead of relying on the old model of the marriage institution. This is easier said than done, and I feel that we've a long way to go. But I am patient. As with any ideology, it starts with one person and expands out like the domino effect. I plan on continuing to be one of the women who push the dominoes over.

("Denny's Tune")
I'm Not Monogamous Anymore, But . . .

Alix Dobkin

SUMMARY. Just months after declaring herself non-monogamous, the author falls in love and finds herself wanting only one woman. Her song "Denny's Tune" playfully contrasts philosophical convictions with heartfelt desire.

INTRODUCTION

Breaking up from my first Lesbian relationship in 1978 broke my heart and dashed my dreams of lifelong partnership. I never was so miserable before. Non-monogamy seemed like the way to avoid such devastating pain in the future. But unfortunately, it wouldn't be that easy. Only a few months after several public proclamations of my non-monogamy, I met Denny (now Denslow). "Denny's Tune" was a joke on myself. I wrote it to highlight the contradiction between my new philosophy and my new feelings.

Alix Dobkin is a singer and songwriter who has been performing primarily for women since 1972. Her albums include *Lavender Jane Loves Women* (1973), *Living With Lesbians* (1976), *XXAlix* (1980), *These Women/Never Been Better* (1986), *Yahoo Australia* (1990), *Love & Politics* (1992), and *Living With Lavender Jane* (1997). Her book *Alix Dobkin's Adventures in Women's Music (Not Just a Songbook)* was published in 1978 by Tomato Publications. All are available from Ladyslipper Music at 1-800-634-6044. "Denny's Tune" is printed here by permission.

Address correspondence to Alix Dobkin, 481 Rich Street, Oakland, CA 94609.

[Haworth co-indexing entry note]: "("Denny's Tune") I'm Not Monogamous Anymore, But. . . ." Dobkin, Alix. Co-published simultaneously in *Journal of Lesbian Studies* (The Haworth Press, Inc.) Vol. 3, No. 1/2, 1999, pp. 185-187; and: *The Lesbian Polyamory Reader: Open Relationships, Non-Monogamy, and Casual Sex* (ed: Marcia Munson and Judith P. Stelboum) The Haworth Press, Inc., 1999, pp. 185-187.

I think many of us try out various relationship styles, political positions and ways of being before we settle into a life that is a true expression of ourselves. I was non-monogamous (actually, it was more like serial monogamy in a time warp) for only a few months, but for some women this is a lifelong choice.

A large part of my Lesbian life has been enjoyed without a romantic partner. I love being single and often wish everybody was.

As we know, Lesbians enjoy an extraordinarily diverse community. It seems to me that the secret to success is to TREAT each other with respect, even when we don't respect each other or each others' choices.

Denny's Tune

I'm not monogamous anymore
But Denny you're so adorable
A one-woman woman I'm not but
We're hot, honey, it's true
I've got to be close to you

How I miss you when you're gone
I'm sleeping with all my jewelry on
Talking on the phone
until the cows come home
Writing corny letters
Wearing your old sweater
It's not what I expected, I stand
Politically corrected

I'm happy by myself at home
Getting a pile of deskwork done
I practice, cook and clean
Familiar old routine
Play seven innings, spend
Time with women friends, then
Time to be a writer, mother
Time to be an entertainer
Suits me fine and it's all mine, but

Triple Virgo, blue-eyed gal
Queen of the prom, you've got your
California family
You've got your Kappa Kappa Key
Queen of Swords, a champion
You're feminist, you're feminine
So organized and logical,
I find you irresistible and when I

Think of our intimacy
Ripples of pleasure flow through me
I stop to catch my breath
I'm very much impressed
But Venuses in "trine"
Still cannot make you mine
Yes life seems contradictory when
Trying to live differently, you see

You have your life, I have mine
Many more years they'll intertwine
With women in our lives
There's drama and surprise
When eye to eye we see
On non-monogamy
So what's this thing we're in for now?
The women are creating how
To be not monogamous anymore . . .

Dinah, Sam, Beth, and Jolyn Say

Merril Mushroom

SUMMARY. As lesbians interact with one another, we relate in a variety of ways through different degrees of intimacy and involvement. Finding and living the way that's right for each of us can be difficult. Lesbians can be judgmental, and the sexual aspects of relating seem to eclipse all other forms in importance, intensity, and the degrees of social ramifications and judgmental responses. This article discusses the experiences of several lesbians in the diverse ways they do their intimate relationships. *[Article copies available for a fee from The Haworth Document Delivery Service: 1-800-342-9678. E-mail address: getinfo@haworthpressinc.com]*

Dinah says that Sam is sexually promiscuous and emotionally monogamous. Beth says that Dinah is sexually monogamous and emotionally promiscuous. Dinah, Beth, and Sam live within a big-city lesbian community that has many different, intertwined, and overlapping social sets. The primary group of dykes that Sam, Dinah, and Beth hang out with are professional white women between 40 and 55 years of age. They are close and loving and very physically demonstrative. They all will hug, kiss, sleep together, cuddle, pet, massage, touch one another. Some of them may or may not have been and/or are or are not sexual with one another. They snuggle in private and in public, in many combinations and arrangements. Their behavior can be very confusing to women who don't know them well or to new women on the scene.

Merril Mushroom is an old-timey dyke. Her stories and essays appear frequently in lesbian publications.

[Haworth co-indexing entry note]: "Dinah, Sam, Beth, and Jolyn Say." Mushroom, Merril. Co-published simultaneously in *Journal of Lesbian Studies* (The Haworth Press, Inc.) Vol. 3, No. 1/2, 1999, pp. 189-196; and: *The Lesbian Polyamory Reader: Open Relationships, Non-Monogamy, and Casual Sex* (ed: Marcia Munson and Judith P. Stelboum) The Haworth Press, Inc., 1999, pp. 189-196. Single or multiple copies of this article are available for a fee from The Haworth Document Delivery Service [1-800-342-9678, 9:00 a.m. - 5:00 p.m. (EST). E-mail address: getinfo@haworthpressinc.com].

189

*   *   *

As our relationships with each other ebb and flow, moving in varied lesbianic configurations of distance and closeness with various other dykes, many patterns of relating are practiced. Some of these are more permissible than others; some even are required. Many kinds of intimacies are expressed, some of which are more acceptable than others. These parameters are neither static nor universal; but, in general, the boundaries are defined in terms of experiences and behaviors that involve sexuality, sexual fidelity and the overlapping transitional area of physical touching, all of which are inextricably involved with one's experience of safety in the relationship.

As lesbians interact with one another, we communicate and relate in a variety of ways and on many different levels, through varying degrees of intimacy and involvement; however, sexual relating seems to eclipse all other forms in importance, intensity, and the degrees of social ramifications and judgmental responses. Sometimes issues of possessiveness and control around sex can cause us to behave in a confrontational or defensive manner. Dykes in social situations are often motivated by what's known as the "threat factor," i.e., the concern of many lesbians who are "in relationships" when first they meet a new dyke as to who your lover is and that you have one; and if you have one and she is not right there next to you, then why not; and if you don't have a lover then will you be after me or MY lover, or, maybe, would you be interested in my single friend Anna who desperately wants to be coupled?

Coupleness is as important in lesbian communities as it is in the general social order. The messages that we get through advertising and other communication media in our culture emphasize the necessity of being paired; that a person is somehow incomplete–not to mention a threat to you and your spouse–if she is NOT coupled, or she is morally deficient if she is MORE than coupled. The purpose for touting these images is not out of any ethical or humanitarian concern but to financially empower white boys who are pushing the products, whether these products be material or spiritual in nature. These boys set the standards for what is desirable in looks and behavior, then make lots of money selling items that will produce or enhance these images. They increase their control by bombarding us with representations of perfectly groomed and proportioned, highly gregarious women whose goals are to attract and keep their mates. Images other than coupleness are often presented as oddities or perversions and designed to amuse or titillate, provoking negative judgments from others.

As individuals and in small groups within the greater lesbian community, we overlap and interface with each other in tangled configurations. As combinations of individuals, we personify every imaginable form of expression in relating. Some of us, from the very core of our beings, have it in our nature to be coupled. This is right for us. We are comfortable with home and family and picket fence, job and friends and hobbies, pets, children. This is healthy for us. Others of us are not so disposed; some of us feel more naturally fulfilled through moving about and being with many different people in many different ways. For some of us, our most significant relationship is with ourselves. Some of us prefer to live alone, some of us couple, some seek community. Dykes come with differences. Among us we may have a wide range of desire for social interaction. We may have one or none or many sexual relationships, solely, sequentially, or simultaneously. Some of us move among overlapping relationships within or even outside our lesbian community. Some of us are very focused within a microcosm of relating. And sometimes we change from one form of relating to another.

Finding and living the way that is right for each of us can be difficult. Peer pressure in the lesbian community is as rife as in any community. Although opinions and practices may change radically from one year to the next regarding what kind of behavior in relationships is socially acceptable and politically correct, lesbians always are quick to tell each other the ways we are expected to behave, especially around issues of monogamy and sexual fidelity—terms which often are used synonymously.

*   *   *

Jolyn says that we need to be partnered so that we can build futures together and create a measure of security. Sam says only present time is certain, and maybe not even that. We should be in the here and now in our relationships, so we don't replay the past or project fantasies of the future. Dinah says that we create our futures differently. Some of us create futures primarily with others, some of us are more inclined toward living by ourselves. Some of us focus our need for a sense of reliability and continuity with one partner, some of us create our futures through intimacy with many others in a variety of ways. And

Beth says that futures can be created in any manner as long as we can trust to dream together.

In the group Sam, Dinah, and Beth hang with, figuring out who is "with" whom can be difficult for women who aren't often in their company. Women in the group use the terms "exclusive" and "inclusive." They prefer to behave toward each other in an inclusive manner, which means that even if they are coupled, they don't necessarily keep to that particular configuration when in social settings. Likely as not, two or three or even more women will be cuddled together in a blob, stroking each others' hair or body, hugging and kissing, disappearing for a walk together. Women who need to know who is with whom, who relate on the basis of single or coupled, sometimes will ask those questions of these women, trying to determine what the relationships are in a way that makes sense. Jolyn recalls her first meeting with the women in this group:

> Bobbie and I had rented this cabin at a campground for the week, and the second day we were there, we were walking in the woods and met these three other dykes. They told us that five of them had the cabin just down the road from us, and they invited us to come watch lesbian videos with them that evening. Well, there Bobbie and I sat, on the couch together, welded at the arms, hips, and knees, my hand velcroed to her thigh, while these five other women were all over the place and all over one another. Bobbie and I couldn't figure out at all who was with whom, and we both were frightened that maybe they all probably were having an orgy together, and wanted us to join in too. Maybe we should stay the hell away from them. (She laughed.) In fact, as we found out later, only two of them were lovers, and only with each other; although some of the women were ex's of each other.

Jolyn feels that we must maintain a focus which is very specific and exclusive, that our energy is diminished if we divide it among too many others in intimate relating, that human beings and especially lesbians really are not capable of loving more than one other person. "How can my lover be with me if she's with someone else?" she says. "When will she have time for me? Anyhow, I need to know I'm special–that my lover keeps what she gives to me JUST for me, and that I don't give anyone else what I give to her either. Otherwise, what will we have left for one another?"

Beth says, "For me, every relationship is special and unique. We give to each other what we give to no one else. Love doesn't have any limit; it just keeps flowing."

"I want one specific partner to share my life with," says Jolyn. "I want someone with whom to build a household. Our combined energy is very powerful."

"I prefer multiple experiences of bonding and community," Sam interjects. "I like the power of combined energies."

"I need to know who and where my partner is," Dinah joins in. "I need some frequency of the physical presence of my intimate companion in order to maintain a relationship. Why be with each other at all if you aren't going to be WITH each other?"

"But that doesn't mean you have to be with each other ALL the time," Sam mutters. "I need my own space, my own life, too. I'm uncomfortable when someone wants to know where I am and what I'm doing every second."

"Secrets?"

"No, it's not that. I get really focused, really into what I'm doing. Telling about it just isn't a consideration."

"Well, what about the trust factor," questions Jolyn. "Suppose you're running around on your girlfriend. Doesn't she have the right to know?"

"You don't 'run around on' someone you're not in a mutual exclusive monogamous relationship with," Sam retorts. "What's important to me is the way someone behaves toward me when we're together, not what she does when we're NOT together."

"Maintaining relationships over time and space is important to me," says Beth. "I really enjoy my long-distance relationships." Beth is intimate with most of her "ex-lovers"–women who now live in different parts of the US. "I don't even think I should be calling them that," she says, "because we still love each other, and we're usually sexual with each other when we're together. Does being lovers have to depend on how much time you spend together?" Beth sees some of these women infrequently, "but it's always like we saw each other just yesterday. Do we have to give our relationship a label because we still may be sexual with each other? That may not always happen or endure. Sex is not the priority. We have deep-rooted karmic connections. Besides, we LIKE being together. We enjoy the hell out of each other."

"But it's not real intimacy," counters Jolyn. "These are not real, committed relationships. You get only the gravy, only the good times. You don't have to deal with the everyday realities of creating a life together, with compromise and decisions and conflicts."

"Bullshit!" Beth is angry. "My relationships are as real and committed as anyone else's. What makes you so qualified to judge what's a real, committed relationship–especially when you seem to require the presence of conflict as necessary to the definition?"

Jolyn nods. "Conflict IS necessary to the definition."

"Why? Since when?"

"How else can we work things out? How else can we resolve our differences except through conflict?"

"We have to struggle so that we know we're alive," Dinah interjects.

"I just don't agree with that," says Beth. "I know I'm alive because of the joy I feel in my heart. I don't need conflict. I don't like to struggle, and I believe we don't have to struggle if we can find balance in wholeness, if we can accept our differences, no, CHERISH our differences. I resent when someone says she's in love with me and then wants me to change and be someone else than who I really am. That makes me think she's really in love with a fantasy she wants me to conform to. Anyhow, if it makes you feel any better, my relationships with my girlfriends are not ALL sweetness and gravy. We still have issues, but sometimes it's more productive to let them go than to put energy into working them out. My girlfriends and I prefer to really enjoy the time we have together, to appreciate each other for who we are. What makes these relationships real and committed to me is that these women will be in my life, will be in my heart, forever."

"Still, you miss the little intimacies that come with being together every day," says Dinah, "like coming home in the evening and talking about today or making plans for tomorrow, just hanging out together like that."

Beth shrugs. "That's the tradeoff, I guess."

*   *   *

When I came out in the 1950s, lesbian relationships mirrored those of the straight society which was the only model we had. We queers presented a domesticated front of butch and femme in a household, complete with marital fidelity, in keeping with the hetero-patriarchal religious requirements underpinning our social structure. And also in keeping with the behavior of our role models, lesbians frequently "cheated" on one another, had affairs, and broke up/got back together. My best buddy usually had a steady girl with an occasional fuck on the side. I preferred to date around and do one- (maybe two-) night stands. Although doing one-night stands was frowned upon as politically incorrect, many of us younger dykes frequently engaged in this practice; although we'd swear each time at great length that we weren't that way and didn't do this.

Through the decades, I've been in many and varied relationships, with sex, without sex, and both. I've seen friends couple and uncouple, triple and un-triple, do-si-do and daisy-chain. I've been scolded, blamed, and praised for my own proclivities and style of relating. I've been applauded and reviled, understood and misunderstood, accepted and rejected. Personally, I really feel in my heart of hearts that the way I do my relationships is nobody's goddam business but my own, and no one else has the right to stand in judgment over me.

I like women, especially lesbians. I've been incredibly blessed with many amazing women in my life–women with whom I've engaged in a wide range of intimacies. I couldn't imagine leaving never to see again any of these dear and precious women. I like to retain a sense of connection, even though years may pass with little or no contact. Sometimes sexual intimacy continues, sometimes not. Always there remains a deep spiritual bond. I also like my own space and my own life. I don't like to live with lovers, don't want to "share EVERYthing" with anyone, nor do I have personal confidences that need to be told. That's just the way I am.

A revolutionary concept is that each of us has the right to be who she is and deserves the support of the community. However, this is all very easy to say, but then what happens in reality when one of us doesn't like the way someone else is, personally, politically, ethically, sexually, spiritually, socially? What happens when one of us collides with someone else, when we feel mistreated, battered, wronged?

If we don't like the way that someone else does relationships, we can try not to engage. Instead, we each must go into ourselves to find and define who we really are and what we really need, then find a way to express ourselves and meet our own needs without offending, betraying, or violating others in our community. This is an extremely difficult undertaking, because always there will be those who are affected by our personal choices of behavior. The best that we can do is to be honest with ourselves and with each other and to allow ourselves and our lesbian sisters the space and freedom for change and self-discovery.

Gays to Marry? Let's Not!

Martha McPheeters

SUMMARY. In the midst of the current publicity about gay marriages, a contrarian viewpoint is presented. Marriage is seen as a legal construct of the state to further its aims of sexism and capitalism. Marriage has lost any connection it may have had to spiritual or emotional bonding. The notion of pair-bonding for life as natural is also disputed. From these perspectives, gays and lesbians and polyamorous types are encouraged to fight for the abolition of marriage, rather than for inclusion in the privileged group allowed by the state to marry. *[Article copies available for a fee from The Haworth Document Delivery Service: 1-800-342-9678. E-mail address: getinfo@haworthpressinc.com]*

I keep half an ear cocked to National Public Radio when they report on gay marriages. Will they be legal? Will all states be forced to recognize them? If anyone should happen to ask my opinion of gay marriages they would get an earful. My first answer would be, "No way, gays should not be allowed to marry." My second statement

Martha McPheeters, PhD, was an academic research neurobiologist for 18 years. Concurrently she was a wilderness educator with various adventure-challenge programs. At the moment she is in a "dream-fulfillment" phase of her life following through on a number of childhood dreams. These range from being a hermit in the Northwoods to paddling the Grand Canyon to trying her hand at wilderness program administration. She has published a string of scientific papers and, more recently, an article in *On My Honor: Lesbians Reflect on Their Scouting Experience*.

Address correspondence to Martha McPheeters, 263 Farm and Wilderness Road, Plymouth, VT 05056.

[Haworth co-indexing entry note]: "Gays to Marry? Let's Not!" McPheeters, Martha. Co-published simultaneously in *Journal of Lesbian Studies* (The Haworth Press, Inc.) Vol. 3, No. 1/2, 1999, pp. 197-203; and: *The Lesbian Polyamory Reader: Open Relationships, Non-Monogamy, and Casual Sex* (ed: Marcia Munson and Judith P. Stelboum) The Haworth Press, Inc., 1999, pp. 197-203. Single or multiple copies of this article are available for a fee from The Haworth Document Delivery Service [1-800-342-9678, 9:00 a.m. - 5:00 p.m. (EST). E-mail address: getinfo@haworthpressinc.com].

would be, "No heterosexuals marrying each other, either! The institution of marriage has caused enough pain and suffering in this world; instead of allowing gays to marry, let's abolish the institution of marriage."

I had a similar answer when the issue was gays in the military. "I agree, no gays in the military, and further, no heterosexuals in the military either." The military has also caused an immense amount of pain and suffering in this world. Let's decrease its membership to zero. Putting energy into recognizing gays in the military is a waste of time; likewise I see it as a mistake for gays to fight for the right to marry. We should instead focus our energy on abolishing marriage.

Perhaps I should clarify my position about relationships among human beings before I start this diatribe against marriage, both gay and straight. I have nothing against intimacy or sex; I believe they are basic human needs. Romantic relationships that respect each individual's rights and do not cause harm to others have my support. I have no concern with the length of these relationships; one night is fine, lifelong is fine. Nor do I have concern with the participants' race, gender, sexual orientation, ethnicity, or disability. My concern stems from the state sanctioning some particular relationships and not others. I find marriage to be state-sanctioned fucking. Why should the state "authorize" fucking for particular people but not for others? This article explores why our sexist, capitalist state does just that. But before those arguments I want to ask, "Is the life-long pair-bonding that marriage tries to enforce even natural?"

We are certainly led to believe that non-human animals have a natural drive for pair bonding. It is true that some species bond in twosomes for life (geese and swans), and some species bond in twosomes for a breeding season (penguins, loons, bald eagles), and some twosomes in hierarchical species stay together as long as the partner maintains rank (wolves). However, the vast majority of species (Wallace, 1980) and almost all mammals get together for brief sex and then part ways (dogs, cats, moose, chickadees, spiders, bears, mice). If we humans were to be truly natural, more of us would do the last. Indeed, it is implausible that rational humans who live over seventy years on average would bond to a single human and have exclusive sexual relations with that person for life.

The notion that lifelong heterosexual bonding is "natural" has come to us from early Christian tradition (McNeill, 1993). To act naturally meant to act according to reason. The biggest reason for relationships was to procreate. The known world was a sparsely populated desert. Power and control came from large families and large armies. From this we have received our messages about the "unnaturalness" of masturbation and homosexuality. It is noteworthy that this tradition encouraged polygamy as not only natural but the best vehicle for ensuring reproduction. Thus the Bible clearly condones polyamory at least for men.

In present times as we struggle with overpopulation, it is appropriate to change the reason people form relationships. Birth control allows us to choose our reasons. If one tasted the pleasures of falling in love and/or lust at the beginning of a relationship, why wouldn't one wish to reproduce those fine feelings repeatedly? In the marriage therapy circuit, there is lots of talk of rekindling the flames of passion. Those flames flow easily if the object is a new person. Rekindling is not necessary. Wouldn't that be the natural way? Additionally, in couples counseling there is often talk that no one person can meet the needs of another. Why do we persist in believing that one person can meet all our sexual needs?

If pair bonding were the easiest, most natural and convenient way to structure human relationships, then we would not need laws prohibiting other forms of bonding. Indeed, it has always seemed odd to me that our first set of significant relationships is often with at least two people–mom and dad. In many cases siblings are present and are extremely important to us, as well. Yet, by the time we reach adolescence, we have been indoctrinated into believing that humans can only deal with one relationship at a time. Pair bonding is presented as the only option by teachers, ministers, television and radio. There are precious few models of long-term relationships with multiple adults, particularly once the relationships become romantic. This has always rankled me, since humans are clearly able from birth to form significant relationships with multiple persons. Life-long pair bonding is not a natural phenomenon.

It is a state-defined phenomenon. Robert H. Knight of the (Right Wing) Family Research Council is absolutely correct when he proclaims: "Marriage is specifically defined legal union of a man and a woman." Marriage, in fact, is the process of getting permission from the government and performing a required procedure in order to get special privileges not available to other citizens who are single. It has nothing to do with a spiritual or religious bonding, which is a common experience available to all (Davis, 1997). In order to make marriage palatable, certain privileges are granted to married people. Heterosexual married couples have a government-approved legal method of (1) paying less taxes than other people by filing jointly, (2) becoming eligible for other people's money through social security, Medicare, and veteran's pensions, (3) holding joint insurance policies for health care and life insurance, (4) visiting sick partners in the hospital, (5) making medical decisions for a partner, and (6) inheriting a partner's money (Singer, 1996). Why does the state want its citizens married?

Pair bonding that requires a license leads to a society that is easier to control and allows easier tracing of genetic lineage. Control comes from having restricted sets of acceptable behavior. By exerting control over a basic human behavior, the choice of a sex partner, all other state control becomes easier. We humans have only a limited amount of energy. If the choice of sexual partners becomes an act of resistance, then how much energy is left for educational reform, political activism or creating new economic systems? By promoting pair bonding, the state has halved the number of "its" entities, and, with sexism, the state need only control the behavior of the men while expecting them to control the behavior of "their" women and children.

The institution of marriage clearly has roots in the exploitation of women. Women were exploited as the lesser creatures needing the protection of a man. They went from the custody of a father to the custody of a husband. The woman provided unpaid labor for the man in exchange for his "husbandry." In today's world the roots have grown stout trunks. We see sexism in traditions like the woman changing her name when she marries, the woman's family planning and paying for the wedding celebration, and the woman's father "giving away the bride." Enforced monogamous marriage also allows a heterosexual male to be more confident of the paternity of "his" children.

The obsession with needing to know the paternity of children may be genetic. However, it dovetails nicely with capitalism's delineation of private property. If a piece of land, a material possession, a slave, or a wife can be considered private property, then it can be exploited, bartered away or exchanged for a different form of private property. Historically, a man owned his wife and children, much like he owned his tools and his clothes. Once ownership was established, no one else could use his tools, wear his clothes or make love to his wife. Her body, mind and spirit became another set of possessions. The thrust of women's liberation has been to equalize the ownership, not to abolish it. Now-a-days a man may feel as confined by marriage as only a woman used to. Women now "own" their husbands, as well as being owned by them.

I distinctly remember my little brother explaining to my mother why he was in no rush to get married. He explained quite articulately that marriage in the 1990s conferred precious few benefits on the man. In his upper-middle class, a woman would come to the marriage with a career and a set of job demands that might mean he had to quit his job and move. She would expect my brother to do fully half of the house-work, cooking and cleaning at some mutually agreed upon standards, most likely higher than his. If children were under consideration, he would be expected to take alternate years off from work, distinctly interfering with his career trajectory and thus his self-worth. To him, it didn't seem like nearly as good a deal as my father got when he married my mom. Mom gave up her career, did one hundred percent of the housework and did all the child raising. My father had a posses-sion that served him well. For my brother, marriage would not be nearly as lucrative. He would need to serve his spouse in equal mea-sure as she served him. Feminism has made marriage more egalitarian today than it was 50 years ago, but marriage still means people "own-ing" each other. As long as the institution of marriage is based on ownership by one or both members of the union, it will continue to thrive in our capitalist economy.

By definition, capitalism cannot exist without private property. Some would agree with me that private property is the root evil in our consumerist, throw-away society. The notion that people can own the means of production, produce something of value, and sell it at a profit is the basic tenet of capitalism. The twisted logic of this tenet is easily demonstrated with land ownership. If I own land, I can grow crops on this land without paying anything for the sunshine, minerals and rain-water (this is called exploitation of the land). Because I own the land, I can even hire someone to harvest the crops and pay them less than their labor is worth (this is called exploitation of workers). Other cultures have existed for millennia without ever assuming the earth (or anything else for that matter) could be owned. Yet our culture of capitalism extends ownership even beyond land to people. The history of slavery attests to that and the institution of marriage continues the thread of ownership.

The other basic tenet of capitalism, which strengthens the institution of marriage, is a dependence upon ever-expanding markets. Growth is the primary measure of success in our capitalist economy. So the system supports myriad benefits for married couples in the hopes that they will raise children, and it offers tax breaks when children join a family. Children are the future consumers. A capitalist system cannot fully back zero population growth and must continue to confer special privileges to whoever or whatever creates new markets.

Family units with blood bonds are the building blocks of competitive nation states. For most of us our first experience with us-them thinking was with our families of origin–a pair bond with kids. The bounds of a family define a societal unit that can view everything outside those bounds as "them." "They" are different from "us" and therefore inferior to "us" in some way(s). This kind of thinking on a grand scale allows whole nations to view other nations as inferior and feel justified annihilating them in war. There is truth in patriotic slogans such as "strong families are the backbone of America."

These days corporations are replacing nations as the units of world power. It is fascinating to watch the ways in which corporations diverge from "family values" and the ways in which they mirror them. Loyalty is less valued as workers become interchangeable and transportable parts in a giant machine. The belief that it is right and natural to "own" another person in marriage is fine preparation for working in corporations which "own" and exploit the earth, human-generated information and people.

Challenging the traditional family structure attacks the roots of capitalism; this explains the strong state and social endorsement for heterosexual marriage and traditional families. Marriage for gays and lesbians challenges this structure a bit because the partners are likely to be equal in power. Parenting may be shared by additional adults confounding paternity rights. The elimination of marriage altogether and thus the sanctioning of polyamorous relationships and multi-adult parenting is a much greater challenge to the current state-sanctioned, capitalism-endorsed family structure.

Discrimination is present whenever one particular group gets societal recognition or privileges that are not available to others. Gays and lesbians are not allowed to marry, and polygyny (having more than one wife) was outlawed in the late 1800s. (Our society's sexist roots have ensured that we didn't even need to legislate that women couldn't have more than one husband. Who would own the woman, if she had two husbands?)

From an outsider's perspective, it is just plain unfair that the benefits of marriage aren't available to everyone. Why shouldn't anyone be able to have a big celebration of their love for someone (or many someones), get a license to fuck, health insurance for their special someone(s) and tax breaks plus all sorts of intangible support? This unfairness is probably why some gays are fighting for the right to marry, but I'd rather fight to end marriage altogether.

In conclusion, marriage is not a natural phenomenon, it is a state-defined institution that has roots in sexism and supports capitalism. Capitalism is an economic system with a host of attendant evils. Our indoctrination as Americans has inhibited our ability to even imagine many of the possible ways of relating that don't involve ownership and exploitation.

I use the following metaphor to help me create new options for positive relationships. I have the idea that marriage is like owning a few cubic yards of air. The air can't really be owned. However, for reasons that were never explained to me, the state wants control of those cubic yards. The state has legislated some very clear guidelines about where my air ends and the next person's begins. It has dictated what privileges accrue from owning air and exactly who may own the air. I put it to you–we can't own the air. It makes no difference if the air is bisexual, gay, lesbian or straight. Our world will be a better place if we let the air circulate in response to the truly natural forces like sun and wind and water. Let's not confine or confound the air with the forces of sexism and capitalism.

REFERENCES

Davis, S. (1997). "Just" married? A contrarian viewpoint. *Loving More, 9,* 32-33.
McNeill, J.J. (1993). *The church and the homosexual.* Boston: Beacon Press.
Singer, J. (1996). For better or worse. *Loving More, 8,* 17-19.
Wallace, R. (1980). *How they do it?* New York: William Morrow.

Canary in the Coal Mine

Teri

SUMMARY. The author explains that lesbians' failure to "succeed" at coupling should be seen as a warning to all of humanity that the institution of marriage is not a viable relationship model.

INTRODUCTION

This appeared as a letter to the editor in a 1996 issue of *New Phazes,* a lesbian newsletter published in Colorado Springs. It was in reaction to an article the previous month encouraging lesbians to work harder at their coupled relationships. That article had referred to the Philip Blumstein and Pepper Schwartz study, described in their book *American Couples* (1983), that suggested that lesbian couples do not stay together as long as married heterosexuals, cohabiting heterosexuals, or gay men.

Dear New Phazes,

I was interested in reading about the study done by Blumstein and Schwartz (Love Matters, August issue) which shows that lesbians have the shortest coupling of any of the major pairings. It's interesting

Teri is an environmental educator, backpacker, and spiritual seeker who has lived in Colorado all her life. She has been a lesbian for nearly a quarter of a century. This article originally appeared as a letter to the editor in a 1996 issue of the newsletter *New Phazes* and is reprinted here by permission.

[Haworth co-indexing entry note]: "Canary in the Coal Mine." Teri. Co-published simultaneously in *Journal of Lesbian Studies* (The Haworth Press, Inc.) Vol. 3, No. 1/2, 1999, pp. 205-207; and: *The Lesbian Polyamory Reader: Open Relationships, Non-Monogamy, and Casual Sex* (ed: Marcia Munson and Judith P. Stelboum) The Haworth Press, Inc., 1999, pp. 205-207.

because at first glance it seems counter intuitive. I would think that because we are so nurturing, therapized, and just because we're women that we would be the MOST successful. Lesbians have the advantage over other pairings of not having stereotyped roles to fight against. We usually don't share income as completely as hetero couples, giving us more autonomy. And we're generally brilliant (and cute). This would seem to predispose us to being great at coupling up. Since we're not, and since men made up this concept in the first place, it seems reasonable to examine the idea itself and not our ability or inability to suppress our creativity to fit into the couple role.

According to my best buddy, Sonia Johnson (1991), 5000 years ago saw the change from the Matriarchy to the Patriarchy. At that time men developed the structure of the soon to be "modern day family." And how powerfully convenient for them. Women were separated from other women and their connection with men was defined almost exclusively as having sex with them. Which is really the only information we are imparting when we say we are in a "relationship," that we are having sex with this person. It would take a man to have such a narrow view of intimacy. This, I think, mightily embarrasses and mystifies us when we stop having sex with our "partner" as is often the case for lesbians after two, three, or four years.

I think lesbians are the canaries in the coal mine of relationships. We are experiencing that coupling is not a whole, workable, or even desirable structure. Don't you intuitively feel that we have the potential to truly have a loving community that isn't harmful to ourselves or to other people and living things on the earth, and that it shouldn't be all that hard to attain? But we aren't doing it. We've been brainwashed into the couple ideal, and when it doesn't work out we wonder at our choices and vow to find a "better" person with which we will surely have the perfect relationship (with years of hard work and couple counseling of course). The structure has been so concretely ingrained in us that we are even hoping to be able to get legally married. I wonder why it is that we are incredulous and envious when we know of a lesbian couple who has been together for say . . . twenty years. But when we mention our parents' endless relationship, we say it not with pride, but usually with the necessity of going to therapy.

How much more loving and enlivening it would be to forget the whole trying-to-be-a-couple thing. We have the capacity for great connections with many people and an ability to make a community where we are not killing the earth. I think one reason we don't couple well is because our unconscious knows that there is no way the world can go on having "single family dwellings" sucking out the life of the earth and unfairly dividing and wasting resources.

I hope we take the information revealed by the Blumstein/Schwartz study to not commiserate further on how we can finally figure it out and be eternally happy with our soul mate or whoever else happens to come along. But to instead know we are wonderful women and if it's not working, maybe it's because it's not workable. Many people, of course, may find it grand and fulfilling to be in a traditional relationship. My view would probably not be of much interest to them. Still, it is our struggle to be obedient to our awareness of life. And for those of us who are always looking for "a lover," I hope we think twice about how to get what we truly long for.

REFERENCES

Blumstein, P., & Schwartz, P. (1983). *American couples*. New York: William Morrow and Company.

Johnson, S. (1991). *The ship that sailed into the living room*. Estancia, NM: Wildfire Books.

Safer Sex and the Polyamorous Lesbian

Marcia Munson

SUMMARY. In recent years, concern about transmission of AIDS and other STDs has prompted people of all sexual orientations to use various safer sex techniques. This article explains why monogamy is not necessarily any safer than polyamory. Research on the low risk of woman-to-woman transmission of HIV and other STDs is described. *[Article copies available for a fee from The Haworth Document Delivery Service: 1-800-342-9678. E-mail address: getinfo@haworthpressinc.com]*

In the age of AIDS, monogamists and conservatives of many stripes have embraced the "reduce your number of partners" safer sex suggestion as an excuse to promote their own brands of morality. The polyamorous lesbian could argue that, over a 10-year period, a serial monogamist might very well have more different sex partners than someone who practices polyamory. The educated lesbian would insist that there are many varied safer sex techniques to choose from. And

---

Marcia Munson is a sex educator who has been leading workshops at various women's music festivals and lesbian gatherings since 1987. She has a BS in Biology and a Certificate as a Sexological Instructor/Advisor of AIDS/STD Prevention from the Institute for Advanced Study of Human Sexuality. Her articles have appeared in the anthology *Dyke Life, On Our Backs* magazine, and the *Women & Therapy* journal.

Address correspondence to Marcia Munson, P.O. Box 40370, San Francisco, CA 94140.

The author would like to thank Stacy, Karen, Louise, and Molly for their help in preparing this article.

[Haworth co-indexing entry note]: "Safer Sex and the Polyamorous Lesbian." Munson, Marcia. Co-published simultaneously in *Journal of Lesbian Studies* (The Haworth Press, Inc.) Vol. 3, No. 1/2, 1999, pp. 209-216; and: *The Lesbian Polyamory Reader: Open Relationships, Non-Monogamy, and Casual Sex* (ed: Marcia Munson and Judith P. Stelboum) The Haworth Press, Inc., 1999, pp. 209-216. Single or multiple copies of this article are available for a fee from The Haworth Document Delivery Service [1-800-342-9678, 9:00 a.m. - 5:00 p.m. (EST). E-mail address: getinfo@haworthpressinc.com].

the health-conscious lesbian would point out that, given the research showing the low risk of woman-to-woman transmission of HIV and other sexually transmitted diseases (STDs), and considering the statistics on traffic fatalities and work-related deaths, a woman is a lot safer in bed, having sex with another woman, than going out to do most anything else.

POLYAMORY VERSUS MONOGAMY: WHICH IS SAFER?

Hardly anyone practices life-long monogamy these days. Instead, people usually experience a series of sexual relationships over their lifetimes. For the monogamous lesbian, the beginning of a new love affair often marks the ending of an old relationship. There may be a period of overlap, as a woman makes the transition from an old lover to a new flame.

For the polyamorous person, the beginning of a new romance does not mean that old involvements must end, though it may mean a shift in time or commitment to existing relationships. A couple might include the new lover in their partnership, and become a triad. A woman might have less time for her primary partner, once she starts a new affair. Or an old lover might become less important, and the new lover might become the primary focus of attention.

The big difference between polyamorists and serial monogamists is that, for polyamorists, a new love affair need not signal the end of old relationships. Communication, negotiation, and intimacy can occur concurrently with several partners. For the monogamist, a period of overlapping sexual involvements may be a time of secrecy, avoiding communication, feeling guilty, and even lying. When a lesbian couple splits up, it is common to agree to a period of "no contact" before they "try to be friends."

Imagine you're a monogamous lesbian. Two months ago you moved out of the house you own with your old girlfriend, to be with a new lover. You're both angry, and not talking. You discover you have an STD. How likely would you to be to break the silence, call your old girlfriend, and let her know she might need to seek treatment? It would be hard.

If you're a polyamorous lesbian, on the other hand, you're probably communicating all along with your lovers about other sexual involvements. You're aware of STDs, and seek diagnosis and treatment for any suspicious genital discomfort. You probably don't cut off communication with an old flame when a new romance begins. A hot weekend fling is as likely to be with an old friend as it is to be with a stranger.

For all these reasons–ongoing communication, honesty, familiarity with partners, and awareness of STDs–polyamory can be a lifestyle conducive to a healthy sex life.

For those who place importance on counting the number of lifetime sexual partners, the polyamorous lesbian may have fewer partners than her serially monogamous sister. Moving in and out of platonic, erotic, sensual, and sexual phases with friends is a common practice among polyamorous lesbians. This recycling of lovers can mean more than one lover in a given month, but fewer total women over a five- or ten-year period.

SAFER SEX TECHNIQUES

A few years ago, in an STD and HIV prevention class at the Institute for Advanced Study of Human Sexuality, the instructor explained why "reduce your number of sex partners" was a poor technique for avoiding sexually transmitted diseases. The real goal, he explained, was to reduce one's exposure to various STDs. He asked us to compare, for example, two people who had sex 100 times in a year. Person A had sex only with their HIV positive monogamous partner. Person B had sex one time each with 100 random people. Person A was exposed to HIV 100 times. Person B was exposed to HIV an unknown number of times, but significantly less than 100. To actually compare the relative risks persons A and B were facing, you would have to take into account some quantifiable data, such as the fact that when used properly, condoms break up to 2% of the time (*Consumer Reports*, 1994). You would also have to consider some hard-to-measure data such as the relative risks of various sex acts engaged in during each sexual episode, and the level of diligence each couple used in practicing safer sex techniques.

Safer sex, he explained, meant either avoiding those sex acts which posed the highest risk, or employing risk-reduction tools (such as latex condoms, lube with Nonoxynol-9 which kills many STDs, oral sex barriers, soap and water to wash hands and sex toys, and fingernail files to smooth the nails and avoid scratching).

For lesbians, the general safer sex rule for avoiding STDs is to wash hands and sex toys well with soap and water (or cover them with clean latex) after touching your partner's genitals, mouth, or anus, before touching your own (or another person's) genitals, mouth, or anus. Also, fingers or dildos should not be moved from anus to vagina without first being cleaned. Vulva-to-vulva rubbing, where the mucous membranes touch, should be avoided if one woman has an STD. During a herpes outbreak, or when another STD is present, avoid mouth-to-genital contact.

Sex is not risky unless one person is infected with HIV or another STD. Since it's not always possible to know whether a partner is infected, some people choose to act as if every person poses a risk, and other people choose to act as if none of their sex partners could possibly have an STD. Most people choose a level of vigilance against STDs somewhere in between these two extremes. With new or unknown partners, there is the risk of not knowing if they have an STD. With multiple partners, there is the risk of catching a disease from one lover, then passing it on to someone else, before realizing you are infected. With old or long-term partners, there is the risk of becoming lax about STD prevention, or presuming disease-free status without actually discussing the topic.

In order for HIV to be spread, live virus from an infected person must get into the bloodstream of a partner (O'Sullivan and Parmar, 1992). This can happen by sharing injection drug needles that have not been properly cleaned between users, or through certain sex acts.

HIV can travel through intact mucous membranes of the anus or the vagina (Phillips, 1994). When scratching or tearing has occurred during penetration, this makes the vaginal walls or the more delicate anal lining even more vulnerable to HIV and other STDs (Norvell, Benrubi, and Thompson, 1984). This is why an infected man ejaculating into an anus or vagina poses such high risk of transmitting HIV to his partner.

A lesbian might move vaginal fluid or blood from an infected partner into herself or another woman with her fingers or a dildo. This is why washing hands and dildos with soap and water, or covering them with clean latex, is important. (Vaginitis due to Trichomonas bacteria, Gardnerella vaginalis bacteria, or a yeast fungus can also be spread between women with unwashed hands or dildos.)

HIV dies quickly when exposed to air or temperature changes; hepatitis (which can also be fatal) is a much hardier virus. Gonorrhea, syphilis, chlamydia, genital warts, and herpes, though not fatal, are other STDs that pose serious health risks to millions of Americans each year. Many STDs have similar symptoms and are difficult to identify without laboratory testing. Any unusual itching, soreness, swelling, growth, or discharge in the genital area or anus might be a sign of an STD. Free or low-cost STD clinics at County Health Departments throughout the U. S. offer diagnosis and treatment of STDs.

Herpes is an STD of particular concern to lesbians because it is highly contagious through kissing and oral sex. Over 50% of adult Americans are estimated to have experienced an oral herpes outbreak sometime in their lives. (This is commonly called a "cold sore.") For the few days before a Herpes simplex Type I outbreak (when itching and soreness occur), during the outbreak (when the actual cold sore appears), and after (until the lip skin is completely healed), oral herpes can be spread to the lips of a partner through kissing, or to the genitals through oral sex. Herpes simplex Type II, a slightly different virus, usually occurs on the genitals but can be transmitted to the mouth.

Oral sex on a woman is not a likely way to spread HIV, because saliva has a neutralizing effect on HIV. But herpes, gonorrhea, syphilis, hepatitis, and chlamydia can all be spread through oral sex. Cuts, sores, or piercings in the mouth can make a person more vulnerable to contracting an STD through oral sex (McIlvenna, 1992).

The key to avoiding HIV and most other STDs is to not let any body fluid (blood, semen, vaginal fluid, or breast milk) from an infected person get into the bloodstream or onto the mucous membranes (eyes, nose, throat, anus, vagina). Intact skin is a good barrier against HIV and other STDs, but cuts, bites, or scratches can break the skin and allow disease to enter the body (Richman and Rickman, 1992).

Some women choose to never come in contact with a sex partner's body fluid. They may avoid oral sex, and always use condoms and latex gloves (Stevens, 1994).

Other women see contact with body fluid as an important intimate connection they are not willing to give up. They might restrict sharing of body fluids to sex with a primary partner, or with partners they know to be disease-free.

Some lesbians see avoidance of sex with men as an adequate safer-sex measure.

Most lesbians refuse to kiss, to use saliva as a sexual lubricant, or to give oral sex when they have cold sores on their lips, recognizing that herpes is very contagious.

ARE HIV AND STDS
A SIGNIFICANT HEALTH RISK TO LESBIANS?

With eight studies published in the 1990s showing the extremely low risk of woman-to-woman HIV transmission, some lesbians believe that safer sex is a non-issue for women who have sex only with women. Other lesbians insist that safer sex is everybody's concern, pointing out that many women who have sex with women (WSWs) are also sexual with men (Hunter, 1995).

Many long-time lesbians criticize the emphasis on HIV and remind younger dykes that, while woman-to-woman sex poses far less risk than heterosexual sex for spreading most STDs, herpes is still a major concern of lesbians.

Safer sex educators explain that, while soap, water, and fingernail files may be adequate safer sex tools at home, latex gloves and oral sex barriers may be essential at a sex club or on a camping trip. It's up to each woman to evaluate the available information on STDs, decide for herself what risk-reduction measures are appropriate–and then be prepared to negotiate with a partner who may have a very different level of concern about safer sex.

In 1994 the University of Turin, Italy published the results of a study of 18 HIV-discordant lesbian couples (Raiteri, Fora, and Sinicco, 1994) which showed no evidence of woman-to-woman HIV transmission during six months of sexual activity (including anal and oral sex, sharing of sex toys, and sex during menstruation) without the use of any latex condoms, gloves, or oral sex barriers. This was the first prospective study on possible woman-to-woman HIV transmission. Previous retrospective studies done in the U. S. had given similar results (Chu, Conti, Schable, and Diaz, 1994; Chu, Hammett, and Buehler, 1992; Chu, Buehler, Fleming and Berkelman, 1990; Cohen, Marmor, Wolfe, and Ribble, 1993; McCombs, McCray, Wendell, Sweeney, and Onorato, 1992; Peterson, Doll, White, and Chu, 1992).

A 1993 survey of 498 Bay Area women who have sex with women, done by the San Francisco and Berkeley Health Departments, found a higher rate of HIV infection in their sample than in the general population of women (Surveillance Branch, 1993). The study found no evidence of woman-to-woman transmission, but it did show that this population of lesbians and bisexual women had higher-than-average rates of injection drug use and sex with gay and bisexual men. This study and other WSW studies with similar results are often cited by groups seeking funding for safer sex education aimed at lesbians and bisexual women.

A 1980 study of 2,345 women done by Dr. Susan Johnson concluded that "the sexual behaviors of lesbians are associated with a lower risk of most sexually transmitted diseases" (Johnson, 1987, p. 805).

Why? The answer is simple: the fingering, fisting, tribadism, and oral sex commonly practiced by lesbians do not move body fluid from one partner into another as efficiently as a penis ejaculating into an anus or vagina.

Considering these studies, and emphasizing that only five cases of suspected woman-to-woman HIV transmission have appeared in the scientific literature since the AIDS epidemic began in 1978 (Rich, Buck, Tuomala, and Kazanjian, 1993), many health activists point to other serious health risks. Each year around 45,000 American women die of breast cancer. Smoking contributes to over 420,000 deaths annually in the U.S. (Castleman, 1996), while traffic accidents claim the lives of around 40,000 people. Each year over 6,000 people die from accidents on the job (Coleman, 1997); ten times that many die from work-related illnesses. These statistics can make the risk of HIV infection seem insignificant to the lesbian who has sex only with other women.

Woman-to-woman sex is relatively safe, compared to activities like driving, smoking, heterosexual sex, or working. This can lead the polyamorous lesbian to conclude that the more lovers a woman has, the more time she'll spend in bed with women, and the less time she'll have for other more dangerous activities.

REFERENCES

Castleman, M. (1996). A life in smoke. *Mother Jones*, May/June, pp. 68-69.

Chu, S., Buehler, J., Fleming, P., & Berkelman, R. (1990). Epidemiology of reported cases of AIDS in lesbians, United States 1980-89. *American Journal of Public Health*, 80, 1380-1381.

Chu, S., Hammett, T. A., & Buehler, J.W. (1992). Update: Epidemiology of reported cases of AIDS in women who report sex only with other women, United States, 1980-1991. *AIDS*, 6, 518-519.

Chu, S., Conti, L., Schable, B., & Diaz, T. (1994). Female-to-female sexual contact and HIV transmission. *Journal of the American Medical Association*, 272, 433.

Cohen, H., Marmor, M., Wolfe, H., & Ribble, D. (1993). Risk assessment of HIV transmission among lesbians. *Journal of Acquired Immune Deficiency Syndromes* 6, 1173-1174.

Coleman, B. (1997) Work injuries, illnesses rival cancer, AIDS. *Daily Camera*, 7/28/97, p. 1.

Consumer Reports (1994). Selling fear. 59, 560.

Hunter, J. (1995). At the crossroads: Lesbian youth. In K. Jay (Ed.). *Dyke Life: From Growing Up to Growing Old, a Celebration of the Lesbian Experience.* New York: HarperCollins Publishers.

Johnson, S. R. (1987). Comparison of gynecologic health care problems between lesbians and bisexual women. *Journal of Reproductive Medicine*, 32, 805-811.

McCombs, S., McCray, E., Wendell, D., Sweeney, P., & Onorato, I. (1992). Epidemiology of HIV-1 infection in bisexual women. *Journal of Acquired Immune Deficiency Syndromes*, 5, 850-852.

McIlvenna, T. (1992). *The Complete Guide to Safer Sex.* Fort Lee, New Jersey: Barricade Books.

Norvell, M. K., Benrubi, G. I., Thompson, R. J. (1984). Investigation of Microtrauma after sexual intercourse. *Journal of Reproductive Medicine*, 29, 269-271.

O'Sullivan, S., & Parmar, P. (1992). *Lesbians Talk Safer Sex.* London: Scarlet Press.

Petersen, L., Doll, L., White, C., & Chu, S. (1992). No evidence for female-to-female HIV transmission among 960,000 female blood donors. *Journal of Acquired Immune Deficiency Syndromes*, 5, 853-855.

Phillips, D. M. (1994). The role of cell-to-cell transmission in HIV infection. *AIDS*, 8, 719-731.

Raiteri, R., Fora, R., & Sinicco, A. (1994). No HIV transmission through lesbian sex. *Lancet*, 344, 270.

Rich, J. C., Buck, A., Tuomala, R. E., & Kazanjian, P. H. (1993). Transmission of Human Immunodeficiency Virus infection presumed to have occurred via female homosexual contact. *Clinical Infectious Diseases*, 17, 1003-1005.

Richman, K., & Rickman, L. (1992). The potential for transmission of Human Immunodeficiency Virus through human bites. *Journal of Acquired Immune Deficiency Syndromes*, 6, 402-406.

Stevens, P. (1994). HIV prevention education for lesbians and bisexual women: A cultural analysis of a community intervention. *Social Science and Medicine*, 39, 1565-1578.

Surveillance Branch, AIDS office (1993). *Seroprevalence and risk behaviors among lesbians and bisexual women: The 1993 San Francisco/Berkeley women's survey.* San Francisco Department of Public Health, San Francisco, CA.

Models of Open Relationships

Kathy Labriola

SUMMARY. This article describes three categories of open relationships: the primary/secondary model, the multiple primary partners model, and the multiple non-primary relationships model. Examples of each type are given, and the advantages and drawbacks of each model are discussed. *[Article copies available for a fee from The Haworth Document Delivery Service: 1-800-342-9678. E-mail address: getinfo@haworthpressinc.com]*

The model of heterosexual, monogamous marriage is sanctioned by society, religion, and the law as the only acceptable type of sexual relationship. As a result, most people have not been exposed to other ways of life. In fact, we are so heavily socialized to believe in the ideals of monogamy and marriage that many people cannot even imagine any other option. While lesbians have traditionally tended towards a belief in monogamy, in reality, lesbian relationships are very diverse. Frequent responses to the idea of open relationships are: "But I've never seen one," "No one I know has ever tried that," and

Kathy Labriola is a counselor and nurse who provides low-fee counseling for individuals, couples, and groups. She has experience assisting people with the challenges of non-traditional relationships, health problems and disabilities, HIV/AIDS, sexual orientation crises, political activism, and class struggle. She facilitates discussion and support groups about health and disabilities, political activism and burnout, and open relationships.

Address correspondence to Kathy Labriola, 1307 University Avenue, Berkeley, CA 94702.

[Haworth co-indexing entry note]: "Models of Open Relationships." Labriola, Kathy. Co-published simultaneously in *Journal of Lesbian Studies* (The Haworth Press, Inc.) Vol. 3, No. 1/2, 1999, pp. 217-225; and: *The Lesbian Polyamory Reader: Open Relationships, Non-Monogamy, and Casual Sex* (ed: Marcia Munson and Judith P. Stelboum) The Haworth Press, Inc., 1999, pp. 217-225. Single or multiple copies of this article are available for a fee from The Haworth Document Delivery Service [1-800-342-9678, 9:00 a.m. - 5:00 p.m. (EST). E-mail address: getinfo@haworthpressinc.com].

"There's no way it could possibly work out." People always ask, "But how does it work? What's it like?"

Many successful models do exist. This article gives an overview of the three types of non-monogamous, or polyamorous, relationships which currently exist, and variations on those models. To begin thinking about new ways of living, it can help to see some examples and to understand the advantages and drawbacks of each model. This may help you to decide whether an open relationship is right for you and, if so, which model may best fit your individual lifestyle. The possibilities are limitless and you can "customize" any of these models to accommodate your needs.

PRIMARY/SECONDARY MODEL

This is by far the most commonly practiced form of open relationship and it is the most similar to monogamous marriage. In this model, the "couple relationship" is considered primary, and any other relationships revolve around the couple. It is most frequently practiced by married people and other couples in long-term relationships. The couple decides that their relationship will have precedence over any outside relationships. The couple often lives together and forms the primary family unit, while other relationships receive less time and priority. No outside relationship is allowed to become equal in importance to the primary partnership. The couple makes the rules; secondary lovers have little power over decisions and are not allowed to negotiate for what they want.

Some couples together pick up a third (and fourth and fifth) person to have casual sex with. This may occur at a music festival, through personals ads, or at a sex club or S/M party. (Among bisexuals and heterosexuals, these couples are often called "swingers.") Both primary partners participate in the sexual encounter, and this can enhance the sex life of the couple. For example:

- *Lori and Dianne had been together for nearly three years when they met Monika at a dance. They were both attracted to her. The next week, they invited Monika over for Sunday brunch. After a playful morning of feeding each other ripe fruit and croissants, Lori and Dianne invited Monika into their bedroom.*
- *Dorothy had long lusted after her friend Devi, but for professional reasons, never let romance enter into their encounters. Then*

one weekend Dorothy, Devi, and Dorothy's long-term girlfriend Loraine were out of town at a conference together. Knowing that Devi and Loraine were attracted to each other, Dorothy encouraged the two of them to have a brief affair. All three had dinner together, and later that night, when Loraine came back from Devi's room and crawled into bed, Dorothy was hungry to hear every detail.

Some couples allow each partner to independently have outside sexual relationships, either casual or long-term. These outside relationships are still considered secondary, and if any conflict develops, the primary couple relationship takes precedence. Often the couple lives together, shares finances, and spends weekends, holidays, and vacations together. The outside lovers usually do not live with them, spend less time with them, and have very little voice in decisions and rule-making. Scheduling is arranged around the demands of the primary couple. Some couples have rules that each partner has veto power over any new lovers that her partner may choose. In other words, if a woman is interested in a new person, her girlfriend has the power to veto that relationship before it starts, for any reason. Other couples allow each person to sleep with whomever they choose, but make rules about how much time they can spend with their other lovers, whether they can spend the night away from home, how far away a potential new lover must live, whether they can spend any weekend time together, and other restrictions. For example:

- *Sarah and Jill are a lesbian couple with a 3-year-old child. Jill also has a long-term relationship with Megan. Jill spends most evenings and weekends with Sarah and their child. Jill sees Megan one or two evenings a week as her schedule permits.*
- *Lynette and JoEllen live together and have a primary relationship. Both have ex-lovers with whom they are very close, and both occasionally have sex with their ex-lovers.*
- *David and Lucy are a bisexual couple who are married and have two children. David has a long-term male lover whom he sees frequently, but he considers his marriage and children his first priority and devotes more time and commitment to them. Lucy has had several female lovers but each one has left her because she insists that her husband comes first. So currently she has no outside relationship.*

- *Denise and Tanisha live together and are committed to their partnership. Denise has a strong preference for S/M sexual activities, but Tanisha is lukewarm about bondage and other activities Denise wants. Denise satisfies her S/M desires by attending S/M sex parties. She also meets S/M partners through personals ads.*
- *Laetitia and Kim have been lovers for ten years, but don't live together. They see each other on designated nights each week, but a few nights each week are their own for work, activities, or an occasional affair. They maintain a high degree of privacy, and rarely tell each other details of their outside sexual adventures.*

The primary/secondary model is popular because it is most similar to traditional marriage and does not threaten the primacy of the couple. For most couples, it is not such a stretch to have outside relationships as long as they know that the most important commitment is to the primary partner. They can live together, have children, be socially acceptable, and "live a normal life." They may keep their outside relationships a secret from friends and family. This model doesn't require making any radical changes in lifestyle or world view. One major benefit for many couples is that they feel secure that they won't be abandoned, because their partner has agreed that outside relationships will be secondary. This is simpler and easier to organize logistically than other forms of open relationships. If there is any conflict over time, loyalty, or commitment, the primary partner always gets priority.

A major drawback of this model is that outside relationships are not so simple or easy to predict or control. Having a sexual relationship with someone else often leads to becoming emotionally involved and even falling in love, frequently causing a crisis in the primary relationship, possibly leading to a breakup. Initiating a sexual relationship means opening the door to many possibilities, and often secondary relationships grow into something else which does not fit neatly into the confines of this model. Many people who become "secondary" lovers become angry at being subjugated to the couple, and demand equality or end the relationship. For this model to be successful, couples must be very convinced that their relationship is strong enough to weather these ups and downs. Conversely, some couples who start with this model decide eventually to shift to some form of the Multiple

Primary Partners Model to allow secondary relationships to become equal to the primary relationship.

MULTIPLE PRIMARY PARTNERS MODEL

While there are many variations on this theme, the key factor is that all primary partner models include three or more people in a primary relationship in which all members are equal partners. Instead of a couple having priority and control in the relationship, all relationships are considered primary, or have the potential of becoming primary. Each partner has equal power to negotiate for what they want in the relationship in terms of time, commitment, living situation, financial arrangements, sex, and other issues. Two variations of the Multiple Primary Partners Model follow.

Polyfidelity Model: Closed Multi-Adult Families

This is a "group marriage" model, essentially the same as being married, except that you're married to more than one person. Usually consisting of three to six adults, all partners live together and share finances, children, and household responsibilities. The partners could be all women, all men, or both. Depending on the sexual orientation of the family members, some or all adults in the family may be sexual partners. This is a closed system, and sex is allowed only between family members–no outside sexual relationships are allowed. Some families are open to taking on new partners, but only if all members of the family agree to accept the new person as a partner. The new person then moves into the household and becomes an equal member of the family. The polyfidelity model was made famous during the 1970s and 1980s by the Kerista commune in San Francisco, which had several households living this model for many years. Currently the most common form of this model is a heterosexual or bisexual triad of two women and one man, or two men and one woman, but many lesbian triads exist. Here are some examples of polyfidelity:

- *Ann, Rachel, and Nathan live together as a family; all three are bisexual. Rachel has sexual relationships with both Ann and Nathan. Ann and Nathan also have a sexual relationship. They have a "sleeping schedule" so that each relationship receives equal time, each spending two nights a week with each partner.*

- *Debra and Holly were very close friends with another lesbian couple, Karen and Elena. After years of spending weekends together camping, bowling, going to the movies, and having potluck dinners, they bought a house and moved in together as a polyfidelitous family. Each woman has sexual relationships with the other three women. Each has her own bedroom and negotiates time with each partner.*

Polyfidelity can be a richly rewarding experience, creating an extended family and intentional community. Pooling resources is economical and ecological, and can reduce the stress of child rearing by spreading the work and the responsibility among several adults rather than just one or two parents. However, polyfidelity requires a very high level of compatibility and affinity among all partners. Everyone must agree on where to live, what to cook for dinner, how clean the house should be, how much money to spend and on what, whether to have children and how to raise them. Most people find it difficult enough to locate one partner they can successfully live with for the "long haul," much less two, three, four or more. Living together as a group decreases privacy and autonomy, often leading to interpersonal conflicts and stress. Living in a group requires excellent interpersonal skills, clear communication, assertiveness, cooperation, and flexibility in order to accommodate everyone's needs. Picking compatible partners and being flexible are both essential for successful polyfidelity.

Multiple Primary Partners: Open Model

This model is very different from polyfidelity in that all partners are given much more autonomy and flexibility in developing any relationships they choose and defining those relationships on their own terms. In the Primary/Secondary Model the couple is the center of power, and in the Polyfidelity Model the entire family group makes decisions together and all must agree. In the Multiple Primary Partners Open Model, the individual is the basic unit of the family and is empowered to make her own rules and decisions. Partners may choose to live together, they may choose to live with one or more lovers, or they may live alone. This model is open, in that each partner has the right to choose other lovers at any time without the approval of any other partner. Each relationship evolves independently of partners' other relationships, with rules and levels of commitment to be negotiated by each individual. No one can veto a potential partner, or "pull rank" and insist on being the number one priority. Here are some examples:

- *Jennifer and Andrea are a lesbian couple who live together. Andrea also has another primary partner, Julia, who does not live with them, but receives equal time and priority. Andrea spends one-half of the week with each woman.*
- *Ricardo and Maria are a bisexual married couple: they spend Monday, Wednesday, and Friday nights together. Tom also lives with them, and has his own bedroom. Ricardo spends a few nights each week with Tom. Maria has two lovers, Erica and Jessica, who she sees frequently.*
- *Carmen is a "lesbian with two wives," as she calls herself. The three own a duplex and are on a weekly rotational schedule. Carmen spends three nights each week upstairs with Tanya, and three nights downstairs with Katy. The seventh day of the week is "Carmen's time," and she can negotiate to spend that time with either wife or have time to herself.*

There is much more fluidity in the Multiple Primary Partners Open Model, because relationships are allowed to evolve over time. Very few rules restrict how relationships grow; changing levels of commitment are possible. However, this model is much less predictable than the others, and may cause anxiety for people who like more structure and prefer a clear hierarchy.

Because all partners are considered equal, each partner can negotiate for what they want. This "processing" requires time, effort, and excellent communication skills. Some people find the potential for conflicting loyalties to be too threatening. For instance, which partner will spend holidays or vacations with you? Will they both go, will they alternate each year, or will you spend part of each holiday or vacation with each one? If one partner is going through a crisis, can they demand more of your time and commitment? If you are experiencing problems in one relationship or feel more drawn toward another partner, what behavior is appropriate? Weighing your own needs and the desires of each partner can be very stressful and confusing. Some people find this model requires too much thinking, problem-solving, and "going with the flow," so they may prefer a more rigid structure such as the Primary/Secondary Model or the Polyfidelity Model.

MULTIPLE NON-PRIMARY RELATIONSHIPS MODEL

While the previous models stress commitment and primary relationships, some people prefer to remain essentially single but participate in more than one relationship. They are not looking for a committed relationship. For them, non-monogamy offers the intimacy, love, and sexual satisfaction they need without the constraints of a primary relationship. This model works best for people who have a serious, all-consuming commitment to something other than relationships: people who are very busy with their work, their art, raising children, or political involvements. Usually they prefer to be involved with people who, like themselves, want less commitment, or people who already have a primary relationship and are looking for a secondary relationship. People choosing this model usually don't make a lot of rules about their relationships, and retain a very high degree of personal freedom and autonomy. They usually live alone and make relationships a relatively low priority in their lives. These are some examples:

- *Rosemary writes lesbian mystery novels. She lives alone and spends most of her time writing in her home office. She has two long-term lovers, Janet and Danielle. She sees each of them sporadically when her work permits. Both Janet and Danielle have primary relationships, so they are content to see Rosemary a few times each month.*
- *Jill is a civil rights attorney working 80-hour weeks at the ACLU. She doesn't have time for a primary relationship, but has two long-term affairs with Jasmine and Betsy, who are also lawyers. They see each other "between trials," when their workloads permit.*

For the Multiple Non-Primary Relationships Model to work, it is crucial to carefully choose partners who will be satisfied with a less committed relationship, and to communicate that clearly to potential partners. This model often is successful if all parties are too busy or too committed elsewhere to want a primary relationship. However, conflict can arise when circumstances change and one person has more time or develops a desire for a primary relationship. For example, when Rosemary finishes her novel she may want to devote more time to a relationship, or she may even desire monogamy. Such a change can prove fatal to the existing relationship. However, sometimes people see this change as an opportunity for growth, and are able to alter their relationship to accommodate everyone's needs.

Choosing the Right Relationship Model

There are many different types of open relationships. Some models will fit your needs much better than others. To identify your preferred model, ask yourself some tough questions:

- How much security do you need to feel safe in a relationship?
- Do you need to feel that you are "number one," or can you share that priority with other lovers?
- How much privacy and personal freedom do you need to feel comfortable?
- Have you been happiest living alone, living with one person, or with a group?
- What pushes your buttons or provokes jealousy or insecurity?
- How much time and energy do you have to devote to relationships?
- What are your expectations of love relationships?

To be happy in relationships of any kind, it helps to know what you want and which model will be most likely to work for you. You must be willing to communicate what you want to potential partners in an honest and clear way. It is best to pick partners who want the same type of relationship model you would choose. Knowing what you want, communicating your desires, and choosing partners who have similar preferences are all ways for maximizing your chances of developing successful relationships, whatever model you choose.

The Flexible House:
A Fairy Tale

Kathryn Werhane

SUMMARY. "The Flexible House: A Fairy Tale" is a fictionalized account of a long-term lesbian relationship, which uses the metaphor of building a house for the development of the relationship. The narrator invites a mysterious third woman into their home, and then must live with the aftershocks the house goes through. *[Article copies available for a fee from The Haworth Document Delivery Service: 1-800-342-9678. E-mail address: getinfo@haworthpressinc.com]*

Once upon a time, long, long ago, I started building a house with a new girlfriend. Today, it's still under construction. The house we're building is flexible, malleable, adjustable. It's not in any one location, or of any particular size. Grant and I have been building it, tearing it down, and rebuilding it for twenty years, although we didn't intend to build anything but a good time at the beginning. From the start we agreed not to limit each other, but to love without ownership of each other's time or pussy. Our emotional boundaries are as flexible as the floor plan.

Kathryn Werhane is a visual artist and an avid reader of lesbian fiction, personal ads, and listings for self-improvement workshops. She is a pagan who practices Buddhist meditation, yoga, sex, art and journal writing to keep herself nominally sane and balanced.

Address correspondence to Kathryn Werhane, P.O. Box 882554, San Francisco, CA 94188.

[Haworth co-indexing entry note]: "The Flexible House: A Fairy Tale." Werhane, Kathryn. Co-published simultaneously in *Journal of Lesbian Studies* (The Haworth Press, Inc.) Vol. 3, No. 1/2, 1999, pp. 227-233; and: *The Lesbian Polyamory Reader: Open Relationships, Non-Monogamy, and Casual Sex* (ed: Marcia Munson and Judith P. Stelboum) The Haworth Press, Inc., 1999, pp. 227-233. Single or multiple copies of this article are available for a fee from The Haworth Document Delivery Service [1-800-342-9678, 9:00 a.m. - 5:00 p.m. (EST). E-mail address: getinfo@haworthpressinc.com].

We met in the 70s, when I was a baby dyke looking for sex and adventure and experience, working hard to wash away the fresh-from-the-farm, midwest girl look. I didn't want a lover, or a girlfriend, or a relationship; especially not a long-term, happily-ever-after one. When I met Grant, I still didn't want a lover, or a girlfriend, or a relationship; especially not a long-term, happily-ever-after one. Fortunately, neither did she. We set out to have fun, to have good times, to have good sex. We dated for two years before we could even admit to having a relationship, let alone a house.

We didn't intend to build a house, but we're both domestic sorts: we both cook, garden, like to be at home, like to have sex in our nest. She's the butch top but she likes to wash the dishes, I'm the bottom (but not very femme) and I take out the garbage, do home repairs. Every few months or years, Grant and I change the rules and rearrange our house, make it larger, smaller, let in other people, add a story, dig a basement, enlarge the windows, cut a skylight, move it to another town or to the country. Or we might change a bedroom into a study, a study into a yoga room, clear out a room altogether just to have a spare room, a bare room.

The spare room never stays empty for long; soon it becomes storage space or a room for a particular purpose; it has a way of filling up, of being used. But a couple years ago we cleaned it out, shut the door, and in our contentment with each other and the rest of the house, forgot all about it. The house got smaller and cozier. We boarded up doors and windows, ignored whole floors, moved it to a quiet street.

Twice in the past, we've had to expand the house to include extra room for me to have other lovers. The first time the expansion was so great the house came close to exploding, the second time it shook and rattled, but settled down stronger than ever. But more often, during most of my affairs, we have only had to add extra doors and windows so I could come and go more easily, to have quick hot fucks with butch women whom I would probably never choose as girlfriends, not even to the extent of bringing them home. Grant is much better behaved in her sexual liaisons. She quietly woos and pursues, seeing her other women elsewhere, so discreetly I'm barely aware of it. She has fun, gets what she needs and wants, without letting her clit direct her life. Unlike me.

I thought I had learned a little bit over the years about how to steer my cunt toward safer targets, so I could have fun but not disrupt the rest of my life too drastically. But last year, suddenly a new lust-love-sex-interest came into my life, the spare room was called into use, the house needed to be enlarged again. With my new lust, a wild woman who called herself Fog, I still remembered those lessons, but felt I was taking a different class in a different school, and the previous lessons were not of much use.

* * *

I invited Fog in, showed her the house, explained the floor plan that Grant and I had been adjusting for so many years, and finally showed her the spare room. I told her it was an empty room, she could move right in. I'd never done that before, but I was that much in lust. I told her we didn't use it, didn't need it, she could have it, that Grant wouldn't mind. Fog stepped inside, looked around, approved of me for having an empty room in my life and in my house, approved of my relationship with Grant, the fact that we could have a house together, a life together, and still have a clean, empty room, light and airy and inviting. She looked around, approved of it, but never moved in.

When she did come over, it was always for a visit, a very short visit. She would bring only her travel toothbrush and her sleeping bag. I would bring in a futon and blankets and pillows and candles, maybe flowers and a pot of tea, and we would have hot passionate wild sex with dildos and vibrators and tit clamps, or with no toys at all, only gloves and lube. We would start slow, lying comfortably on the futon, touching and licking and kissing, then build to hot hungry sex, rolling off the futon onto her sleeping bag on the floor. Fog was a minimalist, even an ascetic, not able to tolerate too much material comfort; sometimes even the smooth floor was too luxurious and we'd roll right out the door into the back yard, then on into the woods behind the house, to lie naked on the twigs and needles and prickly bushes under the pine trees. Only then could she let loose, be wild, really feel.

After sex in the woods, I would want to go back to my own room, to my queen size bed with its down comforter, flannel sheets, feather pillows; she'd beg me to stay, suddenly turning from a butch dyke to a whimpering child, a little girl in need of a back rub and a comforting hug. Somehow, we'd drift back to the room, her room in my house, the home I lived in with Grant, and we'd wake in the morning in her sleeping bag on the floor. She'd sleep late, much later than I, and after awhile when I'd come back to check on her she'd be gone, the room bare again–the futon and blankets folded up against the wall, her toothbrush and sleeping bag vanished with her. She would never tell me when she was going, or where; her sense of privacy was invaded if I even asked. I might not see her again for weeks, but I knew that the day after she left she would call at a time she knew I wouldn't be home, to leave a sexy thank-you message on my answering machine. In her husky sweet voice, she would tell me how wonderful I was, how hot I was, how beautiful and interesting and fascinating and how glad she was to know me, know my luscious body.

Sometimes I think I had dates with her in that room just so I'd get those messages; sometimes they were better than the sex that preceded them. I kept them all, bought a case of sixty-minute incoming message tapes so I could save all her honeyed words. If I didn't see her for a few days and needed a fix, I'd take my own sleeping bag, my vibrator, and a tape player into the bare room, when Grant wasn't home or was busy in another part of the house. I'd play the tapes at full volume, touching myself, reliving the nights with her, crying for her to come back, to fuck me again. I lived for her approval, became addicted to her positive judgments of me. I came to need it, to crave it, to hunger for her opinions of me, my body, my life as I'd created it.

I would never know when she'd be back again, but she would always give me a day's warning with another phone message. In that voice that made my cunt drip with desire, she'd tell my machine how much she was looking forward to seeing me again. But she never gave any clue about where she was, what she was doing. I wondered: did she work, did she have other girlfriends, did she rob banks, did she sleep in the woods?

For months it went on this way: waiting for a call, then getting a call, then a visit and a fuck, then a followup thank-you call. Grant felt a little left out, and would sometimes wander into the spare room. She felt hurt that I would drop anything to spend time with Fog whenever she and her sleeping bag showed up. But Grant had interests of her own–a business to run, short hot affairs with short fat women she met through the personal ads, gardening, cooking, seeing her many friends, and keeping the rest of the house in one piece, a responsibility I was ignoring. And she had me when I wasn't with Fog or anticipating her arrival or recovering from her visits.

In my obsession with Fog, I denied the significance of my relationship with Grant, treated her like a member of my family of origin instead of my family of choice. I didn't want to lose her, I didn't want to move out or change our arrangement, I just wanted space and time to be in the spare room with Fog whenever Fog was interested, and time to pine and mope for her when she wasn't. For awhile I equated the importance of the spare room with the rest of the house, for awhile I denied my love for Grant. I pretended the spare room had been there as long as the rest of the house, that the spare room was as big and strong as the rest of the house.

I wanted Fog to join my family, somehow. I wanted her to be another girlfriend, not the other woman. That cool demeanor of hers gave me the illusion that she could fit right in, become part of the family package: three women, two cats, a flexible home. I denied the depth of my relationship to Grant, in order to try to equate the two relationships. On cold foggy nights, I wondered where this need came from. I was tempted, for the first time ever, to try to have equally meaningful relationships with two women simultaneously. Always before, I had pictured myself as having a primary relationship, and varying degrees of intensity with a second woman, the other woman. What was this need for two real girlfriends? Why now? Was I being a greedy child or was I being mature and wise? Was I ready for this; was this the next step? What relationship did I think Grant and Fog would have between them? Would we all sit down to dinner together? Would we all sleep together, have sex together? I couldn't quite conceive of it, but thought it could evolve in time. One time I introduced them to each other, wanting to see how it felt to be in the same room with both of them together. It excited me, I wanted it. I wanted more of it, I was ready for a relationship that involved all three of us. They were polite, but Grant wasn't interested, Fog kept her distance. It didn't happen again.

For months I lived in nervous anticipation of Fog's visits bracketed by phone messages, but I appeared to lead a normal life, and learned to hide my addiction. I meditated, did yoga, went to work every day. But always, in the back of my mind, was Fog. When I wearied of her continuous presence in my head, when my fantasies wore me down, I'd chant: *she's a girl scout, not a goddess,* while seated in a half lotus, eyes closed, breathing deeply. I needed to remind myself of her human traits, her earthly faults.

Grant was so understanding of it all. She's seen me, in our twenty years as lovers, in a lot of altered states over different women. Each had been unique. At least, she thought, this one comes and goes, and cleans her own room.

*   *   *

On the night of the full moon in September, Fog showed up, announced only by a very brief message delivered in a flat, disinterested voice. It was in such contrast to her usually husky, slow, seductive tones, it scared me. September is my favorite month and I'd been hoping she would come soon so we could share a night during it. Anticipating our naked bodies together in the light of the harvest moon, yet nervous and worried because of her businesslike, impersonal message, I was very anxious, wondering what she would be like, what she would want, what mood she would be in. Whatever it was, I was determined that I would mold and shape and dissolve or grow to fit her needs. During the time of knowing her, I had become quite adept at shape shifting; I was sand, water, clouds, taking her shape. When I wasn't with her, I went out into the world a much firmer person, tall and strong, appearing to be a pillar of strength. Grant softened me, but only around Fog did I willingly crumble. My free will was weakened by her needs.

Under the full moon, Fog arrived, covered in the armor of a hooded sweatshirt, down vest and parka. Her deep-set eyes were in shadow, her pale skin glowed eerily. I ran naked to the spare room, her room, and stood offering myself eagerly in the cold night air. Afraid of her chilly presence, too impatient to wait for her impassive self to warm up, I eagerly began licking and nibbling her cheeks and earlobes, unzipping her parka, her down vest, her sweatshirt. As I grasped for her breasts, she stopped me, slowly pulling all her heavy clothes back into place, one piece at time, torturing me. With no emotion in her voice, she told me that we wouldn't be lovers anymore, told me to take the room back, to furnish it, redecorate it, make it part of my home with Grant.

I was shocked and humiliated; unable to breathe. I wanted to tear down my house, destroy every room. I melted into a puddle around her hiking boots, unable to accept what she was saying. She stepped over me, disappeared out the back door. I felt my life leave with her.

*   *   *

But I will accept it; I will recover, I've done it before. I'll lose myself in my job, get re-acquainted with Grant, plant a garden, meditate, remember how to live for myself, remember how to have a girlfriend who loves me and wants to be with me in our whole house, remember how to have sex without getting lost in the woods. I'll recover my balance, get back my other life, the life that had been swallowed up by the newness, the mystery, the sexual excitement.

I'll recover: I'll act like a nice middle-class woman in a long-term relationship with her one true love, for awhile, for months or for years. Grant and I will act like a couple; no one will question it. We'll work on the house, scale it down, move it to a busy neighborhood. We'll feel honored when her relatives invite me to their weddings, funerals, bat mitzvahs. We'll smile smugly when young lesbians are awed by the length of our relationship. We'll join organizations together at the couple rate, we'll renew our joint autoclub membership, we'll attend lesbian weddings together, we'll fool our friends.

Our coupled friends will think I've settled down, once again, and breathe a sigh of relief for us, for themselves, for the sisterhood of coupledom. They've seen us go through this before, they've held their collective breath and waited for me to get over it, to come to my senses and appreciate what a fine woman I have, what a nice secure life I could have, if only. . . . If only I didn't need more than one woman, one kind of sex, one kind of love, one kind of romance, one master bedroom in one stable house. What they don't see is the beauty of the spare room, the room where other kinds of women with other ideas about sex, romance, relationships, with other needs and desires, can come for visits, or move in for a while. Where other women can decorate it in their own taste, where we don't talk about cleaning the oven or buying cat kibble.

But for now, the room stands bare. Sometimes I dust and vacuum it, polish the wood floor. Sometimes I let the dust accumulate and the air get stale. Sometimes I leave the door to the backyard open, just to see who might wander in; sometimes I leave the hallway door open, to see if Grant will walk in, or a guest at a dinner party. It's there, it's bare, and someday I'll use it again.

Index

Abraham, 40
Academic conferences, 4,44,97-103,
    143
Adam and Eve, 40,42
"Addressee Unknown" (Jay), 4,
    97-103
Adolescents, passionate friendships of,
    78-79,80
Advertising, 2,190-191
Aerial Letter, The (Brossard), 45
Agape, 40
AIDS, 5,40,209. *See also* HIV (human
    immunodeficiency virus)
Allegra, Donna, xv-xviii
Amassalik, 51
American Couples (Blumstein and
    Schwartz), 205-207
Animals
    human dominance over, 41-42
    monogamy of, 44
    pair bonding by, 198
"An Unspoken Hunger" (Williams),
    19
Arnold, June, 13
"As the Women Turn" (radio
    program), 128-129,131-132

"Bad Friend Book" (Sprecher), 4,
    105-110
Banaro, 51
Barnard Women's Conference on
    Sexuality, 44
Barney, Natalie, 173
Beach, Frank, 51
Below the Belt, 106-107
Betrayal, 17,18
Bible
    condonement of polyamory by, 199
    patriarchal concepts of, 40,41-42

Biphobia, 163
Birth control, 199
Birth control pill, 1
Bisexual couples, 219,223
Bisexuality, 4
Bisexual men, bisexual and lesbian
    women's relationships with,
    214-215,221-222
Bisexual women
    fear of non-monogamy of, 158-160
    heterosexual sexual activities of,
    214
    male lovers of, 162-163,214-215,
    221-222
    outness of, 161
    in polyamorous relationships,
    158-164
    in polyfidelity relationships,
    221-222
"Boomer's View of Non-Monogamy,
    A" (Martin), 3,135-142
*Boston Marriages: Romantic but
    Asexual Relationships
    Among Contemporary
    Lesbians* (Rothblum), 81
Breast cancer, 215
Broumas, Olga, 56-57
Brown, Rita Mae, 13

Cabbage Lane, 126-127
Calendar, Christian, 42
Capitalist economies, marriage in,
    201-202,203
Catal Huyuk, Anatolia, 42
Catholic Church, 12,44
Cheating paradigm, 1-2,160
Chicanas, 145-146
Children
    abandonment of, 44
    as future consumers, 202

   235

legitimacy/paternity of, 42,43,
        200,202
    in polyamorous families, 161
Chlamydial infection, 212-213
Christianity, See also Bible; Catholic
        Church; Presbyterian Church
    attitudes towards marriage,
        198-199
    patriarchal concepts of, 40,41-42,
        34
Chukchee, 51
Clergy, sexual behavior of, 37
Clinton, Bill, 37
Collectives. See also Communities
    of lesbian separatists, 13-14
Colorado Springs, lesbian community
        of, 166
Coming out, to family, 112,113,154
Communication, in relationships
    with multiple partners, 3
    about sexually-transmitted disease,
        210-211
Communities,
        feminist/lesbian/women's, 4,
        79,82
    Kerista commune, 221
    Matriarchal Village, 4,125-133
    rural, 4,125-133,166
Condoms, 211
Conferences, academic, 4,44,97-103,
        143
Conflict, 194
Conflict resolution, 4
Coping, anticipatory, 51-52
Corporations, 2,202
Cosmetics industry, 75-76
Cosmetic surgery, 75-76
Counterculture movement, 126
Country communities, lesbian, 4,
        125-133,166
Country Woman, 127
Coupleness, as social ideal, 190-191
Couples therapy, 30-31,137,199
Crete, Minoan, 42
Crushes, sexual, 80
Culture, of sex, 75-76

Dal Vera, Anne, 4,11-22
"Deception" (Kovattana), 88-89
Deer, Cynthia, 3,165-174
"("Denny's Tune") I'm Not
        Monogamous Anymore, But
        . . ." (Dobkin), 5,185-187
Diet industry, 75-76
Dilno, Jeri, 13
"Dinah, Sam, Beth, and Jolyn Say"
        (Mushroom), 5,189-196
Divorce, 44
Dobkin, Alix, 5,185-187
Domestic partnership benefits, 5
Double standard, of sexual behavior,
        2,154-155

Economy
    capitalist, marriage in, 201-202,203
    physical appearance-related
        industries and, 75-76,82
Ecstasy Lounge, 4,49,179-184
Engels, Frederick, 43,44
Environment, effect of patriarchal
        beliefs on, 41-42
Eros, 40
Eugene, Oregon, Matriarchal Village
        of, 4,125-133
Exclusivity, intimacy as, 18-19,21
Ex-lovers, as friends, 80,159,169,210
Exploitation, of women, 200. See also
        Patriarchy

Family
    boundaries of, 202
    coming out to, 112,113,154
    lesbians' relationships with, 112,
        113-114
    patriarchal, 12,206
    polyamorous, 161,221-224
Family Research Council, 199
Family roles, traditional, 2
Family values, 202
Fantasy, sexual, 29,59-61
Fashion industry, 76
Fathers, patriarchal concept of, 42,43

Fear
    of loss and abandonment, 163
    of polyamory, 158-160,163
Feminists. *See also* Communities,
            feminist/lesbian/women's
    condemnation of monogamy by, 44
    lesbian
        during 1970s, 135-136,142
        distrust of monogamy, 13
        radical, 5
"Field" (Broumas), 56-57
Fisher, Catherine, 111-120
"Flexible House, The: A Fairy Tale"
        (Werhane), 3,227-233
Ford, Clellan, 51
Forestry crews, female, 126,127,128,
        129,131
Free love, 1,135,173
Friends
    definition of, 79
    erotic, 169,170
    ex-lovers as, 80,159,169,210
    jealousy towards, 159
    as lovers, 15,16-17,19-20,80,
        106,166
Friendship, 4-5,15,71-83
    definition of, 79-81
    intimate, non-sexual, 77-79,80-82
    obstacles to prioritization of, 75-82
        culture of sex, 75-76
        definitions of friendship, 79-81
        definitions of sex, 76-79
    passionate, 78-79
    polyamorous, 75,82
    sexual, 19-20
    theatrical performances about,
        105-110
Fundamentalism, 40

Gartrell, Nanette, 3,23-33
"Gays to Marry? Let's Not!"
        (McPheeters), 2,197-203
Geography and Plays (Stein), 149
Goddess worship, 40-41,43

Gonorrhea, 212-213
Great Goddess, 40-41,43
Greek philosophers, 40
Guilt, 27,28,137
Gypsy-dykes, polyamorous
        relationships of, 125-133

Haircuts, 145
Hall, Marny
    *Lesbian Love Companion, The:
        How to Survive Everything
        from Heartthrob to
        Heartbreak*, 47,81
    "Turning Down the Jezebel
        Decibels," 3,47-62
Halpern, Ellen L., 4,157-164
Hepatitis, 212
Herpes, 212-214
Herrington, Joanne, 111-120
Heterosexuals, in polyfidelity
        relationships, 221
HIV (human immunodeficiency virus),
        woman-to-woman
        transmission of, 209-210,
        212,213,214-215
Homophobia, 159,173
Homosexuality, "unnaturalness" of,
        199
Homosexuals
    bisexual and lesbian women's
        relationships with, 214-215
    monogamy of, 5
    sexuality of, 5
Honesty, 17,24
"If Love Is So Wonderful, What's So
        Scary About MORE?"
        (Halpern), 157-164
"If This Is Tuesday, It Must Be Dee . . .
        Confessions of a Closet
        Polyamorist" (Gartrell), 3,
        23-33
"Impossible Body" (play), 143-150
Inheritance, patriarchal concepts of,
        42-43,44,200,202
"I'm Not Monogamous Anymore, But
        . . ." (Dobkin), 5,185-187

Institute for Advanced Study of
Human Sexuality, 211
Intimacy, 4
definition of, 18
degrees and types of, 189-190,191,
192,193-194,195
as exclusivity, 18-19,21
in polyamorous relationships, 18,19
Intimate relationships. *See also*
Polyamorous relationships
secrecy of, 17,27,28

Jay, Karla, 4,97-103
Jealousy, 2,3,64,161
journal discussions of, 115,116-119
and positive "other-woman"
stories, 47-61
invisible other woman, 52-56
modular other woman, 50-52
one-time affairs, 48-50
other woman as forever-after
partner, 59-61,62
other woman as permanent
partner, 56-59
towards friends, 159
Journal, of polyamorous relationships,
4,111-120

Kerista commune, 221
Kissing, as herpes virus transmission
method, 213-214
Kitaka, 4,179-184
"Kitaka's Experiment or Why I
Started the Ecstasy Lounge"
(Kitaka), 4,179-184
Kivi, K. Linda, 111-120
Knight, Robert H., 199
Kovattana, Amanda, 3,85-95
"Deception," 88-89
"Lost Thailand," 91-94
"The Lover," 86-88
"Shadowlove," 89-90
"Three," 94-95

"Wild Life," 90-91
Kuhn, Thomas, 151-152

Labriola, Kathy, 3,217-225
Latin-American women. *See also*
Chicanas
monogamy of, 154-155
"Lesbian bed death," 2-3,26
Lesbian community. *See also*
Communities
role of polyamory in, 173-174
*Lesbian Love Companion, The: How
to Survive Everything from
Heartthrob to Heartbreak*
(Hall), 47,81
Lesbian Polyfidelity (West), 5,17
Lesbian relationships. *See also*
Polyamory; Polyamorous
relationships
definition of, 78
duration of, 205-207
heterosexual model of, 194-195
Lesbians
heterosexual sexual activities of,
214
negative stereotypes of, 36
"Lesbians as Luvbeins" (Loulan), 5,
35-38
Life Outside (Signorile), 5
"Long Journey Towards Polyamorous
Bliss, A" (Deer), 3,165-174
"Lost Thailand" (Kovattana), 91-94
Loulan, JoAnn, 5,35-38
Love
free, 1,135,173
romantic, 78
sacred vs. profane, 40
unrequited, 80
"Lover, The" (Kovattana), 86-88
Lovers
friends as, 15,16-17,19-20,80,106,
166
"half-time," 169-170
male, 162-163,214-215,221-222
Lunasea, 106
Lusero, Lisa, 143-150

"Luvbeins." *See also* "Lesbians as
Luvbeins"
definition of, 35-36

Making Out (Schramm-Evans), 5
Marriage, 197-203
"Boston," 78,81
in capitalist economies, 201-202,
203
definition of, 43,199
egalitarian, 201
group, 2,221
heterosexual, 197-198,217
government's endorsement of,
198,199,200,202
monogamous, 43-44
patriarchy in, 12-13,43,200-203
privileges and benefits associated
with, 199-200,203
same-sex, 5,183-184,197-198
Marriage therapy. *See* Couples therapy
Martin, Molly, 3,135-142
Mary (mother of Jesus), 43
Masturbation, "unnaturalness" of, 199
"Matriarchal Village" (Siegel), 4,
125-133
Matriarchy
of religion, 40-41,43
transition to patriarchy, 206
Matrilineal societies, 41,42
Matrilocal societies, 41,42
McPheeters, Martha, 2,197-203
Merging, lesbian, 2-3
Merryfeather, Lyn, 4,111-120
Michigan Women's Music Festival,
173
Military, gays in, 198
"Models of Open Relationships"
(Labriola), 3,217-225
Monogamy. *See also* Marriage
commitment to, 16-18,24,25
as cultural ideal, 158
definition of, 2,43
economic basis of, 2
exclusivity of, 18-19,21

heterosexual
as cultural ideal, 36-37
model of, 154-155
of homosexuals, 5
intimacy in, 18-19
in Latin-American culture, 154-155
lesbian feminists' distrust of, 13
patriarchal, 39-46
prevalence of, 5-6
serial, 2,44,166-167,210
sexually-transmitted disease risk in,
210-211
Mormons, polygamy of, 41
Mortality causes, 215
Mothers
lesbian, 32. *See also* Family,
polyamorous
unwed, 42
Mushroom, Merril, 5,189-196

National Lesbian Conference (1991),
168
Nation states, familial basis of, 202
Neolithic culture, 40-41,42
Nestle, Joan, 5
Networks, of interpersonal
relationships, 158
Never Say Never, 76,80
New paradigm relating, 160-161
New Phazes (Teri), 205-207
Non-monogamy. *See* Polyamory
Nonoxynol-9, 211
Novels, lesbian-feminist, 13

"Onstage," 143
Open Marriage (O'Neil and O'Neil),
1-2
"Open Relationships" workshop, 173
Orleans, Ellen, 3
"Other woman," 170-171
positive stories about, 48-61
invisible other woman, 52-56
modular other woman, 50-52
one-time affairs, 48-50
other woman as forever-after
partner, 59-61,62

other woman as permanent
partner, 56-59
*Our Right to Love, a Lesbian Resource
Book* (Dilno), 13
Outness, of members of polyamorous
relationships, 161
Overpopulation, 199
OWL Farm, 126

Pair bonding, 4,198,199-200. *See also*
Marriage
Paleolithic culture, 40-41,42
Paradigm shifts, 152
"Paradigms of Polyamory"
(Zambrano), 5,151-155
"Passion for Friends, A" (Raymond),
79
Paternity, of children, 42-43,44,200,
202
Patriarchy, 39-46
of the family, 12
feminist lesbians' rejection of, 5
of marriage, 12-13,43,200-203
People with AIDS, fundamentalist
Christians' attitudes towards,
40
Persistent Desire, The (Nestle, ed.), 5
Physical attractiveness/appearance
as cultural value, 75-76,82,190
of lesbians, 145
Plays/theatrical performances
"*Bad Friend Book*" (Sprecher), 4,
105-110
"Impossible Body" (Lusero),
143-150
Poetry, about polyamorous
relationships, 85-95
Polyamorous relationships
long-distance, 139,140-141,167,
168-169,193
long-term, 16
models of, 217-225
choice of, 225
multiple non-primary partners

model, 223-225
multiple primary partners
model, 220-224
polyfidelity model, 221-222
primary/secondary model,
218-221
as occasional affairs ("one-night
stands"), 171-172,195
partners' age differences in, 30,
31-32
scheduling of, 30-31
secrecy of, 160,167-168
stability of, 163-164
Polyamory
definition of, 1
as emotional infidelity, 158-159
fear of, 158-160,163
of feminist lesbians, 135-136,142
of homosexuals, 5
negative attitudes towards, 24,36,
44
new paradigm of, 160-161
during 1950s, 1-2
as option, 20-21
prevalence of, 5-6
purposes of, 4-5
sexually-transmitted disease risk in,
210-211
types of, 2
"Polyamory Quilt, The: Life's
Lessons" (Dal Vera), 4,11-22
Polyandry, 41
Polyfidelity, 5,17,221-222
"Poly-Friendships" (Rothblum), 4-5,
71-83
Polygamy, 41
Polygyny, 41,202-203
Polyphobia, 158-160,163
"Poly Wants a Lover" (Orleans), 3,
63-65
Pornography, 57-67
Portland, Oregon, lesbian community
of, 166,173,174
Presbyterian Church, 37
Privacy, 53-54,55-56,172,220
Prostitution, 43

Queer Studies Conference, Boulder,
   Colorado, 143
Questionnaires, for evaluation of
   sexual affairs, 54-55
Quilts, patchwork, 11-12,15,21-22

Race/racism, 41,145-146,149-150
Rednour, Shar, 5
Religion. *See also* Christianity
   Goddess worship, 40-41,43
   patriarchal concepts of, 40-43,44
Rhomboid Pegs for Oblong Hearts
   (Allegra), xv-xviii
Rich, Adrienne, 116
Roosevelt, Eleanor, 173
Rothaizer, Shoshana,4
Rothblum, Esther
   *Boston Marriages: Romantic but
      Asexual Relationships
      Among Contemporary
      Lesbians,* 81
   Poly-Friendships, 4-5,71-83
Rubyfruit Jungle (Brown), 13

Safer sex, 181,183,209-216
   techniques of, 211-214
Saliva, herpes virus transmission in,
   213-214
San Francisco
   Kerista commune of, 221
   lesbian subculture of, 135,136
Sappho, 173
Schramm-Evans, Zoe, 5
"Seven Poems for Three"
   (Kovattana), 3,85-95
Sex
   culture of, 75-76
   definition of, 76
   equated with love, 35,36
   as sin, 40
Sex clubs. *See also* Ecstasy Lounge
   safer sex practices of, 214
Sex education, 37
Sexism, 41,200

Sexual activity
   double standard of, 2,154-155
   heterosexual
      of bisexual and lesbian women,
         214
      in heterosexual marriages, 78
   lesbian, 76-79,82
   monogamous model of, 154
Sexual Ecology (Rotello), 5
Sexual intercourse, 76,77
   HIV transmission during, 212,215
Sexually-transmitted diseases, 1,2,163
   in men, 163
   prevention of, 211-214
   woman-to-woman transmission of,
      209-210
"Shadowlove" (Kovattana), 89-90
Shame, 115,116-117,118,119
Siegel, Thyme S., 125-133
Sin, sex as, 40
Sister Mae (Arnold), 13
Slavery, 41,201-202
S/M (sadomasochistic) activities, 218,229
Socialization, of lesbians, 76
Spinsters, 78
"Spontaneous Imaginative Life, The"
   (Hetherington, Kivi, Fisher,
      and Merryfeather), 4,111-120
Sprecher, Katherine Matthaei, 4,
   105-110
Stein, Gertrude, 149
Steiner, Claude, 157-158
Stonewall riots, 137
Storytelling, mutual, 50
"Swingers," 218
Syphilis, 212-213

Teri, 205-207
Testosterone, 29
Threat factor, 190
TLC, 5-6
Tribal bonds, of lesbians, 127
"Turning Down the Jezebel Decibels"
   (Hall), 3,47-62

U-Haul syndrome, 3-4
University of Colorado, 143
University of Puget Sound, 143
University of Turin, 214
"Uses of the Erotic, The: The Erotic
    as Power" (Lorde), 82

Vaginitis, 212
Violence, towards women, 75
Virginity, 43
Virgin Mary, 43
Virgin Territory I & II (Rednour), 5

Warts, genital, 212-213
Werhane, Kathryn, 3,227-233
West, Celeste, 5,17

WHO Farm, 166
"Wild Life" (Kovattana), 90-91
Williams, Terry Tempest, 19
Woman Spirit, 127
Women
    and culture of sex, 75-76
    exploitation of, 200. *See also*
        Patriarchy
    heterosexual, lesbians' sexual
        attraction to, 80-81
    matriarchal concepts of, 41
    patriarchal concepts of, 40,41,
        42-43
    violence towards, 75
Work of a Common Woman, The
    (Grahn), 40

Zambrano, Margarita, 5,151-155
Zero population growth, 202